SO YOU WANT
TO RAISE A BOY?

SO YOU WANT
TO RAISE
A BOY?

W. CLEON SKOUSEN

DOUBLEDAY & COMPANY, INC.
GARDEN CITY, NEW YORK

The photographs in this book are from the following sources:
Chapters 1, 4, 5, 7, 8, 11, 13, 24, 27, 31—Harold M. Lambert
Chapters 3, 6, 9, 10, 12, 14, 15, 16, 21, 23, 25, 26, 28, 29—
H. Armstrong Roberts
Chapters 18, 20, 22—Max Thorpe
Chapter 2—Metropolitan Life Insurance Company
Chapter 19—David M. Mills
Chapter 30—Eric Wahleen

Dedicated to the five happy whoop 'n' holler hooligans we are having the pleasure of raising: *David, Rick, Harold, Paul, Brent.*
And to their three loving and patient sisters who put up with them: *Julianne, Sharon, Kathy.*

ISBN: 0-385-02408-8
LIBRARY OF CONGRESS CATALOG CARD NUMBER 61–9555

ACKNOWLEDGMENT

After twenty years of study, writing, and lecturing on a particular subject there are many friends, researchers, and contributors to one's store of knowledge who deserve heartfelt thanks for their help and inspiration. Among those to whom I would like to express special appreciation are:

J. Edgar Hoover, whose interest in youth problems has been one of the nation's greatest influences in focusing attention on the casualties among neglected youth. It was in the FBI, during the years 1944 and 1945, that I received my first specialized training in the field of youth development and juvenile crime control.

GESELL INSTITUTE OF CHILD DEVELOPMENT, where a full generation of the most comprehensive scientific study of child development has been conducted by Dr. Arnold Gesell, Dr. Frances L. Ilg, Dr. Louise Bates Ames, and their many associates. As the foremost center in the world for the study of child behavior patterns, this team has produced a number of noteworthy classics including *Infant and Child in the Culture of Today; The Child from Five to Ten;* and *Youth: The Years from Ten to Sixteen.*

Dr. Sheldon Glueck and Dr. Eleanor Glueck of Harvard University; Dr. Manuel Lopez-Rey of the United Nations staff; The Children's Bureau of the U. S. Department of Health, Education and Welfare; The Scientific Research Associates, Inc., of Chicago, Illinois, who were responsible for the famous "Life Adjustment Booklet" series.

THE DELINQUENCY CONTROL INSTITUTE at the University of Southern California, whose directors and faculty have been good friends over the years; THE INTERNATIONAL JUVENILE OFFICERS ASSOCIATION with whom I had the pleasure of serving as a board member for a number of years.

CONTENTS

CONFIDENTIALLY, FROM ONE PARENT TO ANOTHER

Several years ago I was invited by my professional associates to write a book on juvenile delinquency. Looking back on it now, I think the reason I failed to respond to that request was because my own brood of little whoop 'n' holler hooligans were gradually giving me the sneaking suspicion that what parents needed was not so much a study of juvenile delinquents as a practical catalogue of concrete, cast-iron suggestions on how to raise a family of *non*-delinquents.

So that is what this present study will be about. It is an adventurous attempt to set down as simply as possible the ABCs of child psychology and the XYZs of parental survival. In other words, these are the things I wish someone had been brave enough to tell me when I first started raising my own family.

One may wonder why this particular study is restricted to boys. It is simply a matter of expediency. The plain unvarnished truth is that ten times more boys get into trouble than girls. Obviously, girls have difficulties too, but perhaps we can give them their fair share of consideration in a separate presentation.

In launching a study of this kind we might take considerable comfort from the fact that there are no living experts on the subject of raising boys. There are a lot of students of the subject, but no experts. I once had a friend who was newly out of college, and he boldly proclaimed himself to be an expert, but when I met him a few years later he was a broken man. He said he had

married soon after graduation and when his children came along
they repealed his education. Of course, this was only true in a
humorous and relative sense, but it did emphasize a lesson which
all of us ultimately learn, namely, that there is a vast difference
between a textbook on child psychology and a real live boy—
particularly one who has inherited all the maverick qualities of
his father!

"AM I RAISING A JUVENILE DELINQUENT?"

Here is a question parents usually ask the police every time a
boy happens to get into serious trouble. Just so those parents
with problem boys will not think we are going to leave out
"delinquency" altogether, let us set down a few facts here at the
beginning which may help clear the air before we get on with
the task of discussing the raising of a normal boy.

First of all, it is somewhat reassuring to newly initiated parents
to learn that it is normal to have trouble with their children.
Most young couples start out married life with profound mutual
assurances that *their* children will be different, but, like the rest
of us, they will get standard-brand human beings, and that means
problems. Of course, their problems need not become chronic,
but problems there will be. Growing good citizens is simply an
old-fashioned building process, and nothing worthwhile was ever
built without meeting the fury of many frustrations and doing a
lot of on-the-spot problem solving at the same time.

Studies show that about 95 per cent of the parents succeed in
working out their boys' problems, but there are the remaining
cases where the problems become so complex for both the
youngsters and their parents that they fail to handle them
properly. And that is all juvenile delinquents really are—*young
people with problems which are not being properly handled.*

Parents, police, and youth leaders learn that a juvenile delinquent might be *anybody's* boy. He does not have to be a
special "type" as they used to think a few years ago. He is not a
boy who was raised in any particular part of town or on any
particular economic or social level. He is not a boy with certain
facial features or with a certain variety of skull bumps. He is not

a boy of a particular age (after World War II it was usually age 18 to 19; today it is usually 14 to 15). He is not necessarily a dull boy nor does he necessarily have a dislike for school. He might be active in a boys' organization and even be active in his church. No organization and no family is 100 per cent delinquency-proof.

WHO IS TO BLAME FOR JUVENILE DELINQUENCY?

This brings us to another important point. Naturally, when people observe an outcropping of delinquency in a boy they tend to judge the builders of the boy the same way they judge the builders of a house. If a house has a leaning wall, a cracked foundation, or a leaking roof, people blame the contractors. Because parents are God's contractors for the building of children, people tend to blame them when the product is faulty.

However, none of us can tell from a distance what a certain set of parents have had to work with as they tried to build a boy into a good citizen. Sometimes there are defective timbers, nails without temper, and a disproportionate amount of sand in the concrete. I have seen parents who have given a youngster far more guidance and affection than his pals were receiving and still end up with a young hoodlum.

This simply means that some parents have a much tougher assignment than their neighbors may know about. Therefore, judgment should be restrained.

Still, on the other hand, there are certain parents who are so mixed up in their thinking that they treat their children as unwanted baggage who should be dumped on the schools, the church, or some social agency to care for. When a case study shows that a boy is being raised by parents of this kind we have a completely different problem. The indignation of the community is entirely justified. That set of parents should be subjected to whatever pressures are necessary to help them appreciate their fundamental responsibilities to raise their own children and not dump them on the community.

Finally, there is an in-between type of situation where the parents are sincerely desirous of doing a good job, but their boy's delinquency is the result of a temporary period of neglect. Perhaps the father is unemployed and the mother is trying to help out by working. There may have been illness in the family, or some other misfortune which has attacked the normal stability of the parents. Of course, temporary neglect may also be the result of too much prosperity in the family. The stability of parents may be attacked by excessive social or professional pressures so that they lack both the time and energy to properly supervise a boy.

But whether the temporary neglect of a boy is due to misfortune or good fortune, if the attitude of the parents is basically sound it usually needs nothing more from the police than a polite reminder of their neglect, and these parents will cinch up the slack in their home life and take care of Junior's problems without any further help being required from the community.

The vast majority of the cases coming to the attention of the police fall within this last category. Studies show that where parents try to co-operate with the police, 95 per cent of the youngsters will make satisfactory adjustments and never come to the attention of the police again.

WHAT ARE THE TRADE-MARKS OF A JUVENILE DELINQUENT?

A delinquent is usually a boy who starts out with the same troubles most boys have. He tends to dislike work, doesn't think he has enough money, wants a car, wants more attention, figures he is a social misfit and that certain people don't like him, has trouble in some of his classes at school, and daydreams a lot. I know a boy we will call Joe who is struggling with these very problems, but I think he will make the grade without becoming a delinquent. Here is the reason why. When his boss at the service station bawled him out for being lazy, he felt very angry about it but since then he has been doing better. He also thought some of his teachers had it in for him because he was not getting good grades, but, since his father had a two-hour session with both him and his teachers and he heard in no uncertain terms what it would take to get better grades, he seems to be trying harder. As for daydreaming, he still does a lot of that, but he is beginning to get so busy there isn't much time for it any more.

I also know another boy we will call Jake. Jake has been fired from four after-school jobs. At school he was nearly expelled for cheating on exams in the classes he was flunking. He enjoys "rodding" around in his car to see how many violations he can get away with in between tickets. He enjoys telling people off, and lately he has gotten the idea that it's smart to have a hang-over.

The difference between Joe and Jake is the simple fact that Joe will make it and Jake probably will not. Both have the same problems, but the boys have different *attitudes*. When the first boy was criticized for being lazy he did not like it any more than Jake, but now he's trying. On the other hand, Jake says, "If those jerks don't like me the way I am, it's their tough luck." Jake is beginning to take pride in being a misfit.

With Joe it is only a question of time until people will have forgotten that he ever had any problems. With Jake it is only a question of time until he has acquired a criminal record. At least, that is the immediate prospect unless something radical and revolutionary happens to change him.

Jake is developing the trade-marks of a delinquent:

1. *His problems are becoming a* habit.
2. *His problems are created* deliberately.
3. *His misbehavior is not occasional but* chronic.
4. *His misbehavior tends to make him almost universally* disliked.
5. *His misbehavior is making him almost universally* distrusted.
6. *His conduct is moving in the direction of* serious criminal acts.

WHAT CAN BE DONE ABOUT JUVENILE DELINQUENCY?

Fortunately, we are learning more and more about ways and means of helping boys like Jake. But, better still, we are learning more and more about ways and means of keeping boys from becoming like Jake. In this study we will discuss many of these procedures in detail, but it might be well even at this point to list some of the basic lessons we are learning.

First, parents need to know more about the *normal* development of children so they can distinguish between difficult behavior which can be expected at certain ages and the behavior which is a clear signal of "criminal delinquency ahead."

Second, a great deal more stress must be placed on building and preserving our homes. Every community facility and service should concentrate on stabilizing the home rather than replacing it. Studies show that even when children are raised in deficient homes they turn out better on the average than those placed in institutions. Therefore, children should never be taken permanently from their homes except in the most extreme situations.

Third, the major defect in the training of youth today is their failure to learn respect for society's "barriers." Youngsters get the idea that no one is big enough to handle them—neither their families, the schools, the city, the state, nor even the government. This is the result of setting up standards and failing to enforce them, gently where possible, firmly where necessary. The situation is further complicated by the fact that when families are criticized for letting their children get out of control, most communities do an even poorer job when they take the youngsters over. Many a minor delinquent has developed into a full-fledged, defiant criminal because he found that the juvenile courts and other community agencies were just too busy to keep track of him. Sometimes youngsters who have been picked up and released many times will offer to make a bet with arresting officers that nothing will happen to them on their latest offense. This trend must come to a halt if delinquents are to learn the limits of the law and learn to respect its barriers.

Fourth, lack of discipline in the life of a child creates a sense of insecurity. When parents set up reasonable standards and enforce them, the child gets the feeling he is living in an "orderly world." On the other hand, when he is promised certain penalties for certain offenses and these promises are not fulfilled, a child gets the feeling his world is unstable and falling to pieces.

Fifth, we are learning that criminal conduct has its roots in the undesirable experiences which many children stumble into when they are very young. Therefore, close supervision by a conscientious mother during these early years is of primary importance. Obviously, some mothers have to leave home and work, but all parents should be aware of the tremendous hazard involved in "farming out" children, especially during their tender years.

THREE CHEERS FOR THOSE WHO TRY

Parents raise their children in a whirlpool of congested conflicts. There is the problem of earning a living coupled with deciding *how much* of a living to earn. A father can sell more insurance or take on a second job by ignoring his family and working night and day. Or the family income can be enhanced by Mother working as well as Dad. All parents should answer this question, "How much of our 'extra' income could we sacrifice in order to raise our children better?"

Then there is the problem of maintaining a balanced social life. When a boy and girl get married they each have many friends. To these they soon add clubs, business associations, and various social groups. Before they know it, their social life, club life, or "business contacts on a social level" can blot out the family almost completely. Many a delinquent is a victim of his parents' social life. Parents must decide: "How much social life are we willing to forego in order to raise our children properly?"

Parents also have personal hobbies and personal interests which compete with the family. A mother is a painter, musician, a ceramics maker, or civic worker. A father may be a hunter, fisherman, golfer, make-it-yourself enthusiast, or stamp collector. These personal sources of satisfaction are a delight where they are shared with a family, but often a child finds that his parents have neither the time nor inclination to share their hobbies. A parent must, therefore, pause every so often to ask, "How much of myself am I willing to share with my children?"

Therefore, in spite of earning a living, satisfying social obligations, and gaining personal satisfaction in various hobbies, there must be a slice of time and energy reserved for the most important people in our world. It is a constant battle to carve out enough time to meet the minimum needs of these exciting, demanding, noisy little creatures who swarm about our feet. Three cheers, then, for the people who try!

Sometimes parents become smothered by their own self-sympathy and think that modern parents really have it tough. However, grandparents who pioneered the breaking of raw sod and the building of former frontiers will assure them that they have more blessings than they may have counted. A grandmother will say wistfully, "My, when I was milking cows, churning butter, packing water from a well, making all our own clothes, having children without a doctor, raising a garden, cooking on a wood stove, ironing with a 'flat,' what wouldn't I have given for the things a mother has today! And how fortunate we would have felt to let our children sit together of an evening watching TV, going together to see a movie, or having such nice parks and playgrounds to enjoy."

Each generation has its blessings and its trials. I suppose modern parents have their share of both.

THREE APPROACHES TO RAISING CHILDREN

They say adults fall into one of three groups when it comes to raising children.

The first is the "Cherubic Approach." This is the theory that children are simply chubby little cherubs who have descended directly from heaven and are therefore absolutely angelic and would do no wrong. This theory is held by adults who haven't been around children lately.

The "theoretical child" of poetry and prose is a simple, sweet, unsophisticated little angel. But a flesh and blood child is a curious, noisy, rambunctious ball of fire who is only partly built and therefore acts only partly reasonable. Any adult who approaches children on the theory that they are purely angelic is in for a rude awakening and will probably need an early appointment with a psychiatrist.

The second approach is the "Sledge and Anvil Approach." This is the theory that we build good citizens the same way we build horseshoes—just "heat 'em up and beat on 'em." Many children have survived such homes in spite of the extreme brutality inflicted on them, but a certain percentage of children from homes like this become candidates for Leavenworth, Sing Sing, Folsom, and Alcatraz. As we shall see later, discipline has its place, but brutality does not.

The third approach is the one we each like to think we are using. This is the "Absorption Approach." It is the idea that we should surround our children with the kind of adults we would like our children to emulate, adults who will exhibit the love, interest, kindness, leadership, and ambition which inspire children to become like them and thereby *absorb* them into the exciting, wonderful precincts of the adult world. Such an approach requires that the most important exemplary adults be the parents themselves. After that there are good neighbors, good teachers, good youth leaders, well-trained police, honest business leaders, and people of integrity in government. There are also the movie idols, the athletic heroes, the champions of all types, who likewise have a responsibility to set high standards for the hero-worshiping small fry who get stars in their eyes as they watch from the side lines.

THE MOTHER, THE FATHER, THE FAMILY

In this book we have included three chapters on the most important influences in the life of a child:

The Ideal Mother
The Ideal Father
The Ideal Family

The reader may be surprised to find how many "ideal" qualities his own efforts have produced. Most parents have an inferiority complex. Often they are better parents than they realize. In any event, it may be helpful to realize that God never created, nor has man ever discovered, a better instrument for raising children than PARENTS.

All of us start out amazingly ignorant. It is well-nigh impossible to be trained for parenthood. It works best on a "learn-as-you-do" basis. Colleges find this out when they try to teach unmarried students how to prepare for parenthood. The unmarried student is so absorbed with personal problems growing out of the court-ship stage that there is little room for post-marital problems such as raising children. Fortunately, as Dr. Benjamin Spock has emphasized in his excellent book, *Baby and Child Care,* many of the things parents need for success "just come naturally." Therefore much of the training for parenthood merely gives rational appreciation to the things which the parents instinctively feel already.

This one lesson, however, we must surely learn: All children are different. This brings us to our final thought for this intro-ductory chapter.

THE HORIZONTAL VS. THE PERPENDICULAR APPROACH

Psychologists usually prefer the perpendicular approach in their studies of child development, rather than the horizontal approach. This perpendicular approach consists of taking a particular quality such as "social adjustment" and measuring the level a youngster has reached at his present stage of maturation. Sometimes people will be very advanced in one quality and almost infantile in another. The scientist feels safer in measuring people "up and down" the scale for each of their respective qualities, rather than taking a cross section of a child's behavior pattern and then rating him as "normal" or "abnormal."

On the other hand, the horizontal approach consists of look-ing at a cross-section view of a boy and then deciding how he compares with other boys his age. The cross-section or horizon-tal approach is the one we have used in this book because it is more easily understood by parents. Frequently after a child psychologist has given the perpendicular analysis of a child and explained in great detail just where each of his qualities can be charted on a maturation scale, the parent will still say, "But, doctor, *how* is he doing? Is he normal or otherwise?" This is the assurance the parent is seeking when a crisis occurs, is his child merely "going through a phase" or is he in urgent need of personality therapy? In this book we have also taken the horizontal cross section of many children, so that parents may look at their own son and heir and then decide whether he needs special treatment or just persuasive pressure to keep him climbing up the ladder of life.

With it all must go a gentle word of warning. Since all children are different, the parent must take this study for what it is designed to be, merely a rule of thumb. Most children will follow the normal ebb and flow tides of development we will describe. Others will hold back and then thrust forward in an amazing leap. Each child, in other words, is a bundle of marvelous quantities and qualities which will be unique unto himself.

Parents must therefore approach the task of raising children with a combination of courage and humility. Not at any time during the growth process are they absolutely sure what the final product will be. Instinctively they hope they are building a monumental structure, but the important thing is to do the best they can with what they have and love the child for what he is and what they feel he can become.

Part I   THE BUILDING OF A BOY

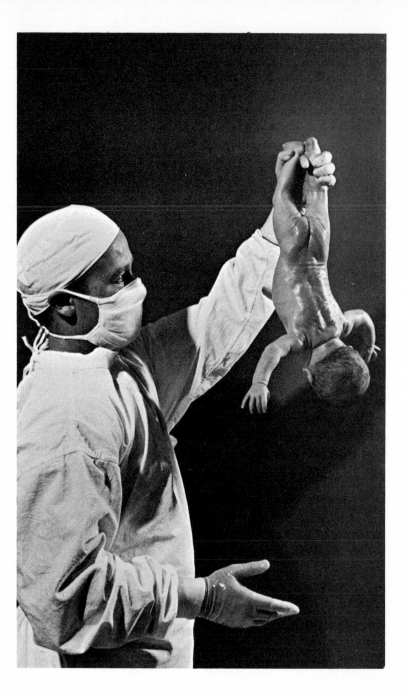

CHAPTER 1

HOW LITTLE BOYS ARE MADE

This is not going to be a chapter about the "birds and bees," but it will include some rather pointed remarks about caterpillars and butterflies. It is logical, no doubt, to associate caterpillars and butterflies with little boys, but in this chapter they are used to help explain how little boys are made.

Of course, not everyone is interested in this exciting process because we who live in the atom-bomb, jet-propulsion space age tend to take so many things for granted. But there is one thing we cannot afford to take for granted: *Life!*

THE SECRET OF LIFE

The secret to this remarkable phenomenon called "life" is hidden deep within its smallest representatives—the single cells. By studying the miracle of the cells we gain a whole new appreciation of life, including ourselves.

Cells do marvelous things. They do not act like machines but like people. They reproduce themselves, they build governments, they take on civic responsibilities, they change assignments to meet an emergency, they set up an army of their own members to ward off enemies, they build themselves into towns, cities, states, and nations.

The most dramatic example of self-government among living cells is contained in the biography of a butterfly. As every schoolboy knows, a butterfly starts out as a caterpillar. A fuzzy caterpillar is a complicated little creature with millions of cells organized together to make its existence possible. At a certain stage the caterpillar grows a tough covering which gradually immobilizes him, and, once he has locked himself inside, he *disintegrates!* Each cell gives up the role it has played to make the skin, hair, legs, feelers, and digestive tract of a caterpillar and becomes a common citizen in a mass of cells which all appear identical. When the time is ripe, these cells all go scrambling back into action again—but in new roles! They re-assemble themselves into a whole new creature with a different kind of body, different mouth, different legs, a new kind of antennae, different eyes, and a glorious spread of magnificent wings which are marked exactly like the original parent butterfly (the one that laid the egg that became the caterpillar that became this beautiful new butterfly).

Herein lies a great secret of nature: Cells are not machines. They display intelligence, organizing ability, reorganizing ability, capacity to follow a plan, ability to intelligently anticipate the future, and, whenever necessary, to choose between different courses of action—adopting one and rejecting the others. It has taken science a long time to discover this fantastic and almost unbelievable fact.

THE MIRACLE OF THE CELLS

In the human body it is astonishing to watch how cells work. In *Man Does Not Stand Alone*, A. Cressy Morrison, former president of the New York Academy of Sciences, describes it this way: "We as human beings are well-ordered republics of billions on billions of similar cells; each cell is a citizen intelligently doing its full quota of devoted service."

When he says each cell is "similar" he means that each and every body cell contains a nucleus of forty-eight chromosomes surrounded by a substance called cytoplasm and covered by a delicate membrane to hold the cell together. But here the similarity ends, because these cells which have built themselves into a human body have had to change their shape to fit the needs of thousands upon thousands of different functions. Of course, in the beginning the developing human embryo starts out with a group of *similar* cells, but when specialization is needed an interesting thing occurs. One of the cells differentiates itself into a kidney cell, for example, and thereafter reproduces nothing but kidney cells. Another differentiates into a type of cell needed for lungs and thereafter it, together with its off-spring, produces nothing but cells for lung tissue. Thus the body develops from similar cells which, at precisely the right moment, become specialized cells and continue thereafter to produce only their own kind until a particular organ or type of tissue is completed.

We know that in an emergency these specialized cells can reorganize themselves as the cells of the caterpillar reorganize themselves to become the butterfly. Dr. Alexis Carrel, in *Man the Unknown,* describes what happens when a bone is broken: "At the seat of the fracture and around it, all structural and functional processes are directed toward repair. *Tissues become what they have to be in order to accomplish the task.* For example, a shred of muscle . . . metamorphoses into cartilage."

And, speaking of adaptation, a remarkable thing happens when the human body gets ready to manufacture a reproductive cell. The female body manufactures an incomplete cell with only twenty-four chromosomes for the female egg, and the male body manufactures an incomplete cell with only twenty-four chromosomes for the male sperm. When these two come together in the female Fallopian tube they "become as one"—a single cell with forty-eight chromosomes!

Now we are ready to tell the story of the building of a boy.

THE FIRST CHAPTER IN A BOY'S BIOGRAPHY

When Mother Nature starts building a little boy she knows precisely what she is about. In nine swift months, a single fertilized cell grows into hundreds of billions of cells—all fantastically and ingeniously organized into units, networks, organs, and systems. To build even one of these complex human creatures is indeed marvelous, but to do it millions of times with scarcely a hitch is miraculous. Every hour approximately 5400 little humans are born into the world, and most of them are perfect specimens. Once in a while something goes awry and a few hundred million cells pile up their work in the wrong place or in the wrong way, but, as a general rule, the powers of life released from the original egg cell permeate the whole cosmic process until finally there comes forth a perfectly formed, beautifully proportioned infant human being "made in the image of God."

The original seed of human life, the fertilized cell in the Fallopian tube, is about as big as the dot over this *i*. In the nucleus of the dot are the forty-eight chromosomes, and these contain thousands of little control gadgets called genes. The genes have the job of determining color of eyes, color of hair, the shape and contour of each part of the body, and so forth, almost ad infinitum.

Since half of the genes come from the mother's side and half come from the father's side, the time of union between the egg and the sperm is a truly monumental moment when the thousands of genes all seek to assert their particular dominance. Some from the father win out and some from the mother win out, until finally we come up with the exact combination which will be our boy. This means that in this first tiny cell every inheritable characteristic of our boy becomes predetermined— from the shape of his toenails to the size and shape of his nose and his ears. In fact, once the gene combination is set up, it becomes "locked in." In other words, when this cell multiplies and produces other cells, each one will carry exactly the same gene combination as the original parent cell.

Just the moment the fertilized egg cell has set its house in order with every gene pattern properly locked in, it immediately goes to work. It starts out by making another cell just like itself. This is a very critical moment, because if this second cell does not remain attached to the parent cell, but breaks away, then we are going to get identical twins! Each cell will build a boy. Of course, there are many twins who are not identical. These are called "fraternal" twins. Fraternal twins occur when two separate eggs are fertilized by two separate sperm cells and result in twins with completely different gene combinations.

However, assuming that the parent cell or egg divides normally, we would soon see additional cells added rapidly. We would also see the egg begin to move down the Fallopian tube to the womb. This is a two-inch journey which takes about three days. By the time the egg reaches the womb it has about sixteen cells. Now specialization will begin. The cells seem to know precisely what to do. The outside cells become flat and multiply rapidly to produce a thin outer layer. The inner cells of the egg are round and multiply more slowly.

By the sixth or seventh day the egg is about the size of a pinhead, and is sending out tiny roots into the soft velvety surface of the womb to secure nourishment from the mother's blood supply.

The round inner cells of the egg now differentiate rapidly. A three-layer disk is formed, and the cells of each layer prepare to produce millions of cells for certain functions. One layer will produce cells for the nervous system, skin, fingernails, hair, tooth enamel, and the lining of the nose and throat. Another layer will produce cells for the muscle, bone, cartilage, blood, blood vessels, kidneys, and tooth dentine. The third layer will provide cells for the digestive and respiratory systems. With all of this manufacturing equipment ready to go to work, the keel for the little human being can now be laid.

About the nineteenth or twentieth day the three-layered disk develops a crease with ridges on either side. The ridges come together at one end. This will be the head. The rest of the disk forms into a crescent shape—the outside of which is the beginning of the spinal column—while small buds appear along the sides indicating the coming of arms and legs.

The tiny body starts to build the two most important organs first—the heart and the brain. By the twenty-first day a tiny heart is forming, and ten days later it will start to beat. The open area in the tiny head is filled with brain cells which prepare to set up signal lines that will stretch down the spinal column and out into the remotest corner of the body.

Usually all of this has happened without the mother even knowing she is pregnant. Sometime after the twenty-first day she may begin to get symptoms, such as missing menstruation, and then she knows the miracle of the cells has begun.

THE SECOND AND THIRD MONTHS

Almost from its earliest stages, the tiny embryo is carefully shockproofed by being suspended in a clear liquid. During the second month the arm and leg buds are growing rapidly. To appreciate the genius of cell construction, one need only contemplate how these millions of cells which keep piling into these extended appendages must organize themselves to form a vast complex of bones, muscles, sinews, supply lines, and signal circuits. It is all done methodically—the arm buds become elongated, then paddles appear with five little buds on each of the paddles. The paddles become hands, the smaller buds, fingers, and the whole arm divides itself into wrist, forearm, and upper arm. An equally amazing process takes place with the leg buds.

By the sixtieth day the embryo is beginning to look like a baby. It is only one inch long from stem to stern (not counting the curled-up legs) and it has nose, mouth, ears, and the beginning of the eye sockets.

During the next thirty days the baby grows to three inches in length and weighs about one ounce. All of the organs of the body begin to become apparent. Eyes and eyelids are formed. The sex of the baby was determined from the very beginning, and the organs typical of his sex now become apparent. By the end of the third month the arms and legs are finished down to the point of fingernails and toenails, and the arms and legs have begun to move about in rhythmical patterns. The mother cannot yet feel this movement, but from our little boy's point of view his behavior pattern of life is already in rudimentary motion.

THE FOURTH AND FIFTH MONTHS

Beginning with the fourth month, the baby is no longer referred to as an embryo but is called a fetus. During the next month he will finally get his full quota of nerve cells—over twelve billion of them. In spite of the number each nerve cell is precious. This is one type of cell which will not be replaced if it is destroyed. What the baby now has must last him throughout life. Other cells, like skin cells, have a longevity of only a few days before they are replaced. Muscle cells are replaced about every eighty days.

During all of this growing and developing, the baby has been completely separated from the mother's nervous system and the mother's circulatory system. Between the mother and the baby is an exchange station—the placenta—which is a platelike organ about eight inches in diameter. There the mother's circulatory system deposits food and oxygen. There the baby's transmission belt—the umbilical cord—picks it up. Because the baby is independent of his mother's nervous system, nothing which she sees, hears, or fears can have a direct effect on the baby.

By the end of the fourth month the baby is big enough to make his waving legs and arms felt by his mother. She perceives the thumps of his tiny kicking feet and says she "feels life." This is called "the quickening." However, it is not the baby that has been quickened but the mother's awareness as she finally feels the gentle knocking of the little fellow who has been growing at breakneck speed and now makes his presence known for the first time.

The baby is finally at the halfway mark. Already he is a well-formed man child. However, he is only six inches long and weighs barely six ounces. The doctor can hear his pounding little heart through the stethoscope and notes that it is pumping away at the rapid rate of 136 times a minute, which is twice as fast as his mother's heartbeat.

THE FINAL PERIOD OF PREPARATION FOR BIRTH

By the end of the sixth month the baby weighs about twenty-four ounces and is twelve inches long. His eyes are almost ready for the light and his eyebrows and eyelashes have appeared. He can even hiccup and sneeze! During the seventh and eighth months, the baby makes his mother aware of his numerous activities. He squirms and stretches and moves about—not only his arms and legs, but his whole body and his head.

From here on it is apparent that the baby has the rudiments of practically all of his faculties. He can use his throat muscles and swallows small amounts of the liquid in which he is immersed. The tiny lungs also expand and contract—inhaling and exhaling the water of his environment as a means of getting prepared for the day when he will have to gulp down air to supply his newborn body with oxygen. The intestines and kidneys are working even though their function is latent. The little mouth also puckers up and makes sucking motions in expectation of the nursing procedure soon to come. In fact, he may find his thumb in the dark and start sucking it before he is born.

The ninth month is the time when the days seem to drag along endlessly. The father, mother, grandparents, and even the baby get desperately anxious. By now the baby is between six and seven pounds, so the mother feels the weight of him. He is around nineteen inches long and likes nothing better than to plant one of his good-sized baby feet on one wall while bracing himself on the other. Or he will get spunky and kick. He especially resents having the doctor prodding about his abdominal home and will frequently kick mightily in protest.

THE BIG DAY

The average baby is born around the 267th day of his gestation, although a fifteen-day variation either way is not unusual. Of course, he has no idea how much fuss and excitement he is creating in anticipation of his arrival. On the other hand, those who wait to welcome him can scarcely imagine the desperate transition he must make. It is the first major crisis in this little boy's existence as he passes from the quiet, dark, and silent world of his genesis to the bright, noisy, threatening world of earth life. His successful arrival is cause for jubilant celebration by parents, friends, and relatives. Nevertheless, in his own personal biography the supreme achievement of "surviving" becomes the monumental victory of his entire lifetime.

Young, inexperienced parents may expect their newborn baby to look like a Christmas doll, but he doesn't. He arrives in the world, red-faced, flat-nosed, and tired. After his first good squawl to prove that he has indeed taken unto himself "the breath of life," he usually wants nothing more than a chance to curl up and rest. And as the new mother looks at the round, tiny wonder child she cannot help but feel proud to have had a part in preparing the way for this new bright jewel of human life. But she knows there was a great power working within her. Without requiring either her thought or direction this little universe of life has developed from a single cell to trillions of cells—all immaculately organized so that he can cry, swallow, eat, hear, smell, see, move, digest food, think, and feel. As the mother cuddles him gently in her arms she knows her baby is indeed a gift of God.

CHAPTER 2

HAPPY AND HELPLESS

The First Year

"They're going to have a baby!"

This is the great news that leaps across backyard fences and skips along neighborhood telephone lines. First, it is told as an absolute secret. A secret is defined as something which is told "to just one person at a time." It is only a matter of weeks before the second stage is reached where everybody knows the secret, although it is still "very confidential." In due process of time, however, the coming event is an obvious historical fact so the big news passes into the third stage of unembarrassed public discussion.

No doubt Providence intended that such a momentous event as having a baby should be enjoyed by the entire community. In fact, it is amazing how many people seem to take credit for the coming event. Grandparents discuss it as though they were the primary parties responsible. Aunts, uncles, friends, and neighbors all talk as though they were in on the planning committee. In all of this, there is nothing personal. It just illustrates how excited everybody gets over the prospect of a new baby.

YOUNG PARENTS IN WAITING

But the young parents have mixed feelings. They are usually happy and hopeful, but filled with wonderment. The young mother-in-waiting gets endless advice from her own mother as

well as from married girl friends who already have babies of
their own.

The young father, on the other hand, usually gets little or no
advice. All kinds of thoughts go tumbling through his head. He
is pleased but worried. The endowment of fatherhood finds him
in one of the most chaotic periods of his life. It is not easy to leap
from the casual, carefree life of being single to the mighty serious
business of gaining a wife, finding a job, finishing an education,
getting into a profession, getting an apartment or home, buying
a car, filling three or four rooms with furniture, and otherwise
laying the foundation for a well-adjusted married life.

Sometimes he looks at his little bride-wife who seems to be
contented and confident, and he wonders how she can trust
him so completely with her future life and welfare. In such
moments of meditation he feels his youthfulness, his inexperience,
and his personal inadequacies. It is also in such moments that a
wise young wife can easily see what is happening and promptly
bolster his "will to succeed" by assuring him that she just *knows*
everything is going to be all right.

WILL THE BABY BE WELCOMED?

The attitude developed by prospective parents toward their
baby can affect his entire future life. Parents-in-waiting need to
resist any tendency to resent the gift of life which is about to be
given them. Every baby should come into the world "wanted."
This is what it means to be wellborn. It means that he will not
only be welcomed, but that down through the years he will be
loved, nursed, taught, guided, fed, clothed, encouraged, and
inspired. This little fellow is depending upon his mom and dad
to love and nurture him through half a lifetime of development.
In the complex and exciting job of raising a boy, no single factor
is more important than the fact that he is loved and wanted.
This not only builds a happy boy, it builds happy parents.

On the other hand, a baby who is unwelcomed and resented
will reflect it in his personality as he begins to mature. The feeling of *rejection* in a human being is one of the most explosive
and destructive forces in existence. It was this very ingredient

which distilled anarchy in the minds of men like Rousseau, Nietzsche, Engels, and Marx; it produced gangsters like those who grew up and poured out of "Hell's Kitchen" in New York; it produces ne'er-do-well Bohemians, criminal psychopaths, and candidates for odd-ball cults like the Beatniks.

Whether one is born in the slums or on Nob Hill is not so important. The key to success is being born "wanted"!

GETTING OFF TO A GOOD START

When it comes time for the baby to arrive, there are a lot of brand-new experiences for everyone concerned. Modern doctors do a lot of advance briefing so a young mother will have a fairly good idea of what to expect. The young father is relegated to the waiting room, where he suffers mostly from not knowing what is going on. Everybody laughs about him "sitting it out," but to him it is no joke. He pretends to read magazines, he paces about the room, he prays, he talks with the more experienced fathers. Then he sees the sign on the waiting room wall: "Take courage! We haven't lost a father yet!"

Eventually, the word finally comes. "It's a boy!" or "It's a girl!" He has stopped caring which, just so everything is all right. After another painful wait (seldom more than thirty minutes) he is taken in tow by a nurse, who may let him catch a quick glimpse of the baby through the nursery window before she takes him to see his wife. The glimpse through the nursery window may be demoralizing. It sometimes takes a lot of imagination to see the possibilities of a future President in a brand-new, red-faced baby. Still, a young father cannot help feeling a certain sense of pride as he looks at the little fellow and says to himself, "Gosh, that's my boy!"

When he sees his wife it seems as though they have been separated for a century. He bends over to kiss her, and she whispers, "Isn't he cute?" He nods, and she exclaims with motherly pride, "At last we have *our* baby."

It always seems like a long time before mother and baby can be brought home, but, once they have arrived, a whole new world opens up for a young father. It is one eternal round of formulas, feedings, burping, and changing. The mother has become adjusted to the day and night schedule at the hospital, but it is a new experience for a father to be in a constant stage of alert—sleeping with one eye open and one foot out of bed! He used to think it would kill him or at least he would be a flop at his job if he did not get a full night of undisturbed sleep. Gradually he learns that young fathers, like young mothers, can adjust to all kinds of temporary inconveniences and still survive.

GETTING ACQUAINTED WITH A NEW SON

Under the new regime, a young father soon learns that a baby takes a tremendous amount of his wife's time and attention. The normal young father will accept this as a mutual venture which will level off as soon as they get past the 2 A.M. feedings and the first few weeks of colic. Under no circumstances will he allow himself to get the idea that he ought to sue this little fellow for alienating his wife's affections. Only an emotionally immature father will generate feelings of jealousy toward his own son. But when this does happen, a young mother finds she has two babies on her hands instead of one.

The mature young father will try to lend a hand wherever possible and learn all he can about this baby business. He gets a big kick out of studying his son and learning from his wife all the things the doctor says to do.

The first thing is learning how to hold a baby. Babies are not only tiny, soft, and helpless, they are hard to hang on to. A new father learns how to hold him with his arms instead of just his hands. He finds a baby should be cradled and cuddled instead of being clutched by the extremities.

A young father soon gets concerned about his little boy's physical well-being and suggests feeding or servicing at frequent intervals. He even supervises the operation occasionally. In the case of a bottle baby the father finds that, with a little patience, he can bottle and burp the baby as well as his wife or mother-in-law. This is a source of supreme satisfaction.

It may take him a while to manage the more complex manipulation of getting his CDS degree—"Changing Diapers Successfully." A father feels a little clumsy at first, especially when it comes to using safety pins. It gives him the shudders to think what would happen if he miscalculated and included a chunk of the baby's pink hide.

BABIES ARE FOR FUN

A few years ago, parents made a chore out of baby care. Today it is done for fun. A baby needs to be enjoyed. He wants to be talked to, smiled at, played with. He cannot be trained or regulated except as Mother Nature provides the equipment, so parents can relax and enjoy this early period. In fact, his physical needs and schedule of operations are "built-in" factors rather than habits to be acquired, so most doctors make liberal allowances for schedules. It also helps to realize that, while babies must be handled gently and kept from rolling off beds, etc., still they are pretty well built for strain. Dr. Benjamin Spock, in *Baby and Child Care,* makes a point of this:

"You have a pretty tough baby. There are many ways to hold him. If his head drops backward by mistake it won't hurt him. The open spot in his skull (the fontanel) is covered by a tough membrane like canvas that isn't easily injured. The system to control his body temperature is working quite well by the time he weighs 7 pounds if he's covered half-way sensibly. He has a good resistance to most germs. During a family cold epidemic he's apt to have it the mildest of all. If he gets his head tangled in anything he has a strong instinct to struggle and yell. If he's not getting enough to eat, he will probably cry for more. If the light is too strong for his eyes, he'll blink and fuss. (You can take his picture with a flash bulb, even if it does make him jump.) He knows how much sleep he needs and takes it. He can care for himself pretty well for a person who can't say a word and knows nothing about the world."

EARLY LESSONS IN CHILD PSYCHOLOGY

Perhaps without quite realizing it, all conscientious parents become students of child psychology. They want answers to at least two questions:

1. *Considering his age, is my child developing normally?*
2. *What causes him to do some things which seem abnormal?*

Since child psychology is simply a study of average child behavior for each particular age, the experts recommend that parents keep the following basic facts in mind:

1. *Qualities in normal children develop at widely different rates; he will be fast in some things, slow in others.*
2. *Rapid development in a normal child does not mean brilliance nor does slow development in a normal child imply dullness.*
3. *The speed of physiological development is "built in" by the original gene pattern. Parents cannot control it any more than the child can.*
4. *Parents should accept a child for what he is—an individual—and help him reach his maximum potential regardless of whether it fits the exact pattern of other children or not.*

In this book, we shall describe the profile of children at various age levels, but this is simply a cross-section study. This must not be anything more than a guide in comparing a specific boy with the average profile for boys his age.

The so-called abnormal behavior of a growing child is usually personality thrust which is *normal for that age*. It simply manifests a boy's anxiety to reach a higher level of activity by breaking down existing barriers or limitations. If a boy and his parents handle these thrust periods properly, they do not become serious problems. Usually, periods of exceptionally strong personality thrust come at 2½, 4, 6, 8, 11, 14, 15, 18, and 19. However, a boy may get behind or in front of his group and set up a different thrust pattern. Once a parent has memorized the characteristics for each age group, it is not difficult to see where a particular boy fits in.

PORTRAIT OF THE FIRST SIX MONTHS

A baby can do lots of things the first day he is born. He will do many more things just as fast as Mother Nature gets the equipment built. This process of building equipment is called *maturation.* It has to do with the construction of physical machinery which takes nearly twenty-four years to complete. Behavior is influenced to a remarkable degree by the amount of working machinery available at each particular age level. Therefore, in raising a child, parents are *not* dealing with a miniature adult who just needs potatoes and gravy and training. They are dealing with a human personality whose body *is not all there!* The margin of tolerance in child training must always make allowances for equipment which is still non-existent or nonfunctioning.

A baby develops from the head downward and from the inside out. The first muscles to show strength, and control will be in the head and neck. During the first month, a baby can raise his head, the second month he can lift up his head and chest, during the fourth month he can sit with support from a pillow, and by the sixth month he can sit in a high chair.

His hands go through a similar development. During the first three months he reaches but misses. By the fifth month, he can reach out and grasp a still object. The sixth month, he can grasp a dangling object.

His eyes are very difficult to control at first, but by the third month the twelve tiny muscles which turn the eyes are strong enough to swing the eyes back and forth with considerable skill. He picks things out for special study. He fixes his gaze on his hand or rattle. He can follow the movement of his mother as she crosses the room. He can begin to distinguish between different people.

His vocal chords are used during the first six months for crying, chortling, and cooing. For two months he cries out with the first little hunger pain. He also cries at the slightest discomfort of wet diapers or being too hot or too cold. Gradually this kind of crying becomes less intense. Feeding time or the need for servicing is preceded by a period of fussing, with his cry being used as a last resort when his small reserve of patience is exhausted. After a month or two he also cries before going to sleep. This is because he is fighting sleep. This will be an established characteristic the rest of his life. As the years pass by, his mother will notice that he becomes irritable whenever he is tired. After he grows up and marries, his wife will notice the same thing. Fatigue and irritability go together as the body hungers for sleep and the wide-awake mind resists it.

HOW THE WORLD LOOKS FROM A BABY'S POINT OF VIEW

If you shut your eyes and plug your ears, you suddenly become aware that the thing which is *you* is inside. This intelligent ego or "I am" looks out through the windows of the eyes, reaches out through the leverage of the arms and hands, moves about with the mighty muscles, bones, and sinews of the legs. As an adult you feel rather at home in the world because you have seen and felt so many things, but as a baby you had not seen, heard, or come to understand anything. Consider, therefore, the marvelous process by which a human intelligence reaches out to discover, interpret, and enjoy the world.

Because the intelligent ego—the part of us that says "I exist"—is buried away in silence and darkness, it must rely exclusively upon the vast network of organs, muscles, and communication systems to discover what is outside. At birth, the physical system is so sluggish that signals are barely perceptible. Sound comes through merely as noise. The eyes register light but not objects. Gradually the ears become more sensitive to sound so that the intelligent ego distinguishes between pleasant sounds and frightening or irritating sounds. The eyes become stronger and begin to send a more accurate signal to the brain defining form, color, and movement. The millions of sensory nerves on the skin register heat, cold, and pressure. The taste buds, consisting of five separate systems, register sweet, sour, bitter, salty, and metallic tastes. The nerve endings on the roof of the nasal passages distinguish six kinds of smells: spices, flowers, fruits, resin, scorching, putrification.

All of these signals go pouring into the brain where they are recorded, evaluated, and used by the intelligent ego to find out just what is going on "outside" and just what "it" wants to do about it. It helps to watch yourself dealing with a new experience to see just how the intelligent ego works. This process of "watching yourself think" is called introspection. Supposing you are visiting Africa for the first time, and while walking down a jungle trail you hear a high-pitched scream far above you in the treetops. You immediately begin talking to yourself "inside." You say, "What is that? Is something about to spring upon me?" Your eyes range through the treetops, trying to find the source of the noise. Trained fingers grip the powerful gun and hold it in readiness. Then you hear the scream again. The eyes shift to the place where your ears indicate the noise is coming from. "There it is!" The screamer turns out to be a medium-sized multicolored bird with a long beautiful tail. The image flashed to the brain indicates no long claws, no powerful beak, no frightening size. The intelligent ego does not recognize the creature from any past experience, but classifies it merely as some kind of bird which does not appear dangerous. The decision is made not to shoot. This is typical of how each of us learn "about the world." When we recognize how complicated we are and how much we depend upon our sensory machinery for accurate signals, we can better appreciate the handicaps of a baby whose machinery is just beginning to function.

PORTRAIT OF A BABY DURING THE SECOND SIX MONTHS

By the age of 6 months, the muscles in a baby's neck and shoulders are sufficiently developed to support his roly-poly head. The nerves and muscles in his arms are also gaining strength and tone so that he can not only grasp things, but change them from one hand to another. The fingers are the last to develop, but, by the time he is 9 months old, each finger is an instrument for probing, poking, pinching, and pulling. It is interesting to watch him use his fingers to "feel things." His brain is gaining impressions of rough, smooth, hard, soft, wet, hot, cold, or ticklish for each of the objects he grabs.

Usually by the seventh month he can sit alone, and a short time later he will stand with help. By the time he is 10 months old he begins to creep. Shortly afterward, he becomes a scooter. Sometimes he uses the posterior slide, sometimes the crab crawl, but either way he's mobile.

By this time his leg muscles have developed until he literally aches to be up on his feet. He bounces up and down on his mother's lap and pulls himself up by the bars of his playpen. He is only a few months away from walking.

The eyes have been going through a similar development. During the second six months, they send through good images, so that a baby can distinguish different members of the family and respond accordingly. He may be startled by the sudden appearance of a stranger and set up a real howl of alarm, especially if the stranger tries to give him the coochy-coo treatment while lisping baby talk. In time he will warm up to a stranger, but only after a proper security check.

The vocal chords, tongue, and lips are gradually co-ordinating so that by six months a baby will entertain himself with jabbering and cooing. At around the tenth month he will say his first word—usually "mama" or "da-da." This delights new parents no end.

The second sixth months is a real adventure stage. He tries his luck at all kinds of things; sitting, scooting, standing, talking, feeling, and tasting. This last item perturbs parents. As the little fellow starts maneuvering about the floor, he latches onto everything and immediately puts it in his mouth. This will include rug fuzz, bits of paper, mousetraps, dropped food, sticks, and dirt. Nothing is sacred. It has to be tasted.

THE FIRST BIRTHDAY

A 1-year-old can look back on a year of furious achievement. He has more than doubled his weight. His brain has increased about 30 per cent in weight, and he is no longer the helpless little bundle of humanity that he used to be. He can now say several words, and he can understand simple commands. He recognizes the signals in different tones of the human voice. He can circulate around the house on all fours or his seater, and he can pull himself up to examine books, ceramics, or doilies on couches or coffee tables.

He has a wider interest span than previously, and can amuse himself with simple toys for long periods at a time. He likes to watch people and will lie still while being changed just because he wants to see what is happening.

The parents may not know it, but the gentle, lovable, helpless age of the first 12 months is not only ending, but also the honeymoon period that went with it. Junior is almost ready to move out into the happy hunting ground of a harum-scarum 1-year-old.

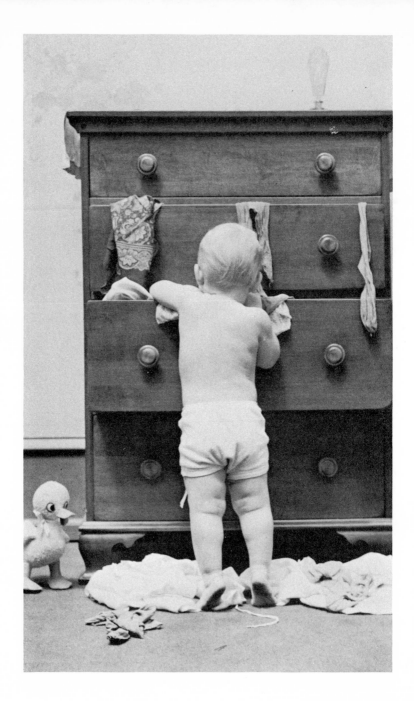

CHAPTER 3

THE CHUBBY LITTLE CHERUB

Patterns and Problems of the 1-Year-Old

Puppies, little pigs, colts, calves, and chicks all have their "cute" stage. Babies have theirs between one and two.

"Chubby Little Cherub" describes a boy during this period. He is curvaceous, well padded, and dimpled. Right after his evening bath, when he enjoys scooting around the house in his birthday suit, his radiant, roly-poly body has all the pink softness of a figure in a Renaissance painting.

He also has the personality to go with it. This is one of those periods when parents get more than they expect. They are accustomed to the helplessness of the previous year and are amazed at the rapid advancement during the Chubby Cherub stage. Almost before they know it, he can walk, talk, start feeding himself, help with his clothes, get into all kinds of mischief, and play the part of the family social lion.

THE MOBILE MIDGET

The two most significant qualities of a Chubby Cherub are mobility and independence. He starts the year as a scooter-creeper-crawler, but by his thirteenth month he is pulling himself up and using furniture or his stroller to circulate around. Often during his fourteenth month, he has that exciting, breathless experience of actually standing alone. He knows he is playing the daredevil as he balances precariously on his two little flat feet and responds to the bravos of his proud parents. Once he has practiced a few stand-ups by himself, it is just a matter of days until he stumbles forward and takes those first few steps. By fifteen months, he may be toddling.

A toddler does not walk erect. He leans forward with shoulders hunched, stomach protruding. His arms do not swing back and forth but spread out and back. His posture implies that he feels "falling" is part of "walking," so he maintains a state of preparedness for any unexpected collapse.

However, once a Cherub has achieved toddling status, nothing is sacred. Flat surfaces seem to arouse his utter disdain. Therefore, he takes to climbing. Before his parents even realize his capabilities, he has "cased the joint" upstairs and down. Soon he will be up on chairs, then climbing pulled-out drawers and, the next thing they know, he will have explored the most remote parental hideaways. During the latter part of the Chubby Cherub stage he has a particular proclivity for finding loaded guns, rat poison, paint thinner, lye, powerful medicines, and secretly hidden Christmas presents.

A Cherub's pride in being able to get around independently is exhibited on out-of-door excursions when he is around 18 months. If parents hold out a finger for him to grasp, he often shrugs his shoulders and swaggers away with total indifference. At age 2 he may be willing to take a parental hand just for the sake of companionship, but there is a certain air of condescension in it.

He also exhibits his independence by preferring to push his carriage or stroller rather than ride. He will push it forward then backward. When there is a shopping tour or a trip around the block he may once more express interest in riding. It is too early for a tricycle for riding. He will be nearly 3 before he can pedal such a vehicle.

A BABY'S HOUSE

Perhaps it is appropriate at this point to mention a word or two about the house. When Junior becomes a toddling Cherub, something begins happening to the house. Of course, when the baby first arrived, everything became partly his, including the house; but now a Cherub acts as though the house were all his. In fact, he will be nearly 6 before he learns how to share the house with his parents. For the present, fine books, ceramics, doilies, pots, pans, perfumes, potted plants, pianos, chairs, records, dishes, and dainties are all monopolized as part of his own exclusive personal domain. One suspects that the reason he climbs so much is simply to find out what else the folks may be hiding from him. In any event, he must scrutinize every single item as though he were the U. S. Bureau of Standards. Every object coming under his scrutiny must be tried, tested, tasted, and, where possible, destroyed (how else can you test things?).

Some young parents have heard of the destructive proclivities of a 1-year-old and so they decide to *train* their boy to be different. They resolve to teach him how to appreciate nice books, expensive vases, beautiful needlework, mahogany furniture, fragile drapes, and delicately designed wallpaper. Usually, after their third bottle of tranquilizers, they give up. It usually happens some night after they go through the house surveying the crayon artwork on the wallpaper, the sagging "lifetime" furniture, the little marks, scars, and stains that defy removal. They decide to throw themselves on the mercy of their pediatrician, "Why have we failed?" The good doctor has some sage advice: "Don't surround a child with things he lacks the capacity to understand and protect. Furnish the house so the baby can enjoy it, and so you can enjoy the baby!"

He may point out that for those who are determined to defy nature, there is the gruesome prospect of continually replacing books, vases, and ceramics; of continually refilling the overturned wastebaskets; of constantly finding the bathmat pulled from the tub into a heap on the floor; of finding doilies, newspapers, magazines, or anything on a table, pulled off; of discovering every dresser drawer raided, every linen closet shelf denuded.

One set of experienced parents declared, "When we were first married we resolved that no child of ours was going to force us to change our way of life by having to put away all of our expensive wedding gifts and nice things. Today, however, at our

house, you will find that below shoulder level it is like the Sahara Desert!"

They also added, "When we were first married our hardwood floors looked like the top of a grand piano. Today, the top of our piano looks like the floor!"

Perhaps this is a bit of humorous exaggeration, but nevertheless a house in which babies are being raised is not an art gallery, a stuffy museum, or a showplace. It is more like a factory where you expect a certain amount of confusion and clutter as part of the "production process."

BEGINNING THE "DO IT YOURSELF" STAGE

All through the Chubby Cherub stage we see evidence of a desire to be independent. When a 1-year-old has a dish of food placed near him he will seize it and throw it, but often before he is 2 he will demand the spoon and try to feed himself from the dish. He only gets what food clings to the spoon, but he tries. The same spirit arouses him to action when his pants are wet or soiled. He sets about to get 'em off right now.

Part of the baby's do-it-yourself learning process includes the discovery of gravity. He is tremendously fascinated as he watches his toys fall from the high chair. Usually his mother promptly returns the toy and he gets the idea this is a game. Eventually he will substitute food for his toys. He likes to watch the effect of gravity on things like potatoes and gravy. They splash. The game of gravity is exciting as long as his mother continues to pick up the toys or mop up the food. He thinks it is interesting the way she grunts every time she stoops. If he has his way, she will soon be in a stooping stupor.

DEVELOPING A SOCIAL SENSE

A tiny baby can be scared by a stranger, but by the time he reaches the Cherub stage he is real folksy. He trusts people and uses his favorite word of "Ma-ma" to greet everything that wears dresses and calls out "Daddy!" to the milkman, postman, or any other kind of man. He does a lot of jabbering at people.

As far as he can tell, they are jabbering at him so he jabbers right back. He gets so he can interpret voice tones and facial expressions. He tries to mimic these. When people laugh, he laughs. He often watches his mother when she talks to him and she finds herself talking to him as though he understood every word.

In the early Cherub stage he can be placed in a backyard playpen with a few fit-together toys and be happy for a couple of hours. Later he needs to be on the front porch where he can see the people and cars go by. Gradually his eyes are reaching out where later his feet will want to go.

A Cherub's growing social sense, together with his "do it yourself" sense, make him want to participate in getting things done. He develops an embryonic sense of duty. It pleases him to do his little part. He will insist on closing a door, fetching a pair of house slippers, closing a cupboard, turning on the TV or radio, flushing the toilet, or using his pudgy little hand to mop up a puddle. He will participate in "putting things away"—especially things that have a container, like Tinker Toys or blocks.

However, when it comes to other children, neither his social sense nor his sense of duty will aid him. He pulls, pinches, and pushes them as though they were something inanimate. He will treat them as play*things,* but not play*mates.* If there are no adults he prefers to play alone.

THE BEDTIME PATTERN OF A CHERUB

Children never appear more angelic than when they are asleep —especially a Cherub. But to achieve this angelic state can be exasperating. Usually the chore of getting him ready for bed comes between six and seven o'clock just when dinner and many other tasks are pressing upon his mother. She therefore tends to give him "the bum's rush," and he knows it. He takes a little while to wind down.

At age 1 he may wind down while nursing a bottle. If he is extra tired, he may fall asleep without a whimper. By 15 months the ritual of "kissing and covering up" is well-nigh useless since he winds down by walking around the crib and having a jabber session with himself from twenty minutes to two hours. When he finally curls up, it will be in some remote corner of the crib—seldom where he's supposed to be, because he goes to sleep accidentally while still trying to resist.

By 1½ he may insist on something to play with or talk to while settling down. This may be his teddy bear, his shoe, a toothbrush, or some rubber toy. In addition to this he may whimper for attention from his mother. When she finally breaks away from stirring the gravy, cutting up a salad, broiling steak, or some other dinner-getting operation, she usually has a note of exasperation in her voice as she hurries to the crib, demanding, "What's the matter?"

A Cherub discovers that it helps to have some alibi. He therefore uses whatever comes off the top of his head. Sometimes he wants a drink, sometimes it's "toidy," other times he wants a cracker, nose-blow, cover-up, or a kiss. If it's "toidy," he is often unsuccessful the first time, although he may have sensations of real need. After the second or third attempt (with his mother's temperature rising with each new failure) he is finally successful, and then goes to sleep with deep sighs of relief and a strong sense of accomplishment.

Between 21 months and age 2, his presleep demands continue to grow. This is a good time to get his motor into neutral by telling him simple little stories. At first playing "This little pig went to market" on his toes is sufficient. Later, he loves to hear his mother tell about the Three Bears and talk to him even when he has only a vague idea of what she is saying. The rising cadence in her voice is exciting to him, and the soft, level tones are soothing. She uses the first to get his attention and the latter to lull him away into slumberland.

If a Cherub is highly active by natural construction, he may use his presleep period for jumping, bouncing, rolling, and tumbling. He may also insist on seeing his father for a "hug and a kiss," especially if he has been put to bed before the head man gets home from work. A little boy at this age is very responsive to his father. He likes the change after being with his mother all day. However, if he is distressed, depressed, or in some kind of trouble, only his mother will do. If he could talk he might say, "Nothing against you, Dad; it's just that fathers are for fun. Trouble requires the know-how of a mama."

Wake-up time for a Chubby Cherub is a time of slow, pleasant awakening. He lies very quiet for twenty to thirty minutes talking softly to himself. Then his little fingers become active. He may suck the thumb on one hand while picking fuzz off the blanket with the other. Pretty soon he will get up and start where he left off the night before, playing with his teddy bear or toys. Or he may take a casual stroll around his crib by going hand over hand around the sides. It is surprising how long he can remain contented when he first wakes up—even when he's wet.

PECULIARITIES OF A CHUBBY CHERUB

There are several humorous and peculiar qualities which pop up in the personality of Chubby Cherub.

He is particularly sensitive about his indelicate tendency to embarrass himself with wet or soiled pants. Parents usually add to his worry by also urging him to do better. Dr. Arnold Gesell mentions what can happen when a little fellow at this stage of life is caught in the company of a telltale puddle: "The child will point to the puddle and say 'ooh-ooh' as though it were quite awful; and when asked, 'Who did it?' he may blame it on the cat or his grandfather."

Another peculiarity is his tendency to be a stripper. Beginning at about 21 months, a Cherub likes to undress himself. Every neighborhood has seen a sedate young mother frantically running out into the backyard to scoop up a little Cherub who is brazenly strutting about the yard with nary a stitch. Later he will do the same thing in the front yard! If given half a chance, he will stroll down the middle of the main thoroughfare. He thinks he's baby Godiva without a horse.

A Chubby Cherub is also like a little bug on a hop stick. He is so fascinated by all the new things he is learning to do that he jumps about from one activity to another. He runs over and grabs a doll, hugs it, drops it, or drags it by one leg to an electric wall plug; the plug is scrutinized. It has such fascinating little holes that something ought to be found to stick into them. He goes looking for something but is distracted by a magazine rack. He bungles through a couple of the latest issues, tearing out a random page here and there. He then goes to check up on his mother but, while wandering through the house, manages to pull a lot of gismos and gadgets to the floor like doilies, newspapers, a blanket on the couch, or a pillow on the bed. An electric clock catches his attention so he takes it down to see what makes the second hand sweep round. He pounds on it to make it stop, and then with great gusto throws it to the floor. Going through the kitchen, he spies the cat which secretly thinks of him as "the mad mauler." In the nick of time she makes a belly-to-floor takeoff that propels her out of reach. He chases her briefly but is easily outmaneuvered because at this age he cannot turn corners without falling down.

Finally, there is the instinctive response to rhythm which makes a Chubby Cherub want to dance. He looks like a little elf as he starts to swing and sway with the TV, radio, or when someone starts to sing. If an adult catches him at it he may immediately stop. On other occasions he will watch older children dance and try to mimic them.

THE CHUBBY CHERUB'S JOY OF LIVING

As he approaches 2 a Cherub is showing signs of getting on in the world. He is usually around thirty-three inches in height and pushing the scales up to approximately twenty-seven pounds. If we sit down and count the words he uses, it may surprise us to find nearly 275. They will be mostly names of things, persons, activities, or predicaments he gets into. Some slow talkers (with equally brilliant futures) will postpone their vocabulary building until a later time.

We notice that he sometimes rushes in with the breathless announcement that he has to go to the bathroom. This is a welcome development for his mother, but she must not expect this control to be complete for several months yet. She will notice how he likes to hear her enthusiastic approval when he wakes up dry, but he must not be told he is "naughty" in case he happens to be wet. At this stage, control is almost entirely physiological and must wait until further maturation of muscle and nerve centers before the mind can exercise genuine control.

He will still suck his thumb, but the doctor says we don't worry about that any more because scientists have found out that thumbsucking is a natural instinct rather than a bad habit. It will pass in due time. The doctor assures us that, unless Junior's thumbsucking becomes excessively prolonged, it will not damage his mouth, teeth, or personality. As Dr. A. P. Sperling puts it: "Thumbsucking relieves an infant's tensions and stimulates the sensitive membranes of the mouth pleasantly. When children are overtired, sleepy, hungry, sick, or teething, the amount of finger-sucking increases. Thumbsucking will not cause 'buck' teeth or facial deformity if the habit stops before the age of six. Scolding a child for thumbsucking will make him feel guilt, which he will try to relieve by more thumbsucking. It is more effective to keep him well fed and to provide him with adequate toys to occupy his hands and fingers."

By the age of 2 we are accustomed to having our Cherub dart about the house in one continuous orgy of curious exploration and ceaseless activity. Therefore we are non-plussed when he suddenly turns dawdler. This usually occurs when we want him to eat, get undressed, go to the bathroom, or do any number of things which are gradually being identified in his mind as *tedious*. This resistance to the routine things of life is a new insight, which is necessary for him to feel before he can move up to the next level of being reconciled to the disciplines of orderly living. *Nearly all phases of human progression begin with an initial period of resistance.* Dawdling during babyhood is a symptom of mental growth, although parents may become convinced that it is Junior's attempt to shorten their own span of life.

A Chubby Cherub will always be remembered for his joy of living. He is an acrobat and loves a rough and tumble session with his dad; he is a clown and will dance and jump and clap his hands; he is a comedian and will gurgle and guffaw at his own antics. He likes to go up and down stairs, and when in a hurry will do a little step dance on each stair before ascending or descending to the next. Every muscle in his body seems to shout, "Spring me, boy, spring me!" Even his little tongue aches to exercise itself and all the while his legs are rodding around the house and his little hands are roaming about in every sort of Cherubic mischief, his slippery little tongue will be burbling away with a lot of nonsensical jargon, salted and peppered with an occasional bit of English.

A 2-year-old is gaining in muscular control. He can string beads, make scissors snip paper, turn a picture book a page at a time, pile blocks twice as high as he could at 18 months, and sometimes hold his glass of milk with one hand. He still has trouble with a spoon, but clearly indicates that he's going to make that scoop shovel work if it takes him another year, and it nearly does.

All in all, the age of the Chubby Cherub is a gloriously happy and lovable one. It sets the stage for the great new era which lies directly ahead, the "Age of No Reason."

CHAPTER 4

THE AGE OF NO REASON

Patterns and Problems of the 2-Year-Old

When a boy has reached the age of "no reason" his parents may think he has reached a stage of "no mind." They can explain things to him, get him to agree completely, and the next thing they know he's doing the very opposite. "Why doesn't he mind?" they wail. "Why doesn't he carry through with what he agrees is right?"

They may even go so far as to secretly wonder about his brain power. "Is he normal?" Time will teach them that he has plenty of brain power and it is geared to one of the most active mental periods of his entire lifeline. They will also discover that this is a period when Junior just loves to hear his mama explain what she wants out of life. He hopes she gets it. Meanwhile, back at the playpen, Junior wants out so he can get his!

PORTRAIT OF A TWO-YEAR-OLD

A robust 2-year-old is motivated mostly by what tastes good, looks good, feels good, sounds good, or smells good. His brain power is designed for the almost exclusive purpose of satisfying his own physical needs. To be dry, well fed, not too hot, not too cold, well entertained, and well rested, these are the objectives of his entire immediate existence.

No doubt Providence intended that this should be a year of self-centered dynamics. A baby has a lot of ground to cover between his twenty-fourth and thirty-sixth month among men. Vast improvements in walking and talking are in order. This is the year he will learn to run. This is the year he will learn nearly all of the rudiments of his parents' language. And if his parents thought he was a curiosity bug last year, they will think he is a full-grown super-snooper this year. It is one continuous round of climbing, searching, testing, and checking. As a graduate from the Chubby Cherub stage, he is more methodical about emptying drawers, giving everything a good shake, messing things up more completely. As he cases the kitchen cupboards he removes all the pots, pans, trays, lids, food grinders, and salad choppers. He likes to fit things together. He pounds on them, slams them together, patiently puts pans inside of each other, and then takes them out again.

He continues to examine all the good books in the house to test the durability of their paper and binding. He is intrigued with a book that tears easily. Tearing out pictures is especially satisfying.

Last year he was curious about electric light plugs, but this year he is drawn toward them with a hypnotic allure. He loves to put nails or hairpins into the cute little holes.

Last year he broke ceramics accidentally. This year it is deliberate. They are so shiny, slick, and pretty. He finds them fun to handle, but after a while he uses an improvised hammer to see how tough they are. Small bits go flying off, or huge chunks crack or break away. This is most interesting.

When it comes to people, this is the year of playing the recluse. Last year he was friendly toward visitors. This year he embarrasses his parents by racing away or, if they pull him back, he stands in the middle of the room like a scared little elf, pigeon-toed, finger in mouth, chin on chest, eyes glued to the floor. And he cannot be jollied out of it. But he loves children. Last year he pulled, poked, and punched at children as if they were toys. This year he is delighted with children his own age and greets them by jumping up and down for joy.

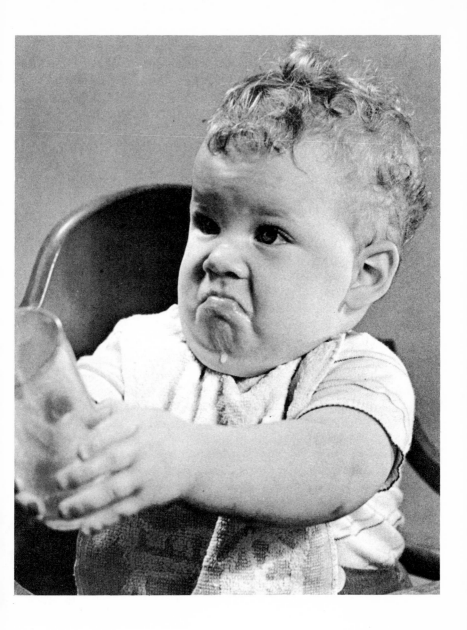

THE DISCOVERY OF HUMAN FREEDOM

Much of the tribulation of the "age of no reason" is the adjustment of both the parents and the boy to this business of learning how to deal with freedom. Early in life, a child learns the exciting independence of "doing just what he feels like doing." This thrilling discovery of human freedom is soon overshadowed by a second discovery: "There is no freedom except under law."

This simply means that when people are living together, common freedoms must be protected by a law or nobody has any freedom. A good example of this is the freedom to use a public highway. If everybody were allowed to do whatever he felt like doing, then some would drive to the right, some to the left, some would weave back and forth. The freedom to drive on the highway would be lost to all. Therefore, the traffic laws do not take away freedom, they protect freedom of the highway from being destroyed by the thoughtless and the selfish. And this is why we have so many laws, *to protect our many freedoms:* freedom to buy, freedom to sell, freedom to invent, freedom to travel, freedom to enjoy the privacy of one's home, freedom from crime, freedom from fraud, freedom from attack by a foreign nation, freedom of speech, freedom from slander, freedom to worship, freedom to assemble, and so forth.

This, then, becomes the object of civilization, to teach a child to enjoy all the freedom possible, but to do it within the law. To achieve this a child must learn two things:

First, a child must know that if he disobeys the law there is a force *outside* of himself which takes hold of him and leaves some kind of impact on him so that he can remember to refrain from destroying the freedom of his neighbors in the future. With adults, this is usually a fine or imprisonment. With children this "outside force" rests in the parents to minister discipline when it is necessary.

Second, there is an *inside* force—inside of each human being—which we try to develop until each person provides his own discipline and chooses voluntarily to live within the law. This second principle is simply "cultivating a sound moral and ethical sense." Naturally, it is far better to raise a child to live a peaceful, orderly life because he wants to rather than because he has to. However, self-control and self-government usually take many years to develop. There are several reasons why a little fellow between 2 and 3 has difficulty with "freedom under law."

First of all, he is by natural construction all for freedom but not much for law. His spirit of the jungle must gradually bow to the legally protected freedoms of an orderly society. He begins by learning to obey the rules and regulations of his own family.

In the second place, a boy of this age is suffering from certain mental limitations which make it difficult for him to concentrate on more than one thing at a time. If he comes running into the house with a live angleworm, it is literally impossible for him to remember the rules about never slamming the doors and never walking on mother's newly scrubbed floor. Anyway, doors and floors are not as important as angleworms.

The third thing which bothers a boy is the fact that the rules and regulations always appear to be somebody else's idea. In middle childhood he is able to put it into words as he thrusts out his quivering chin and says, "Ain't this a free world?" He simply means that his idea of a free world is doing what *he* wants to instead of worrying about "all those darn rules that somebody else is always making up!"

HOW A TWO-YEAR-OLD LEARNS TO MAKE CHOICES

In view of what we have said thus far, it will be easy to understand why psychologists say that solving a boy's problems at this stage usually calls for direct action rather than long parental lectures. A good example of what they mean will occur when a mother tells a 2½-year-old not to go into the street. He listens, understands, and then deliberately disobeys. If he were able to explain why, he would simply say, "I wanted to."

"But Mommy doesn't want you to!"

The toss of his head and shrug of his shoulders is Junior's way of saying, "Well, you live your life and I'll live mine!"

A mother learns that when a little fellow races away toward

the street, it is no time for moaning about his disobedience or "reasoning" with him. Instead, she races after him, swoops him up in her arms, and firmly returns him to safety. Her little boy suddenly realizes that "the outside force" we mentioned a moment ago has just taken over.

The presence of this outside force, "parental supervision," is extremely important during this particular period because a boy has a highly efficient system of locomotion but not the judgment or experience to go with it. He therefore stumbles into all kinds of danger. This is the age when irrigation ditches, busy streets, old wellshafts, and abandoned refrigerators all have an alluring fascination. This is no time to turn a little fellow loose and assume he will have sense enough to take care of himself. His choice of activities between 2 and 3 need the watchful eyes and ready hand of a nearby parent.

Of course, there are a few choices a 2-year-old will make which a parent can't do much about. A good example often occurs at mealtime. A mother will labor all afternoon to fix a nice dinner, and then after everyone is seated around the table she suddenly discovers that Junior is rejecting the entire menu and holding out for crisp bacon and coddled eggs. Or, if he is offered strained green beans, he may just happen to be hankering for strained yellow carrots. And a strained, tired mother may learn from experience that there is nothing disgraceful about putting the beans back in the refrigerator and getting out the carrots. If she tries to reason with him or insist that he eat the beans, he is likely to respond by suddenly seizing the dish and dumping the whole mess on the floor. It is his way of saying, "Scuttle that stuff and get out the carrots!"

Sometimes a mother will present the problem to the family doctor, and she may be surprised to hear him suggest that, where eating is concerned, it is all right to go along with his whims.

"And *spoil* him?" she gasps.

"No," replies the doctor. "He just needs to be assured that he is capable of making choices of his own. A few months from now he will welcome suggestions." Thus we learn to be parents.

THE AGE OF TANTRUMS

We have called the period of 2 to 3 the "Age of No Reason." Perhaps it would be more accurate to call the age of *his* reason. As we have mentioned earlier, he resents having to make his brain available to his parents. Parents therefore learn various techniques to get Junior to do what they want him to do by making him feel that it was his idea in the first place.

Nevertheless, there are times when no strategy seems to work as a parent locks horns with the dictatorial defiance of a robust 2½-year-old. At first a boy will try to argue back with his meager vocabulary of two hundred words. When he fails to get his point across he feels abused, frustrated, imposed upon, and ready to explode. Eventually, he discovers a method of arguing back with a stubborn parent which produces results. This consists of throwing himself on the ground, kicking his toes into the dirt, and screaming so fiercely the neighbors think his mother is murdering him. From experience Junior learns that this gets a marvelous reaction from his parents. He notices how their dignity disappears, how their voices tremble. He hears them plead, beg, and bribe him to please stop. It is infant blackmail. It is called a tantrum.

The child psychologist will assure the frenzied parents that there is only one known cure for a tantrum and that is by *distraction*. The first step is to try and make the desired response reasonable to *him*. For example, "Come on, let's go in the house and wash our hands *because Daddy's coming home!*" If this doesn't work, the only alternative is to go into action. A wise mother will simply pick Junior up bodily, flowersack him on her hip, and pack him into the bathroom. In between open-mouthed bellows she will wash his face and hands with a nice warm cloth and then transport him to the kitchen. There, the change of scenery or the smell of good food will usually stop the howling. In this respect, he may be very much like his father!

So the key to dissolving a tantrum is not discussion, but distraction, unless, of course, the discussion involves a distraction. Experience soon teaches parents what works best for each of their children.

Occasionally, parents who are raising healthy boys find themselves pressed beyond the brink of endurance and resort to a form of distraction which is applied a few inches below Junior's tailbone. This should only be used as a last resort and only after Junior is well aware from two or three warnings that the lightning is eventually going to have to strike. New parents will often be amazed to see how much good a well-applied, well-deserved spanking can do. It seems to release a lot of tight springs, and the little fellow who has just had the treatment will often return in a few moments to put his arms around the parent who did the spanking and act as though nothing had happened. In a subtle way, it has taught him that he lives in an orderly world. It is also the way a child learns that he "matters" to his parents.

THE FOOD STRIKE

Somewhere between 2½ and 3½ a boy will go on a food strike. Not only will he refuse to eat, but his loving mother thinks she can see the visible and tragic effects of his food strike. She sees the roly-poly baby fat and dimples begin to disappear, and her baby starts to take on the characteristics of a string-bean pole. Frantically, she starts begging him to eat. Father joins her for a duet. They try to spoon-feed him, they even eat the majority of it themselves, trying to prove how good it is. Then they get to the desperate stage where they start promising him double desserts, staying up to see the late TV show, or going to see his favorite movie cowboy at the Saturday matinee. Many of these bribes are over his innocent little head, but he definitely has a hunch that he is unexpectedly in a very strong bargaining position.

When the frantic parents finally go to the doctor to see whether this new phenomenon is caused by worms or germs, they usually get the answer that all is well. Mother Nature is simply using Junior's surplus baby fat to make into bone and sinew. While this is going on, his appetite is about as dainty as a hummingbird's.

At times it would be more appropriate to compare it to the dodo bird—extinct. The parents are assured that, when the time is right, Junior will return to his victuals with great gusto. Meanwhile, his food strike may continue for as much as two years.

THE AGE OF RITUALS

We should also mention that during this period when the little king is imposing his omnipotence upon the whole family, he is likely to come up with one more oddity—he displays a passion for certain rituals. He must have a certain spoon, his birthday cup and his blue dish, and they must be arranged a certain way, or he will not eat. When he goes to bed he must have his old worn-out crib blanket, his armless, dragged-about, one-eyed doll, and the hall light left on with the door open, or he will not go to sleep.

He even has to go to the bathroom a certain way. He has to be enthroned a certain way, with his favorite little chair, or a certain toy to hold during the operation. And he may insist that everyone leave until he is ready for them to return.

The doctor tells anxious parents that these rituals are important to him because it is his first appreciation of "living in an orderly world." At the moment he is doing all the ordering, but it makes him feel so good when everything is just right that parents can hardly help but go along with him, as they should. Another year or so and the importance of these rituals will have begun to fade.

THE IMPORTANCE OF T.L.C.

It is during the thrust period of age 2 to 3 that parents must remind themselves occasionally of the importance of T.L.C.—*tender loving care.* This is a term used in children's hospitals and elsewhere to designate a kind of soul medicine which is to be given to children in liberal doses every day.

Of course, it is also true that frequently a child is in need of love and understanding when he is the *least* lovable and *least* understanding himself. Age 2½ is a period of perpetual motion for a boy, and frequently parents spend most of their time "shushing" him or giving him the "don't" treatment:

"Don't go outside!"

"Don't tip over the chairs!"

"Don't climb up in the cupboards!"

"Don't turn up the TV so loud!"

"Don't eat stuff off the floor!"

"Don't dump your Tinker Toys in the living room!"

"Don't take off your clothes!"

"Don't go to the bathroom outside!"

"Don't slam the door!"

If parents are not careful, their energies all go into "don't" and they forget to take time out every so often to swoop up the little guy for a shower of hugs and kisses.

T.L.C. can also be good medicine—if used in time—to head off a tantrum. Therefore, parents learn to watch the psychology of a 2½-year-old and detect the first signs of a rising storm. They notice that during one of these moods he is easily antagonized and that if they can jolly him a little and otherwise get his mind off himself by going for a ride, to the store, watching TV, or playing a game, the storm signals will often pass. On the other hand, if the winds in his brain begin to roar and the waves of anger and defiance beat against the shore, the parent may have to ride out the storm; at least, ride it out as long as it can be endured. But then, if all the distractions and lures available to the parent fail and the little dictator finally has to be shocked back into a state of reality with a little paddling, the storm must be followed in due time by a liberal dose of T.L.C. The child will usually indicate when he is ready to be loved and comforted, but if it is not forthcoming within a reasonable time, the parent will want to go to him and make the first conciliatory gesture.

When children love, it is "all out," and love should be reciprocated by parents in the same spirit. A child can easily detect someone who "just goes through the motions" of being a loving parent. They sense the genuine love of the parent who tells them stories, exhibits interest in a tower of blocks being built, draws pictures for them, or wrestles them around on a soft bed amidst shouts of glee and hilarity. Then, in addition to that, they feel a warm glow inside when they are just picked up and hugged. They may kick and resist when first picked up because the parent has interrupted what they were doing, but if they have just done something extra cute or lovable, it is a good time to follow the natural instinct to pick them up and tell them how wonderful you think they are.

END OF A PHASE

By the end of the "Age of No Reason," we have a remarkably developed boy. In spite of all the fuss and fury, the tantrums and teasing, he has been moving along rapidly to a new comprehension of life which will soon become satisfying to both himself and his parents. Our "baby" is passing from infancy to early childhood, and with it will come the first tiny glimmers of warm and glorious light portending the dawning of Junior's "Age of Reason."

CHAPTER 5

THE BEGINNING OF CHILDHOOD

Patterns and Problems of the 3-Year-Old

As each little fellow completes his third year of life on earth he will suddenly change his personality from that of a caterpillar to a butterfly. It comes as quite a surprise to his bewildered parents. They will be struggling valiantly through the tantrum stage and wondering why their cute little boy can be such a hoodlum at times, when unexpectedly it happens. Without logic or explanation, Mother Nature unceremoniously plops Junior clear up on top of a brand-new behavioral plateau. In later life all the parents can recall is that one morning they awakened with Junior looking up at them from his tiny world of childhood as though to say, "Relax, folks. Everything's going to be all right now!"

Immediately, his parents are astonished by his sudden coming of age, by his new comprehension, his spirit of co-operation, his obvious desire to gain approval. They notice that he has acquired a new skill in dressing himself, feeding himself, and otherwise entertaining or taking care of himself. His tantrums become far less frequent. They even discover they can *reason* with him on almost any subject. Naturally, his parents can't help bragging a bit. As they contemplate the almost unbelievable transition they confide to each other, "Well, just look what we did!"

PORTRAIT OF A THREE-YEAR-OLD

However, Mother Nature gets most of the credit for what happens to Junior as he "comes of age" at 3. All through his growing-up days he will have brief periods of *arriving*. Age 3 is one of these. He gains more confidence—on his feet and in his head. He can run, turn corners, and dodge. When he walks he stands erect and his arms swing naturally back and forth. He does simple tricks on furniture or the tricky bars. He does acrobatics on the living room rug.

He is also quite a talker and he can understand grownups better. His vocabulary will be several hundred words now—sometimes as many as a thousand. And his mother becomes fully aware of it as he bombards her with questions from morning until night. By actual count, children have been known to ask as many as three hundred questions in a single day! Many of these questions start out with "why." He is not really asking for explanations as much as dissertations. He wants to be told about life and about things.

"Why do elephants have long noses?"

Some mothers may think they should go into a long explanation, but a wise mother will simply say, "Isn't it nice that elephants have long trunks so they can reach out and get a peanut from your hand?" Immediately, 3-year-old Junior is all ears. "And when an elephant is in the jungle he uses his big long trunk to reach up into the trees for food, or pick up grass from the ground. He even uses his trunk to drink water—like a soda straw!"

In between question sessions, a 3-year-old darts about the house with boundless energy. If there is a stairs he runs up and down in a breathless frenzy. His constant "on-the-double" running about has little immediate purpose, but his eyes and ears take in everything. In fact, his ears can hear many things his parents will miss—the distant bark of a dog, a faraway factory whistle, the faint wailing of a siren. He races about the house grasping anything which happens to be loose. And he tries to do something with any and all seized objects. What he wants it to do is usually in violent opposition to what it was made to do. He is death on goldfish at this age. He will wreck an aquarium of expensive tropical fish in a fifteen-minute orgy of squealing, splashing delight.

This is a period when color, shape, and sound are becoming important. A particular toy truck is a favorite because it is red, or a certain set of building blocks is always out and underfoot because he likes their shape. He enjoys music. Sometimes an automatic record player will lull him into a pleasant nap when nothing else will even keep him in bed.

He likes good company too, especially grownups, and delights to have them respond to his antics. For this reason he is often remarkably obedient and "reasonable," which comes as a shock to the people who just herded him through the "Age of No Reason."

All in all, a 3-year-old is still in part of his "cute" state. It is not only his looks but the personality and poise which go with it. From Junior's point of view, the adult reaction he gets at this stage is favorable. He can tell by the tone of adult voices, the way they call attention to things he is doing, the frequent approval and commendation—all these combine to tell him that his star is ascending. He likes it.

STORYTELLING TIME

A 3-year-old lives in a dramatic world of make-believe. It is a fantasy world where the imagined things are as exciting as the real ones. He loves stories—especially fairy tales. And the more familiar the story, the better he likes it. Parents discover that they can tell him the same one over and over. He also likes favorite stories read repeatedly. This is frequently safer than trying to tell them, because Junior has a mind like flypaper and he is very sticky about his facts. If a story is varied one iota, there is an indignant interruption as Junior explains to an exasperated parent precisely what happened.

Most children at this age can take "scary stories" without becoming upset, but parents must watch for the first signs of his waking up with nightmares or displaying other symptoms of an overstimulated imagination. This is a great time for ghosts, goblins, sea serpents, and bears, which is all healthy mental development so long as it remains part of the world of fantasy. If it starts getting over into the world of reality, it is time to put on the brakes.

Not only will a 3-year-old listen intently to retold stories but he will often respond to memorizing rhymes or short action stories which he can tell in Sunday school or when company comes. This is good training and teaches a child to have stage presence. It will stand him in good stead if he continues such training up through the years.

CONTINUING THE "DO IT YOURSELF" STAGE

Because he is more inclined to work patiently at things instead of blowing his tiny preschool lid as he did with the slightest frustration during the "Age of No Reason," Junior now gains many new skills. He learns how to make buttons fit buttonholes, he can manage the zipper on his jeans. He can lace his shoes, maybe even tie them. He takes pride in going to the bathroom alone. He can eat by himself—although the proffer of parental help in getting down "just a few more bites" is often accepted. He can fit together large jigsaw puzzles made for his particular age.

A 3-year-old likes to throw things—clods, rocks, blocks, or a ball. What he lacks is accuracy, and a reckless rock seems designed by fate to smash the nearest window. Ambitious fathers with competitive sports in mind may work doggedly with a 3-year-old to make a pitcher out of him. But Junior at this age is a lobber. He can't seem to get the right stance. He tries out several. In the excitement of trying to get the ball launched he may do a momentary toe dance, then crouch, stand, skip, or run before finally lobbing the ball a total of perhaps seven feet. The force of it may turn him around and cast him to the ground.

Junior is also a primitive artist at this age. What he draws is strictly impressionistic, but he has names for his creative efforts. If you don't agree with a particular name, he will gladly choose an alternate. His drawings are at least half scribbling, but he thinks you should easily see "the man," "the horse," or "the fire engine." By age 4 his drawings will be quite easily recognized for what is intended.

THE ARRIVAL OF FATHER

A boy "discovers" his father during his baby days, but by age 3 he catches a new image of the big boss. Father has become somebody to go places with; he tells bedtime stories that have villains, heroes, and desperate plots that leave a 3-year-old pop-eyed with excitement. When he goes on trips he brings home "treats." If Junior can catch him in the right mood, he plays and romps. Matter of fact, a father is a mighty handy gadget to have around the house. In the mind of a 3-year-old, Father has arrived.

Of course, a father gets a big charge out of this wonderful new relationship with his boy, but he has to be careful not to carry it too far. He has to watch his stories, so that they don't have too much grownup blood and thunder in them. The level of conflict in "The Three Bears" is about right. Father also has to be careful about too much roughhousing or a pretended chase. All such doses of exhilaration should be spontaneous and brief. A boy will beg for more, but the excitement of being pursued or rolled and tossed around over a long period of time can shoot enough adrenalin into his blood to keep him awake half the night. Then when he does go to sleep he conjures up bears, lions, and wolves which trigger nightmares and screams that awaken the whole household at 3 A.M.

Fathers tend to be "kidders," and most children enjoy a little of it. But too much kidding becomes teasing, and teasing can make a 3-year-old revert to tantrums. A boy at this age is also too young to interpret sarcasm. An irritated father may try to work off a load of steam through a few sarcastic remarks—half in fun, half in seriousness. A 3-year-old boy usually senses the antagonism but misses the humor.

It is also necessary to be careful about laughing at a 3-year-old. If he is clowning or doing acrobatic stunts, he loves to hear applause and laughter. But if he is struggling to make his half-pint vocabulary tell about some terribly serious situation, it is disastrous to laugh at an accidental mistake. He knows the setting is not humorous, therefore the laughter is interpreted as being ridicule. He senses that he is making a fool of himself and may immediately start crying or run some place and hide. Often parents are confused and surprised by this reaction and enthusiastically assure Junior that what he said was *cute*, but this is beyond his comprehension. He can draw only one conclusion. He goofed!

This is also the time when an enthusiastic father must restrain himself from overindulging a little fellow. It is so exciting to see his boy beam whenever he is given a surprise treat that some fathers pull all the stops. A boy has enough intelligence by age 3 to be easily spoiled. If this happens, he starts begging, bargaining, and throwing a fit if he doesn't get his way. Some fathers who lavish things on their children are really spoiling themselves. They overindulge a child because of the personal pleasure it gives them and completely overlook what it is doing to the 3-year-old personality of a son.

THE DUTIFUL THREE-YEAR-OLD

One of the most obvious changes in a boy between 3 and 4 is his desire to fit in, to do his part, and to take care of himself. This is why he exhibits so much more patience in trying to tie his shoes, put on his clothes, or set up a stack of blocks. To him it is important that he *do his duty*. Parents may misinterpret his intensive efforts and fear that he is building up to an explosion of frustration as he used to do so often at 2½. They therefore rush forward at the slightest provocation and try to help. This, most 3-year-olds resent. Only when they have proved to themselves that they just cannot possibly manage will they welcome help.

Of course, parents must intercede without an invitation if something dangerous is in progress—using a butcher knife to whittle, running with a pair of scissors, climbing a twenty-foot ladder, and so forth. Most of the time, however, a 3-year-old can do amazing feats without getting hurt—it is just the extreme situations such as teasing a dog, trying to cross a highway, or playing near ponds and ditches which demand parental intervention.

A child's sense of duty at this age makes him far more responsive to discipline than before. He almost expects it and is disappointed when he knows he deserves something but nothing happens. He is also quick to point out derelictions of others who are not conforming—even his parents. He may protest violently if his mother has been training him to observe the traffic lights and then pulls a sneaky jaywalk herself.

WHAT ABOUT "SLOW" CHILDREN?

We might also mention that by the time certain children are three years old their parents become aware that they are slow when compared with youngsters their own age. They seem slow in learning to walk or learning to talk. Often they refuse to be housebroken, bed broken, or thumb broken.

When we present these problems to our doctor, he will examine the little fellow and, unless there is some abnormality, tell us to relax. He tells us that "slow-growing" babies often excel as adults. Some of the world's greatest athletes were late learning to walk. Some of the most accomplished public speakers were late learning to talk.

This means that the patterns of behavior we have described as "normal" for particular stages of development are flexible rather than fixed. And it is Mother Nature (rather than parents) who must decide when a child will change from one state to another. It therefore becomes the role of the parents to go right ahead enjoying Junior for what he is, without trying to force activities on him until Mother Nature has given the clear signal of "Ready now!"

A 3-year-old may worry his parents when he is observed eating with his left hand rather than his right. It used to be considered desirable to let this trend continue for fear the frustration of a change might cause Junior to stutter, but today many doctors agree with Dr. Abram Blau who wrote a book, *The Master Hand.* This book provides considerable evidence that right- or left-handedness is not inborn but is acquired through habit. He recommends that parents tactfully help the child from the very beginning to use his right hand. However, if there is a very positive preference for the left hand and all attempts to make the change create violent antagonism, then it is thought best to let the matter go.

SOCIAL SENSE OF A THREE-YEAR-OLD

As we have already suggested, Junior is getting along much better with people during this stage of development. He is cautious about adult strangers but feels an affinity for his contemporaries. He tends to explore the neighborhood and is delighted when he finds another child down the street who is about his own age. On first meeting they will do fine for only about twenty minutes. Then one or the other decides to test this new friendship by pushing, pouring sand on the other's head, grabbing away a toy, or even trying to take something home. After they have become better acquainted and know one another's tolerance limits, they can play well together for two or three hours.

Children at this age cannot cope with a group situation unless it is under supervision. They prefer to play with only one or two at a time. If it is a cold season of the year so that playtime must be conducted inside, parents may expect the social situation to deteriorate rather rapidly. On the other hand, a 3-year-old can play outside with a little neighbor boy for two or three hours and have little or no difficulty. This is because the play can be built around running, jumping, climbing, and working at all kinds of make-believe careers—firemen, robbers, policemen, cowboys, jet pilots, and space men.

Junior's growing social sense is also reflected in one negative aspect: he cannot keep a secret. He loves to share secrets with everybody, children or adults. This can be devastating around Christmas time when he is an expert at snooping into all the odd places and gets the supreme satisfaction of telling the whole world what he finds.

But even adults should remember the psychological principles involved in "telling a secret." Psychologists say it is common to tell a sworn secret because:

1. *It may give the person an elated feeling of power to share the secret.*
2. *It may give relief to a person who "can't wait to make someone happy" by telling about a secret in which the listener is involved.*
3. *It may not seem as important to keep the secret as it was to the original informant.*
4. *It may give relief to a person who has a guilt complex and feels compelled to tell unpleasant secrets about himself.*

It takes a long time for a human being to discipline himself against the impulse to tell secrets. The 3-year-old is just beginning to enjoy the fun of telling. It will be some time before he can hold down the temptation to pass along big juicy gobs of gossip. In fact, many people never achieve it.

NEW CLOTHES AND INVISIBLE FRIENDS

Junior's awakening social sense also tends to make him very pleased with any new clothes he gets, especially shoes, shirts, pants, or pajamas. He enjoys strutting about and calling attention to the new acquisition. He may even demand to take his new shoes to bed with him or have them on a chair nearby. This sense of "pride in possession" almost always makes him rebel against another child wearing his clothes. At 5 this may not bother him so much, but at 3½ it is intolerable.

We might also mention Junior's social propensity for invisible friends. This does not happen to many children but it does to some. It is more likely to happen to children who must play alone much of the time. The strong instinct for companionship causes them to make up a friend. Parents will hear their pride and joy talking to this unseen pal. Junior may share everything with him and exhibit great solicitude toward this invisible playmate. Sometimes this playmate is an animal—a rabbit, dog, or other friendly creature.

Obviously, such a development is a worry to parents, but their doctor is likely to reassure them and tell them that such things are not rated as abnormal. He may even warn them to relax and enjoy Junior's imaginary pal because the latter may be around off and on for several years; sometimes as late as 8 or 9. It is all part of a boy's growing appetite for pleasant social relations. Experts have observed that when a boy is lonely he can have almost as much fun with a make-believe friend as a real one.

THE AWAKENING OF THE SPIRIT

The depth of interest and perception in the 3-year-old is tremendous. There is a great curiosity about life and all cosmic reality. As we have mentioned earlier, it is a time when a child likes to hear things explained. Parents must be careful and accurate in their explanations, but nevertheless strive to keep the discussion understandable and interesting. This is a good time to begin creating an appreciation for the omniscience of God and the responsibility which each human being bears toward Him for their personal conduct. If done properly, this can assist a boy throughout his life.

When a 3-year-old is taken to church he may surprise his parents with his instinctive response. He cannot understand the service, but often he will like the soft music and the quiet order of the church. If he becomes restless, a pencil and piece of paper will usually keep him occupied and quiet. At home a child of this age will enjoy having his parents help him as he says his prayers, and with proper encouragement this can become a most helpful pattern in his life. In fact, the parent who takes the time to awaken the spirit of a boy to the great realities around him will usually find it paying rich dividends in later years.

SUMMARY

It will be clearly seen that this golden age of the 3-year-old is good for parents as well as their little boy. It is a time when Junior is at peace with the world. He loves life, he loves his parents, and he feels good about himself. He is learning how to play with other children and learning how to do things which were impossible just a few months ago. It is a time of immense satisfaction for parents, and if their doctor happens to be handy he may say, "Enjoy this, folks. It won't last long, and the next stage is a whing-dinger!"

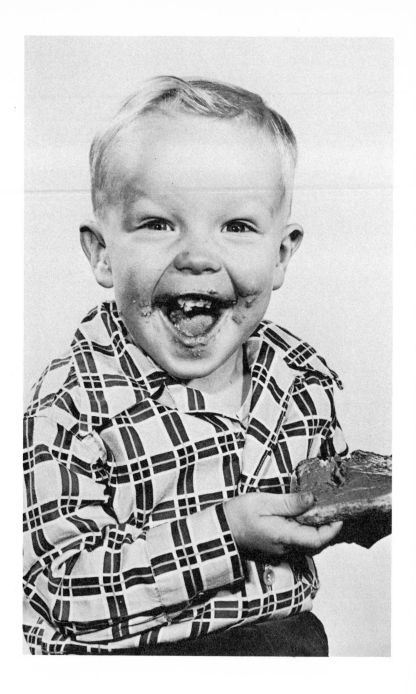

CHAPTER 6

THE ME STAGE

Patterns and Problems of the 4-Year-Old

It is certainly a tribute to the wisdom of Providence that parents are only exposed to the scratchy side of child psychology a little at a time. The pleasant period we described in the last chapter is one of those interludes between two scratchy patches. It separates the thrust period of 2 to 3 from the thrust period of 4 to 5. From the parents' point of view it is a welcome intermission to allow them to catch their breath and recharge their batteries. However, in some children this temporary armistice does not last long; a good percentage of them will push over into the "Me Stage" several months ahead of time. Parents can tell from the sudden change in climate that Junior is letting them know: "Ready or not, here I come!"

THE FOUR-YEAR-OLD'S POINT OF VIEW

It is usually some time after 3½ or perhaps a quarter to 4, and just as Junior is getting nicely adjusted to all the little "duties" and "habits" of a model child, that something happens. He acts as though he had just made a terrible discovery, and immediately there is a reaction.

The experts say it is triggered by something which first happens in the minds of parents—*they start taking Junior for granted.* They are rejoicing in the fact that he is "becoming such a little man" and are going right ahead pushing Junior up the road of self-sufficiency. All of this is precisely the way Providence planned it, but it creates a series of pressures on Junior which eventually alert him to what is happening: he is feeding himself, dressing himself, going to the bathroom by himself, and generally taking care of himself. Like a bolt of lightning from a clear summer sky the idea suddenly crackles in his brain: "Say, I am being kicked out of the nest!"

With nostalgic anguish he recalls the good old days when his parents let him be a baby; when they fed him, dressed him, fondled and coddled him. When he fell down and scratched or bumped himself they rushed over, swept him up in their arms, anointed his bruises, and kissed away the hurt. Now, when he falls down and gets a scabby nose, all they say is, "Get up, Junior. Be a little man!"

This scandalous development convinces a 4-year-old that life has reached a monumental crisis. Almost instinctively he takes decisive action. He determines to bugle a retreat and get back to his baby days as fast as possible. Overnight he starts acting like a baby. He whimpers, pulls tantrums, asks for a bottle, starts wetting the bed occasionally, wants someone to feed him, help him lace his shoes, help him take a bath, and he may go back to sucking his thumb again.

It is the beginning of a campaign to force his parents to return to "the good old days." Psychologists call it a period of centrifugal dynamics when Junior appears determined to make himself the center of the universe. The "Me Stage" has arrived!

We should point out, of course, that Junior doesn't resort to his baby ways every moment of the day. In fact, if he is pleased with the way things are going, he can be a very self-sufficient, grownup little fellow; but if something goes wrong, or he feels neglected, the baby act is whipped out with a draw from the hip that is lightning fast.

REACTION OF PARENTS TO THE "ME STAGE"

The natural reaction of most parents to the "Me Stage" is to interpret Junior's sudden collapse as a tremendous catastrophe which must be recouped at all costs. They double the pressure to make Junior conform the way he did so beautifully during the previous few months. The fact that he does not respond is maddening, since they know he can do it. Obviously, he is just being stubborn. "Like his father," the mother soliloquizes.

It helps if the mother remembers how she used to cure his tantrums when he was 2½ years old. The same principles of distraction will work now. It also helps if both mother and father remember that the attention he demands when he is bossy, rambunctious, and belligerent is just what Mother Nature ordered. A 4-year-old needs a lot of warm, personalized attention. If parents see a rising storm brewing, they can frequently head off the cyclone by creating a new interest focus for Junior— taking him for a ride, telling him how he can work *with* one of his parents to earn some money for a treat, telling him a story, or suggesting that he invite a friend over.

They also discover that sometimes Junior will not respond to any suggestion because he is testing the psychological barriers of his parents. He wants to find out just how far he can go before involving himself in a pants-warming session. Oddly enough, he may be disappointed if he is not allowed to probe the situation to its logical conclusion. A young father who has been pressed beyond the limits of human endurance by a pestering, probing 4½-year-old may resort to the laying on of hands and then feel remorseful about it. But after Junior has had a good healthy cry, he will frequently come back to his father just as though nothing had happened. The tight springs are all unwound and Junior seems to feel great. The father learns at this stage what he first encountered at 2½—that when a little fellow starts teasing for a fight he feels better after the situation has culminated according to plan. Of course, the need for taking direct action should be avoided if at all possible, but in those few cases when Junior absolutely will not respond to anything else, a well-deserved impression on the posterior of his personality has definite therapeutic value.

PORTRAIT OF A FOUR-YEAR-OLD

Contrary to outward appearances, the true picture of a 4-year-old is not a throwback to 2½ but a period of adventurous growth pointing toward a new plateau of achievement. Mother

Nature has endowed him with a brand-new set of insights. The very fact that he resents the pressures and responsibilities of life is a new insight to which he must now learn to reconcile himself. He will buck and pitch for a year or so until he settles down to the load. This bucking will happen again at 9, 11, 15, 18, and 19.

He has also become aware of many other new powers which are difficult for him to manage. He has learned to wander off on exploratory adventures. He knows what it means to unlock the backyard gate and run away. He can throw much straighter now and has probably smashed one or two windows—not accidentally but with malice and premeditation. He is learning how to use the language of his parents and likes to chatter continuously with his two-thousand-word vocabulary. He has also learned how to use words to sass adults, to alibi, to tattle, to tell big stories.

Parents should be quick to make an issue out of sassing. An alibi containing an element of deceit should also be straightened out, so that Junior learns even at this early stage that his parents like him better if he tells the truth.

Tattling is designed to build up a confidential relationship between the boy and his parents, so they need to handle it accordingly. To tell a boy he is a tattletale destroys the very thing the boy is trying to build. It is better to show a keen interest in his report and then suggest to him how you think the complaint should be handled. In those cases where a boy is exaggerating or making up stories to alarm his parents, it may help to tell the story of the shepherd boy who kept shouting, "Wolf! Wolf!"

In summarizing the qualities of the normal 4-year-old, Dr. Arnold Gesell describes him as "voluble, dogmatic, boastful and bossy." This is not an overstatement. Young parents might also add that he is egotistical, self-assertive, flamboyant, and frazzled. "He is out for blood!" Time, however, will demonstrate that he is simply trying to learn to control a lot of new powers and for the moment he has more speed than direction. In wild glee he lunges out to see just what lies within his perimeter of achievement. As one would suspect, this creates a feeling of physical insecurity and emotional dislocation.

THE AGE OF INSTABILITY

One of the places where this shows up is in his sleeping habits. A year ago he could sleep soundly. Now he gets up in the middle of the night and takes exploratory excursions throughout the house. Often he will end up with his pillow and blanket sleeping on the couch. He may even curl up on the rug in front of a heater vent. This tends to worry parents but, like most of his other childhood problems, "This too will pass." It may help him settle down for bed if he is furnished with his teddy bear and told a story which is interesting but not too exciting. During this period of instability he tends to have nightmares and is particularly sensitive about bears and lions. It is also helpful to have his bed in a darkened corner of the room so a hall or closet light can give him some light but not keep him awake.

This is also the period when a little fellow may want some help if he awakens in the middle of the night and needs to go to the bathroom. The help consists mostly of merely being with him and then tucking him back in bed.

Lack of stability in a 4-year-old shows up in his art. He will start to draw a horse and end up with an elephant or a camel. His imagination is fluid and creative. He lacks goal posts toward which to drive and therefore enjoys just cruising around. When he plays doctor he can use blocks as a satisfactory symbol for bottles, stethoscope, a knife, or part of the patient. Later on a block would be completely rejected for such purposes.

This same fluid quality of intellectual threshing about accounts for many of his tall tales, his exaggeration and his propensity for using maverick words like "namby-pamby," "gooshy-wooshy," "dumby-bunny."

His physical maturity, on the other hand, is not nearly so fluid. He has definitely stabilized many of his growth processes. He can throw a ball overhand, he can trace a straight line or cut on the line with scissors. He has better control of himself and can sit for a long period while doing something with his hands. Much of the clumsiness has gone out of his arm, leg, and trunk movement. He has become quite graceful.

His social maturity includes the vocalizing of everything that pops into his head. He asks questions by the hundreds. He loves to hold conversations of teen-age length on the telephone. He enjoys dressing up in adult clothes and copies adult manners in speech, stride, and stance. He also enjoys playing with a boy his own age for several hours at a time. However, more than one little friend can lead to mayhem. With a 4-year-old "two is company, three's a mob."

THE PROBLEM OF VISITORS

Another place where the social propensities of a 4-year-old come apart at the seams is when the family has visitors. He immediately tries to take over and demands the complete attention of the guests as though they were his own exclusive charges. He gets their attention by the devices in which he specializes. He does acrobatics. He peeks around door jambs and shouts, "Boo!" He pounds on the piano. He climbs up on the windowsill behind the curtains, he brings out all his toys, he gets another child to chase him through the house amidst shrill shrieks of attention-getting clamor.

The more his parents plead with him to "show the people what a nice boy you are," the more he plays the scallywag. He cunningly surmises that somehow or other he has his folks caught in a psychological trap. He notices that they are trying to be on their good behavior and impress the visitors that this is a well-run household. He concludes that under the circumstances they would hardly dare scold him, let alone paddle him, so this means he can pull all the stops without fear of reprisal.

New parents soon learn that if they are to preserve any semblance of a reputation with their guests, they had better get Junior off the set. No compromise will work. If the visitors try to satisfy Junior by giving him a little polite attention, it merely feeds the flames. If they casually compliment him on his growth or acrobatic accomplishments, he snatches up the conversation and brags away at a jet propulsion clip. A 4-year-old would far rather brag about himself than have somebody else do it.

Experienced parents usually conjure up some kind of device

to get Junior watching TV in the playroom or get him otherwise occupied so that the visitors will come and go without becoming a "Me Stage" casualty. Sometimes Junior can be worked into the picture for a brief spell after the visitors have become settled and the stimulating greetings and "how-do you-do's" are dispensed with. This is the stage which is particularly difficult for a 4-year-old to handle without feeling he is the star of the show.

FIBBING AND SNITCHING

As we have already mentioned, a 4-year-old is experimenting with a variety of new powers. These include his talent for making up stories and his "pride of possession" which will frequently include other people's possessions. These two propensities sometimes give parents the impression that they are raising a psychopathic liar and a congenital kleptomaniac. Fortunately, however, a little fellow of this age does not think of himself as "lying" or "stealing," and the worst mistake an adult can make is to tell him he is a "liar" or a "thief." If he ever gets the idea that he is either a liar or a thief, he is likely to wear it like a badge and continue his practices just because of the new status it gives him.

Junior's fibs at age 4 are really exercises in creative imagination:

"Mommy!"

"Yes."

"I just saw a dragon."

"Oh, Junior, you didn't see any dragon."

"Sure I did. It was big as a house. Had horns and burned a fire in its nose."

"What did you do?"

"Well, I just stood and watched. I was very brave."

"What happened to the dragon?"

"He went down a gopher hole!"

Parents soon learn that if they pretend to enjoy Junior's tall tales and refer to them as real good "stories," he soon gets the idea that his folks are pretty smart and they can tell when it really happened and when he is just making things up for fun.

As for stealing, all a 4-year-old knows about it is that he saw something, wanted it, and took it. At this stage he thinks "possession" is "ownership." He has practically no real sense of property rights.

"Son, where did you get that red toy truck?"

"Oh, I found it."

"Isn't that Bobby Smith's red truck?"

"No, he threw it away. I found it on his lawn."

"Don't you think Bobby will feel badly when he finds out you have taken his truck?"

"Oh, I won't tell him!"

At this point a parent may have visions of raising a gangster. However, the recommended remedy is simply to let Junior play with the acquired toy for a while and then go with him to return it to the neighbor boy. By the time he is 6 he should have a fairly clear idea that he is not supposed to take things which belong to other people.

THE FACTS OF LIFE

Most new parents assume that when Junior gets to be an adolescent they will have a nice long talk with him about the facts of life. They feel comfortable in the thought that this task is still a long way off. This will account for the apoplectic reaction of a friend of ours who was recently in the process of shaving when his bright little 4-year-old came walking into the bathroom and said, "Daddy, how do we get babies?" He looked down at the innocent upturned face and said, "Oh no, son. Not so soon!"

But our friend learned from his doctor that this was all very normal. The doctor said that between 3 and 6 children have a genuine sexual awakening, and it involves both physical and emotional responses. It is the age when they become very curious about themselves, about the opposite sex, and eventually about babies. Hence the question put to our friend. The doctor suggests four rules:

1. *Be very matter-of-fact about it.*
2. *Do not tell too much and do not excite more curiosity with provocative answers.*
3. *Use accurate scientific terminology when referring to physical processes.*
4. *Give the child the feeling that you will be glad to discuss this subject with him whenever he has a question.*

Many fine books are available for parents which suggest ways and means of explaining this important part of life. All the authorities agree that the simple direct approach is the best. Modern youth is too sophisticated to have respect for fairy tales. This is even more true as the child matures.

The story is related of a sixth grader who was told by his teacher to get the facts of life from his home. He asked his grandmother where she came from, and the grandmother said her folks found her under a cabbage leaf. He asked his mother where she came from, and the mother said a stork brought her. He then said, "Well, where did I come from?" The mother said she opened the door one morning and there he was on the doorstep. The student returned to school to report. "Teacher," he said, "we haven't had a normal birth in our family for three generations!"

When a 4-year-old is asking about "where babies come from," it is simple curiosity requiring a simple explanation. "Babies? Oh, they come from their mothers."

"But how do mothers grow babies?"

"They grow them in a special place which God made for growing babies. It is a warm pleasant place not far from the mother's heart."

Many months later he will want to know how the baby got into this special place, and he is usually satisfied when he is told that the baby grows from a tiny cell that was part of the mother already. He may return in a few more months to ask, "But how is the baby born?" Unless he is 7 or 8 it is usually best to simply say that a special passage is provided when it is time for the baby to be born. However, older children respond to a chart or illustration in the family doctor book showing the marvelous mechanics of human birth.

Somewhere along the line there will be questions about the place of the father. The fact that the baby will not start to grow until the mother and father share their love with each other is usually sufficient in the beginning. When a youngster is 9 or 10 he can begin to appreciate the naturalness of marital relations as the "highest expression of love between a mother and father." Once more the family doctor book will be helpful, but terminology should be scientific rather than colloquial and the entire matter should be treated in a very casual, matter-of-fact way. This is certainly the time to stress the sacredness of the human body and the necessity of showing respect and love for that future sweetheart whom Junior will marry by keeping himself circumspect and not sharing himself with anyone until after his marriage.

With a little forethought, all of these problems can be handled in a delicate but highly satisfactory manner for all concerned.

SUMMARY

In spite of the challenge which the 4-year-old represents, his parents will learn with the passing of time that it is a genuine period of growth and not a backsliding reversion as they thought at first. In fact, with their later children they will feel much greater confidence in dealing with the "Me Stage." Experience will have taught them to simply ride it out by keeping a little pressure on Junior mixed with a lot of affection and personalized attention. In this way he will gradually realize that he doesn't have to work so hard to get attention. As soon as he can begin to take himself for granted, he will start having frequent flights of "being good" just as he used to be in those heavenly days between 3 and 4.

CHAPTER 7

FIVE IS FUN

As one might suspect, the age of 5 marks a happy new plateau of maturity. Five is alive, five is fun. The intensity of last year is seldom evident. Junior has discovered that he doesn't have to fight his parents for their love and attention. He takes himself a little more for granted, and this is the golden key which opens the door to each important stage of "arriving." Parents notice a new refinement in his personality and also big boy attitudes which make him far more compatible with adults this year than during the "Me Stage." A father, however, will notice that a 5-year-old is still his "mama's boy" and depends upon her for his comfort and companionship in most situations. He also notices that occasionally Mother Nature allows Junior a fleeting return to the "Me Stage" with its tantrums and centripetal dynamics. Both parents are relieved when Junior finally settles back down again. Shortly thereafter Junior will convince them once again that Five can be fun.

PORTRAIT OF A BOY BETWEEN FIVE AND SIX

It will be recalled that last year Junior was a jumping jiver. This year he has much more poise with obvious improvement in self-confidence and behavior restraint. His muscle tone, sense of balance, and signal circuits have improved in quality. He can walk on top of a narrow stone wall without falling. He walks up and down stairs like an adult, a step at a time. He can climb

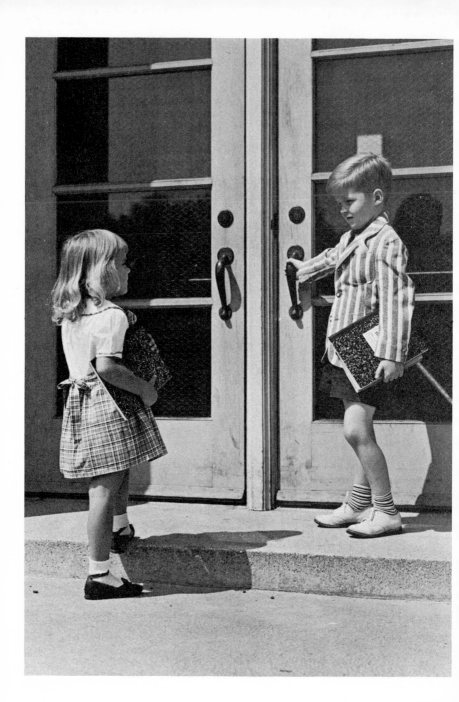

trees, fences, and tricky bars with skill and dexterity. He can ride his tricycle for an hour or more without tiring. He may ask Santa Claus for a pair of skates. He shows considerable ability to analyze problems, to reach decisions, and to make selections. This year he likes to complete each task before starting another one. He can be trusted with simple errands and small work tasks if his parents will work with him.

By this time a boy will usually exhibit a positive inclination to use one hand to the exclusion of the other. He will favor the dominant hand in eating, drawing, pointing, and throwing.

Even Junior's appetite will usually settle down at 5. He should be a fairly good eater by now. Sometimes, however, he likes to have his parents do a little hand feeding toward the end of the meal. If left to his own devices in between meals, he will feast perpetually on cookies, leftovers, or make-it-yourself jam sandwiches. A mother who wishes to assure herself of a hungry boy at the supper table will reserve the two hours just before mealtime as closed to nibbling.

A 5-year-old is not as experimental as he was at 4. He likes to try a few new things but will spend far more time getting intimately familiar with old things. He will play house for a whole morning or afternoon, going over the same procedures time after time. He will sit for long periods behind the wheel of a car and chortle away with make-believe motor noises as he takes an imaginary ride. He will play at his father's profession of carpenter, schoolteacher, auto mechanic, or storekeeper to further familiarize himself with patterns of life which seem closest to him.

He is not gushy over strangers but neither will he race away and hide as he did a year ago. He will gradually warm up to visitors and may sit observing them in quiet contemplation until he has worn off the novelty of having the newcomers around. His social sense among children his own age is enthusiastic and friendly, but he is not capable of expanding group play beyond two or three.

Junior is developing his sense of duty and the importance of gaining approval. He can carry out some projects to completion and gains personal satisfaction by imitating adult dress, adult

behavior, and adult conversational expressions. He will usually
pick up a few swear words about this time, but has little
conception of what they mean. A recent conversation between
two boys of this age produced the following:

"What is damnit?"

"Oh, damnit is a bad word."

"What does it mean?"

"It means a crazy old coo-coo boo-boo."

A MAMA'S BOY

Under normal circumstances a 5-year-old will display a particularly warm attachment to his mother. He is very concerned
if he cannot find her when he comes in from play. He wants a
close working relationship with his mom and constant assurance
of her approval. When things go wrong he wants her physical
and spiritual medication. He likes her to talk with him, to
explain things, and tell him about the multitude of exciting,
mysterious things in life. His dependence on his mom is apparent
when he has a nightmare. He may resist all efforts of his father
to comfort him and will insist that his mother take over. This
may be disturbing to a father but it is only a characteristic of
the age. The love of a 5-year-old son for his dad can be perfectly
normal and still he will call on his mom when trouble arises. Ten
years hence it will be different.

A mother notices that a boy of this age likes to go places with
her. It may be to the store or just walking over to the neighbor's.
A boy likes to feel a chummy relationship with his mom, a
feeling of sharing and doing things together. If a mother is wise
she will take advantage of this. In the normal course of events,
it may not last long. It is between 5 and 6 that a mother may
find her son sharing his love more completely than at any other
stage of his life.

GAB AND GRUB

Two qualities of a 5-year-old compete with each other. One is
his desire to talk and the other is his reawakening passion for

food. As a result, he tends to mix gab and grub. It is a common sight to see a boy of this age trying to talk at top speed while eating a huge plate of potatoes and gravy. At other times, he may worry his folks by maintaining a jet stream flow of talk but allowing his food to get cold. This is usually due to the fact that most boys at 5 only want two good meals a day and will dawdle with the third. Later in the year he will devour the third meal and mix in plenty of gab as he does with his other meals.

If a boy at this age is one of those who turns out to be a slow eater, he nevertheless will usually clean up his plate if given time. The growing instinct to "complete the job" is budding in him, and therefore he usually persists until his plate is empty.

It does little good to worry too much about the table manners of a 5-year-old. He may eat with a fork or spoon. By 6 or 7 his table manners will sharpen considerably, and by 10 he can be a little gentleman. At 5, however, the main thing from his point of view is to get the victuals down. If allowed to serve himself, he is likely to scoop out Paul Bunyan portions. If others give him less, he may complain loudly. But even at this age a boy can be very particular about a napkin. He even may refuse to continue eating without one.

and if he has not attended Pre-school.

KINDERGARTEN

Starting kindergarten is a big event for Junior, especially if he is a first child. Somehow it seems easier to make the adjustment if an older brother or sister is already going to school. But in either event the new adventure can be better accepted if there has been an enthusiastic buildup some time before. Two factors help the average youngster get started in school. First, if he is "taken" by a parent for a day or so, and, secondly, if there is some other youngster in the kindergarten whom he already knows.

However, it is not uncommon for a 5-year-old to start out the day with: "I'm not going to school today." This is almost inevitable if he has been allowed to watch early morning TV cartoons or has just received a new toy or a new pet. Home is where he wants to be. Early morning TV for children—especially young children—is a distraction and should be avoided. As for the pet or the toy, it can usually be arranged with the teacher to have Junior take it to school for the "show and tell" session. In fact, if Junior is rebellious about going to school, it may help to have something special occasionally which he can take for "show and tell."

It is also helpful if parents can take time to have Junior describe all the things he did in school. He should be encouraged to sing the songs he learned or repeat the stories he heard. This is not easy for him, and all the family will have to give him a patient hearing as he struggles to remember. The object, of course, is to give him the satisfaction of sharing the school experience with the family. This can become an important factor in getting him to "like school."

School activity on the kindergarten level is mostly "learning with play." Learning letters is associated with interesting objects which the letters represent. Counting is made a game. He learns a few words "by sight" which appeal to him—words that have dramatic and meaningful sounds like rip, roar, rush, crash, plop, etc., and words that he identifies with people like Mother, Father, Tom, Bob, Jane, and Joe. However, it is not desirable to force the reading of a 5-year-old. Physiologically, he will be better prepared at 6.

The boy in kindergarten is not particularly social. He will sit at a table with several others but will insist on some individual activity such as drawing, working in clay, or making a sand mold. Children at this age will carry on a lively conversation even though they are working on different projects.

Age 5 is an ebb-tide year and therefore an ideal time to get a boy oriented in school. If he waits until the next year by skipping kindergarten, he is likely to have a more difficult time because it will be a year of personality thrust. Age 5 is a period when a boy wants to please people. He wants to fit in, be helpful, and conform. This may be one of the reasons he is so quick to alibi if he makes a mistake. It is not uncommon for a child in kindergarten to say, "Look what you made me do!"

It is this same sensitivity which makes it necessary for parents to avoid any possibility of the child getting a rejection complex.

ROOTS OF THE PSYCHOPATHIC PERSONALITY

In some homes a real tragedy occurs at this stage through the reckless and unsympathetic treatment of a youngster. A harassed parent may express by word or action that a child is a nuisance. Some parents will even violate the most elementary common sense and tell a child, "We never really wanted you and we're sorry we've got you. If you don't behave yourself, we'll send you away to an orphan home." If a child ever starts absorbing this kind of mental poison, both he and his parents— perhaps even the whole community—are in for a bushel basket of trouble. Psychologists have learned that if a child gets the idea that he is disliked, disowned, and unwanted, he will often start developing a psychopathic personality and spend the rest of his life trying to "get even" with society.

Sometimes a grade school youngster will break out a score of expensive windows or commit other acts of vandalism, and everyone wonders what would motivate such abnormal behavior. Nine times out of ten it will be discovered that the child is lonely, rejected, and resentful. Breaking the windows is retaliation. The child may not even know specifically whom he is trying to get even with. He just knows he is unloved and unhappy. Recently the mother of such a boy stopped work so she could be home to give her boy more attention and affection. He had broken two thousand dollars' worth of plate-glass windows.

Every parent should know that a child with a rejection complex will usually become a social misfit. The vast majority of the criminal population in our jails and prisons are this kind of misfit. They have normal brains and healthy bodies but they have a twisted, cynical outlook on life. As a matter of fact, they fight life and become their own worst enemies. As time goes on they become highly susceptible to the escape of alcoholism or narcotic addiction. They can't even stand themselves. They are called criminal psychopaths.

Under careful psychoanalysis, most of them can trace their complex, curdled personalities to a period in early childhood when they somehow got the idea that nobody wanted them.

They therefore grew to maturity with personalities that were twisted, tormented, and deformed.

The needs of a child during early childhood are therefore much more important than many had previously believed. Neglect or mistreatment during early childhood can lay the foundation for sixty-five years of existence as a human misfit with its trailing sorrows of drunkenness, divorce, dissoluteness, and crime.

PREDICTING DELINQUENCY

For many years, Sheldon and Eleanor Glueck, a Harvard University husband-wife team, have been studying the case histories of serious delinquents, and they discovered that the seeds for the delinquent personality have usually been sown by the age 6. They found that if five questions about a certain boy are all answered in the negative, then the development of a delinquent personality in that boy can be predicted with almost mathematical certainty. Here are the questions:

1. *Did this child get affection from his mother during the first six years?*
2. *Did the child get affection from his father during the first six years?*
3. *Did the mother adequately supervise the child—did she make it her business to know where he was and what he was doing all the time?*
4. *Did the father provide proper discipline—being neither too lax nor too strict?*
5. *During his first six years was there cohesiveness in the family—a lively sense of unity and belonging?*

The reason these five negative factors can foreshadow a psychopathic criminal even as early as age 6 is because, if they are *continued,* this is what they will almost invariably produce. However, just because they were present during the first six years does not mean that the child cannot be changed. With a lot of patient effort he can be rerouted. The problem is that many parents or adults wait until several years later to make the change. Often this is too late. Even at age 6 the impact of these five factors will be so impressed on a child's mind that the fruits of a rejection complex will begin to show in his behavior. A rejected child is a retreating child. Instinctively he fights back—not for improvement but for vengeance. He resolves to get even. This gets him into deeper trouble, produces more forced retreats, triggers more retaliation. It is chain reaction operating in a vicious circle of perpetual motion.

It becomes the task of the parent or teacher of a rejected child to somehow break the chain.

This is done by providing the positive ingredients which were lacking during the first six years:

1. *Seeing to it that he begins to enjoy some mother love. If he has no natural mother, this must be provided by some generous woman who enjoys his confidence—a teacher, Sunday school instructor, foster mother, perhaps later a Den Mother.*

2. *Seeing to it that he begins to enjoy some father love. Here again, if he has no natural father or his natural father is incompetent, this love must come from a substitute source. A boy is not balanced unless he has both kinds of love—from a father as well as from a mother.*

3. *Seeing to it that the boy is given proper supervision. He should get the feeling that he is important to his folks and they want to know where he is and what he is doing all the time. Of course, it should be done in such a way that he doesn't get the feeling that they mistrust him or think he is a "bad boy." He should get the feeling that they are just interested in him and want to know where to call him if something exciting happens in which he might like to participate.*

4. *Seeing to it that a boy is disciplined when he truly needs it. This means that discipline must not be too lax or too strict. It should be reasonable, fair, and consistent. We will say more about this in a moment.*

5. *Seeing to it that there is unity and cohesiveness in the family. A boy likes to feel he is part of a going concern—a real sharp outfit. He resents being identified with a collection of people under one roof who fight, quarrel, and brawl.*

The Harvard University team found that if these five positive factors are present they build personality resistance to criminal behavior. If they have been missing during the first six years, we have to provide carefully administered therapeutic doses during the next six years to prevent this boy from growing up to be a misfit.

DEVELOPING A PHILOSOPHY OF DISCIPLINE

We have already mentioned discipline briefly, but it needs to be considered in more detail. Discipline and love are team mates. Either without the other is a distortion. If there has been any one single weakness in the structure of American society which stands out above all others, it is our failure to apply sound principles of discipline. This is particularly true in the social setting of the American family.

Recently a prominent judge began to ask why it was that many European countries had very little juvenile delinquency. In those countries poverty is rampant, the standard of living is low, contagion for crime is everywhere, yet the families are able to hold their children in check.

The judge came to the conclusion that the magic element which had made this possible was authority in the family. Therefore, he wrote, "Let's put Father back at the head of the home." This doesn't mean that the father becomes a dictator—it simply makes him the president of the firm. In harmony with this basic idea other principles necessarily apply:

1. *Reasonable standards of conduct are laid down and agreed upon.*
2. *Firm and* consistent *enforcement of these standards is made the rule.*

3. Within the framework of these disciplinary boundaries copious quantities of affection and love abound.

Now, the question arises, how do we keep the activities of the family within the boundaries we have set up? Experience teaches us that love alone will do it 90 per cent of the time. But what about the other 10 per cent? There is where we strike a cultural vacuum. For more than two generations we have promoted the idea that love should also be the cure for those who smash down the barriers of the family or of society. Authorities are beginning to feel that this is where we made our mistake. We failed to provide genuine discipline when circumstances called for it. Obviously something is wrong when the American juvenile crime rate is skyrocketing to a level which is rapidly setting a world record. Authorities are beginning to ask parents to recognize that *discipline means restraint*—gentle restraint where possible, firm restraint where necessary. For nearly two generations this has been missing from our way of life, and society is beginning to pay a terrible toll.

It will be recalled that during the "Age of No Reason"—2—the doctor said we should try to rock along with Junior and help him establish his self-confidence. However, between 3 and 4 the doctor said reasonable standards of conduct should begin to be set up. This seems fine until our 4-year-old suddenly decides to smash them down. Now it is a good time to turn to a competent psychologist for help. He will probably come forth with a few simple rules of *applied* discipline:

1. Be sure the rule is reasonable for a child of that age.
2. Be sure he understands it and realizes there is a penalty for deliberate violations.
3. Make one or two allowances for a possible lapse of memory but caution him concerning the future.
4. If another violation occurs shortly thereafter, always apply the expected discipline.

WHAT ABOUT SPANKING?

The next question is whether or not family discipline should include an old-fashioned spanking once in awhile. More and more parents are beginning to find that it has remarkable therapeutic qualities. If it is used, here are some suggestions:

1. *Reserve it for exceptionally serious situations.*
2. *Be sure the child knows why the punishment is being given.*
3. *Be sure it is applied where Mother Nature seems to have intended it.*
4. *Get your own emotions under control so the spanking is not harsh or abusive.*

It is suggested that discipline *not* include pinching or slapping. Where a deserved spanking will release tensions, pinching or slapping increase them.

CONCLUSION

Most parents remember the life of a boy between 5 and 6 as happy, lovable, and satisfying. They remember that physically he was gaining poise and muscular skill, mentally he was full of curiosity and enthusiasm for learning. They remember his favorable reaction to kindergarten, once he became accustomed to it. They remember what a great relief it was to get beyond the "Me Stage" and have their boy take himself a little more for granted.

They might even remember a few of the chinks in his armor—his fear of wolves, bears, and bad men, his fear that something might happen to his mother, his occasional tantrum, his anxiety to have the comfort of a doll or teddy bear when he went to bed.

But the over-all picture is a happy one. Most parents remember that "Five is alive, Five is fun."

CHAPTER 8

SIX IS FULL OF TRICKS

We now come to a period of human development which is like the month of March—it comes in like a lamb and goes out like a lion. The parents will have barely become accustomed to that pleasant interlude of self-confidence and co-operation which characterizes age 5 when all of a sudden Junior's personality seems to split at the seams. The force of powerful new maturation pressures make him blow steam in all directions.

Parents tend to lose patience with a 6-year-old because he is such a confusing mixture of baby and boy. Sometimes he is lovable, understanding, and responsive; other times he is almost as bad as he was at 2½. By this time the parents will have seen enough of this boy's personality to know that he can be just wonderful if he wants to. Why, then, does he go berserk every so often? Parents sometimes get to thinking that his contrariness between 6 and 7 is cold-blooded, deliberate, and premeditated. This, of course, is not the situation at all.

In fact, by the time a boy has reached the tricky age of 6 his mother and father should have observed the interesting and intricate cycle of rising and falling tides in human development. Age 1 to 2 was a year of happy, lovable, cuddly babyhood; age 2 to 3 was a year of incoming tides with enough smart-alecky independence to make them call it the "Age of No Reason"; age 3 to 4 was an ebb tide with sweetness, self-confidence, and obedience exuding in all directions; age 4 to 5 was another year

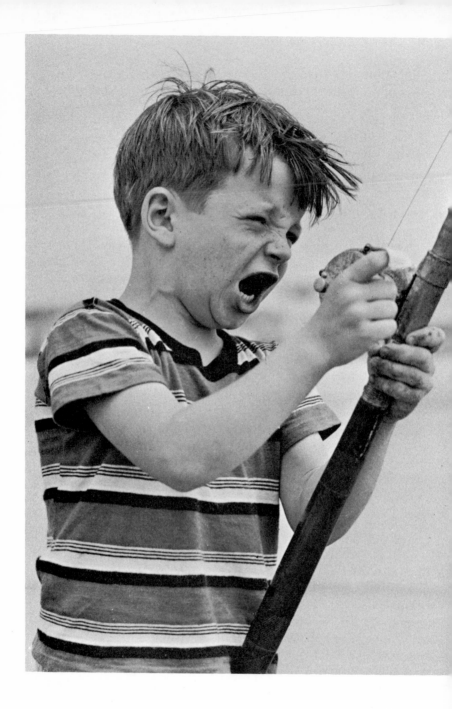

of thrust with enough wild rambunction to equip an African rhino; then age 5 to 6 turned out to be an ebb tide—just in time to get him started in kindergarten. This brings us to age 6, and experienced parents should expect him to start blowing his gaskets again.

PORTRAIT OF A BOY BETWEEN SIX AND SEVEN

By the age of 6 the average boy has reached well over half his final height. His original weight has increased four to six times and is approximately one-third of what his weight will be as an adult. The circumference of his head has reached nine-tenths of its final size, and his heart is now about five times heavier than at birth. He is losing his first temporary teeth and gaining his first permanent ones. All of his faculties are developing rapidly, and he requires twice as much oxygen per unit of weight as an adult. He gets tired easily and needs around eleven hours of sleep.

All of these forces of growth in a boy are reflected in his behavior. First and foremost he appears to be a wiggle-worm. He acts as though every part of his anatomy were attached to springs or someone had put itching powder in his breeches.

Even when he's sitting he puts out more energy than a whirling dervish. This should give parents some idea of what to expect when he's taken to church, and what his teacher will be enduring each day at school. He wriggles and writhes. He is so uncomfortable in one position that the teacher may see him pulling faces, jerking his arms about, striking some nearby boy or girl just to get a rise out of them. He wants to wrestle, run, jump, and holler. He longs to climb, crawl, pull, and push.

Not only are the muscles of his arms, legs, and trunk shrieking for action, but the muscles in his jaw, tongue, lips, and larynx are just as dynamic. As a result, he is a jabber-puss. He talks incessantly.

With all this loose energy being thrown around, parents may get the idea Junior will accomplish something. Unfortunately, this is not the way he feels about it. What he wants is continuous, uninhibited action without worrying about any particular accomplishment. Consequently, he appears clumsy and lacking in skill as he impatiently attempts to pile up some blocks or manipulate a toy. When he tries to use a saw it usually bends and binds. If he tries to pound a nail, he bangs a finger. If he tries to put on a pair of roller skates, they require so much adjustment and patience that he often abandons the effort in a frustrated temper tantrum.

As one would suspect, all of these qualities combine to make a 6-year-old a good beginner but a poor finisher. This is not only true of his play activity, but it is true of his eating, dressing, bathing, or almost anything else he is expected to do.

Qualities of this age also make him easily distracted. He shifts easily from one thing to another. Nevertheless, he is not inattentive, which may puzzle adults. While he is going through acrobatic gyrations and giving the impression of complete indifference to everything around him, his sharp little ears may be listening to everything. His alert and observing senses of sight and sound pick up things like a hungry little vacuum cleaner.

THE AGE OF FRANTIC EXTREMES

The forces of maturity thrust we have already described would indicate that a 6-year-old has a tremendous zest for life. But, as we have already said, much of this zest is motion without direction. Therefore, his reactions often seem to be out of focus. He seems to be perpetually launching some kind of crash program to obscure his problems instead of methodically working them out. His parents observe that his emotions continually run to extremes. If his feelings are hurt, he cries like an infant. But if something pleases him, he may tremble with excitement. At the movie matinee he shrieks and squeals with glee or stops up his ears and covers his eyes in terror.

At home his mother notices that he exhibits strong affection for her at one moment and then shows violent resentment the next. This is Mother Nature's way of preparing a boy to leave the nest—to prepare him for weaning and detachment. This will commence around age 7.

In dealing with children his own age, a boy is equally vacillating. He says he cannot stand to be away from some little pal, yet when they are together it may be only a matter of minutes until there is quarreling and hitting, maybe even biting and kicking.

The insecurity of a 6-year-old is also displayed in his constant attempt to gain attention and build his personal status in the eyes of others. He brags, exaggerates, and struts when describing his own accomplishments. The most casual compliment about a brother, sister, or playmate may cause Junior to quickly point out that he is far better.

His anxiety to "be somebody" also accounts for the fact that he is very responsive to praise. He devours it. Of course, praise should be given judiciously, and only when it is deserved, but bragging up a 6-year-old can often achieve miracles. It is simply a question of emphasizing the positive in him.

By the same token, we might suspect that criticism will be resisted or totally rejected. Experience verifies this. Junior goes on the defensive the moment any faults are called to his attention. Nevertheless, this must be done occasionally, but parents will want to be extremely careful how the criticism is worded. Nothing must be said to give a 6-year-old the idea that he is inherently "no good." This is what he will think if the parents say, "You are a naughty, ungrateful, disobedient boy!" The parents will get far better response if they talk about what he did: "*That* wasn't a nice thing to do!" A boy can take a lot of pressure concerning personal conduct as long as he knows it can be improved and changed, but if people say *he* is "no good," then he starts playing the role of the bad boy and says he cannot change.

IN THE BLACK OF THE NIGHT

The unsettled state of mind in a 6-year-old makes him a likely candidate for nightmares, phobias, and fears. He expresses concern that "somebody is under my bed," he is afraid of the dark, fears dark closets, witches, ghosts, and goblins. He can work himself into a lather if he awakens during a thunder and lightning storm. The wailing night winds can speak to him in the haunting echoes of entombed voices which moan their message of portending disasters.

It does little good to try to shame a 6-year-old into being brave. He may hide his fright because of his fear of a scolding, but inside of him the fear writhes and rattles like a nest of snakes.

The better way is to avoid the things which aggravate his fears. Avoid scary stories, horror movies, and sensational TV shows for the time being, and concentrate on more tranquil topics. This is a good time for travel stories and explorative adventure. A good stand-by is telling him what it was like when he was a baby. He loves to hear about himself, his brothers and sisters, his mother and father.

As in previous stages, his fear of the dark is temporary. If a closet light is left burning with the door slightly ajar, or a tiny night light is allowed to cast its soft, shadowless glow across the room, he will usually be satisfied and gradually drift off to sleep.

It might also be mentioned that when he has a nightmare he generally responds best to a lot of T.L.C. (tender loving care) from his mother or father. It permits his highly imaginative little brain to be brought back to reality while the ugly night vision fades into oblivion. The fears which produce nightmares may also be allayed by the presence of a large stuffed animal. Even live animals help. During the bombing raids in Europe, it was observed that children overcame their fears by comforting a kitten or puppy and assuring these little bosom pals that everything was going to be all right. The same principle is applicable to imaginary fears. Many a boy with the 6-year-old jitters has talked himself out of it while trying to comfort some small pet.

STARTING THE FIRST GRADE

All we have said thus far about the 6-year-old helps to explain his behavior as a first grader. A 6-year-old is usually all activity. He remembers the good time he had in kindergarten. It also means learning to read and write. At this stage of development, most modern youngsters are tired of asking others to read comics or children's books. They long to read for themselves. They also want to write. They have probably been printing their names in capital letters ever since kindergarten, but they are now anxious to write words. A group of 6-year-olds think of going back to school the same way they thrill over the prospect of going to the circus. It means lots of fun, lots of acts, and big new surprises.

The rude awakening comes about the second week. Although it was very exciting the first few days, gradually it dawns on Junior that the teacher brags the most about the pupils who *finish* their work. The drudgery of finishing a task is such a trial to a 6-year-old, still he hungers for the commendation of the teacher. For several days he battles back and forth between his dislike of having to finish assignments and his passion for praise from his teacher. He may become worry-weary and eventually run down his battery. Often the teacher will notice that absenteeism is increasing after the second week. Usually there are lots of colds or other minor illnesses. Gradually, these are less frequent so that by the middle of the school year Junior seems to be less fatigued by the strain of a full day at school. He also seems more reconciled to the fact that, while school is lots of fun, it also involves what one first grader called "a lot of mean old work."

The adjustment of each human being to the "drudgery of work" is not an easy task. Nevertheless, the "joy of work" does not come until after a person can take drudgery more or less for granted. So the first grader gets a tiny taste of life's important lesson: we do lots of things, not because they are fun, but because they just *have* to be done.

The teacher softens the blow of this reality by including a great variety of activities in each school day and making each activity as exciting as possible. Tolerance for drudgery or "getting a job done" is facilitated where the rewards of the task are not postponed too long. "As with seals, so with scholars." They want their goodies after every act. This may seem like a bribe, but it is more accurately described as "the realization that rewards come through effort."

LEARNING TO PLAY ON A TEAM

It takes a boy several years to learn that some things are more fun if done together. At this stage he responds best to simple games that stress a lot of individual activity. Tag is a favorite game. Gradually he will develop a team spirit. This spirit comes first in games, later in work. It is important to appreciate that individual self-realization must precede co-operative team work. We notice that a youngster gets very little vicarious satisfaction from watching other children drawing, building, molding, or making sandbox castles. He wants to get in and do it himself, in his own way. Only after he is certain that others will be a help and not a hindrance does he voluntarily invite them to work with him on a finger-painting mural or to help build "the biggest sand castle in the world."

At school the experienced teacher will know that some youngsters resist team play because of natural timidity or lack of basic skills. The highly critical attitude of classmates often aggravates the situation. It is necessary for the teacher to give each timid, backward student special attention to avoid that terrible feeling of complete rejection. A child can stand the taunting of a few classmates if he is sure that *somebody* cares about him.

The teacher can often assist the timid student by helping him shine in some special way. She may have to tutor him a little so that he *can* shine. This requires extremely careful, patient handling. Nevertheless, it can be done and must be done if society is to be spared the presence of one more frustrated, rejected human being who may spend his adult life trying to get even through crime or some other anti-social behavior.

FIRST GRADE BEHAVIOR PROBLEMS

Being a wiggle-wart and a jabber-puss, a 6-year-old does not respond too quickly to the quiet sanctum of the halls of learning. He has to learn to keep noise down to a dull roar, gradually acquire the gentle art of whispering instead of shouting, and learn how to stay in his seat during work periods. It is difficult for him to remember to hold up his hand when he wants attention or to wait his turn when answering questions.

To alleviate tensions and stimulate adjustment, the wise teacher intersperses play activity with work projects. She includes oral recitations with study periods. The quick shift from one thing to another is the natural inclination of the first grader so the teacher does not have to worry about his resenting interruptions. Later on, such interruptions are resented, but in the first grade a change is always welcomed.

A 6-year-old is not a good loser. He is too concerned about winning so people will think well of him. At the same time he doesn't mind competition, he welcomes it; but it had better be the kind of competition where there is an opportunity for everybody to win part of the time.

Adults also need to remember that a 6-year-old has great difficulty handling feelings of guilt. He will frequently fib if accused of anything directly, but is easily induced to tell the truth if approached indirectly. For example, if a teacher says, "Johnny, tell me how you accidentally happened to tear your book?" he usually interprets this as a sympathetic request for an explanation and finds it easier to tell exactly what happened.

A 6-year-old may still have a fuzzy sense of property rights. He may take things even though they are of little value to him. It is necessary to remind him continually how badly he would feel if someone took his things. A boy who has been doing a little snitching himself is nearly always the most intolerant and critical of others who have committed the same offense.

STUTTERING

This is the age when some children have speech problems. In fact, the dynamics of 6 may aggravate a child's stuttering. Parents may have noticed this problem occurring as early as 4, but it may now start developing a pattern which is almost habitual. Since most stuttering is the result of emotional strain which creates mental blocks, parents can follow a few fundamental rules to assist a child in outgrowing his problem:

1. *Don't nag.*
2. *Help him gain self-confidence.*
3. *Avoid calling attention to his speech.*
4. *Be a patient listener so that he doesn't have to work so hard to communicate. Keep your own conversation slow and casual.*
5. *Avoid interrupting him or helping him during a speech lapse while he is trying to get out the next word or syllable.*
6. *Exhibit interest in what he says rather than how he says it.*
7. *When he is trying to describe something, show by your own relaxed attitude that he can take it easy.*
8. *Without making a major point of it, have him practice words containing unusual or difficult sounds.*
9. *Do not insist that he say things a certain way—such as preceding any request with "please." The important thing is to get the feeling of freedom in expression. The refinements can come later.*
10. *Without pampering or overindulging a child, help him gain a feeling of being loved and wanted; help him overcome unnecessary fears and failures.*

Some children will stutter or stammer because of a physiological defect requiring clinical therapy. Even those with merely psychological problems may need clinical help before they can overcome their defect. Some of the help from the clinic may be getting the parents to understand the underlying causes of stuttering so they can relieve the emotional strain in the home which is causing or contributing to the problem. Many parents can get help from a nearby university or college if the speech department includes a children's corrective speech clinic.

THE ROLE OF THE PARENTS

Parents are the biggest thing in the life of a 6-year-old. They must not overlook their role. A 6-year-old loves to come home from school and show off his achievements. He proudly displays the drawings, coloring, braiding, and writing he has done. When his father comes home, he wants to repeat the demonstration. After he has learned to read he wants to bring his books home just so he can show his parents what miraculous skill he has acquired. Parents must be sensitive to the spirit in which this is done. It is his moment of victory. He must not be robbed of the triumph just because he misreads or mispronounces some of the words. The important thing is that he is now on his way, and he hungers to hear his parents say, "You're coming along fine!"

The law makes it the task of parents to keep Junior in school. They will find this easier all during his academic career if they take a warm interest in what he is doing at school. A telephone call to his teacher can help untangle occasional problems. Parents may become perplexed by the fact that a 6-year-old will love school one day and dislike it the next. The fact is that on those days when he gets some reward or recognition he thinks school is the greatest, but a day of disappointments will clabber his personality. Knowing this, parents can make a little extra fuss over him on the blue days and give him a novelty item to show the teacher or the class so that he will have something pleasant to anticipate when he returns to school.

It is often toward the end of the first year that parents find a boy fighting school the hardest. Unless he is ill, there should be no question whatever as to whether or not he will go to school. It is part of the role of the parents to hold the line. If handled properly, Junior will gradually give up trying to argue his parents into letting him stay home. If, by any chance, they let him win the argument or they capitulate to his nagging and begging, the experts predict "stormy years ahead."

THE PRELUDE TO PARTING

Because a 6-year-old is still part baby he tends to spend a lot of his play time right under his mother's feet. He is still very dependent upon her love and encouragement. Sometimes a mother will feel that her 6-year-old will drive her to distraction with his questioning begging, and constant hanging onto her. She often wishes that somehow she could cut him loose from her apron strings.

Within twelve months this will happen. Mother Nature will not only cut those apron strings, but send her boy drifting away from the home hearth. In later years a mother may recall with fond reminiscence the days when Junior was her constant companion. Once he has started to drift away on his own, a mother notices some gradual changes in their relationship—both psychological and spiritual. Never again is a boy likely to be quite as close to his mother as he was at the spritely age of 6.

SEVEN REACHES TOWARD HEAVEN

A 7-year-old has just come out of the blustering, chin-jutting panic period which usually engulfs most 6-year-olds. Often parents find themselves so exhausted and exasperated that they can hardly contain their relief as Junior slips into the ebb tide of 7. For the next few months there will be a quiet breathing spell as Junior regroups his energies and takes a new look at the world. Parents notice that, whereas he formerly acted as though his major career were to wreck the world, he now seems anxious to fit into it. He is suddenly rational and reasonable. He asks intelligent questions and, what is more important, he listens to his parents as though he thought their answers were intelligent.

By now the 7-year-old has seen enough of the world to arouse a passionate spirit of curiosity. He starts wondering, "What's out yonder?" He begins to relate things in terms of time and space. He learns to "tell time" and read a calendar. He has developed a fairly good sense of direction. He chooses one or two pals and starts exploring, first the neighborhood and then the town. Parents need to see that he satisfies this curiosity under a certain amount of supervision. Up to this time his home has been the major part of his universe. Now home becomes merely the headquarters base or point of departure for his exploratory expeditions. What a 7-year-old can't explore with his feet he tackles with his mind. He starts projecting his questions out into space so that before long his mind will be knocking on the doors of

heaven. He wants to know about life, about death, and about God. These questions cannot be postponed. Wise parents will be ready with some carefully prepared answers. For the moment his comprehension is shallow, but it is the ideal time to lay a foundation. He wants to hear about new ideas, new people, new places. At the beginning of each day a father looks down at his 7-year-old and feels like saying, "Well, little man, what now?"

PORTRAIT OF A SEVEN-YEAR-OLD

This is a good year. It is exciting to watch the visible growth, the co-operation, and the pleasant exchange of affection between parents and a 7-year-old. This is the year a boy seems to slow his pace sufficiently to ask, "What is life doing to me?" He seems to sense that his inner urges are carrying him into unknown regions, and there is a spirit of caution and questioning in it. He isn't blindly reckless and frantically dynamic the way he was last year. He is hungry for counsel, explanations, and demonstrations. His father says, "I think Junior listens to me better than he did last year." Age 7 is a year of good listening, good thinking, and therefore good intellectual focusing.

At this stage, a boy has a very definite desire to fit in. He is sensitive about acceptance. Last year he wanted status and identification. To win a place in the sun he was willing to sacrifice his personal reputation. This year he wants status plus acceptance. He wants people to like him. He is much more polite when he wanders into the house of a neighbor. He is quick to tell himself and others what is right and what is wrong. He develops a strong sense of propriety and of modesty. "Don't look at me," he says, as he undresses or goes to the bathroom.

He is secretly self-critical and likes to have adult approval before starting some new project. It is as though he were saying to himself, "I know what I want to do, but will *they* want me to do it?" Because of this ritual of making frequent requests for approval, parents must be careful not to refuse the request unless they have a good reason. It is easy to get the "no" habit. If the answer is "no," there should always be a reasonable explanation to go with it.

With the passing of time, parents soon learn that age 7 is a very fragile age. His newly visible qualities of maturity sometimes lead parents to take too much for granted. Actually, these new maturity traits are mere sprouting buds. Therefore, he can be easily imposed upon. He does not understand nearly as much as his upturned face and deep wistful eyes seem to reflect. He will agree with his parents after a hurried conversation when he does not really comprehend the most elementary aspects of what they are saying. Parents are deceived by the situation when Junior turns obediently to try and do what he thinks they have asked him to do. Inside, however, he may be a seething vat of brooding confusion. He is further confused when his parents swoop down on him and say he isn't doing what they told him to do at all.

Every so often the pressures on a 7-year-old will cause him to collapse and he will backslide to his babyhood days. This may give his parents butterfly stomachs, but he soon warms up again to restore their sagging confidence.

ASPIRATIONS OF PERFECTION

An outstanding characteristic of age 7 is the passion for perfection. Last year achievement was not very important. This year it is paramount. Junior becomes a repeater. Whatever he does must be done over and over. He erases and corrects, he traces and retraces. If he hears a story, he must have it repeated over and over until every detail is part of him. This new quality in his personality makes a 7-year-old resent interruptions. No longer is he indifferent to distraction as at 6. He wants to finish whatever he starts. He is slow to come to meals because it always interrupts something. If a TV show is in progress it will take a team of horses to pull him away. He always wants to "see how it ends."

Without quite realizing it, a 7-year-old will create frustrations for himself by setting his sights on the stars. Sometimes he comes home completely deflated when he doesn't get a 100 on his school papers. Parents must intervene to assure him that his 78 or 85 is "still pretty good." If his progress is abnormally low, then it is a signal for his folks to give him some concentrated attention. The old saying that "nothing succeeds like success" is particularly true of a 7-year-old. An occasional failure is good for him but he needs to succeed a lot of the time. Continuous failure will leave scars.

FIBS, SELF-PITY AND SELF-RIGHTEOUSNESS

Because a boy is very defensive about his failings during this period, he may alibi and fib after a series of boo-boos and then go into a deep black mood of self-sympathy. He tells himself, "Nobody wants me," and "I guess I'm no good." During a neighborhood fracas his little playmates add to his anguish by assuring him that he is definitely no good. This hurts his heart more than a sharp blow would hurt his head. He comes home crying. It is not the frustration cry of his baby days. It is the sobbing of injured pride. And sometimes he comes home with a bloody nose and a black eye. In his effort to "be somebody," he occasionally takes on another somebody who is bigger than he can handle.

But all that he suffers at the hands of his contemporaries does not soften his own reaction to them. At the slightest provocation he pours out his own wrathful disdain upon them with satisfaction and relish. During this period of middle childhood, boys are quick to criticize, cruel in their thoughtless accusations of each other, and constantly surveying the world with a lordly air of supreme self-righteousness. This sometimes obnoxious superiority must be handled carefully by parents. It is a form of overcompensation to cover up feelings of inadequacy. If parents try to trim a 7-year-old egoist down to size with sarcastic quips or disparaging comments, they only add to his sense of inferiority and thereby agitate his continued construction of a defensive front.

Parents can help a boy acquire self-confidence by simply analyzing each of his changing moods. When he is on his high horse of self-righteousness, remind him of the need for charity, and when he is on the low road of self-condemnation, remind him of the many fine things he does and what a great man he is going to become if he just keeps trying.

THE SECOND GRADER

This should be a good year for a boy at school, especially if he has a teacher who loves and understands 7-year-olds. He likes to have her come by his desk. He gets a special thrill if she touches him. He asks lots of questions up at the desk just to be near her. When he is called on to recite he likes to hear her say his name.

A 7-year-old is beginning to appreciate that "home" and "school" are two different institutions. During kindergarten and the first grade he liked to think of school as merely an extension of home, which in many ways it was. Now, however, he senses that home is one thing, school is another. In some cases a youngster will store up his papers, drawings, and art craft without feeling the need to take each one home the way he used to. If parents have a 7-year-old loafer and the teacher does not give them a call, they may be shocked when he brings home a pile of papers at the end of the term.

"But, Junior, why didn't you tell Mother?"

"Tell you what, Mommy?"

"Well, that you were doing so poorly in school?"

"Oh, I *like* school!"

"Well, these papers don't show it."

The mother promptly calls the teacher, and she may be surprised to find that the parents weren't aware of Junior's problems.

"I thought you would know from his papers," she may say.

"But I didn't see his papers," the mother responds. "He's been hoarding them."

This dramatic unfolding of events may be very disturbing to a 7-year-old gold bricker. "Everybody was so nice to me, I thought I was doing fine."

It is time for this type of boy to learn that there is still a very close connection between home and school; and there is a very close connection between achievement and acclaim. Of course, it would be a mistake to try to push a boy beyond his natural limits, but once his potential capacity has been determined he should be encouraged to rise to that level and, where possible, surpass it. Achievement is usually 75 per cent attitude, and many youngsters with ordinary capacity have become extraordinarily successful just because some teacher or parent put stars in their eyes.

Second graders are usually better readers than spellers. Often they will guess at words or substitute similar words as they plow through a text. They like to hurry along to "get the story" without worrying too much about unfamiliar words or the interpretive significance of periods, commas, or paragraphs. In both reading and writing, a second grader wants to be sure to have time to finish. He is always worried about being interrupted before finishing. The teacher may alleviate this tension by advising the class in advance how much is to be written or read.

In writing, some second graders are anxious to do script instead of printing. Because a 7-year-old is supercritical of himself, he will hurriedly wipe off the blackboard or erase from his paper any errors or crooked lines. Age 7 is strictly an erasure age, and he is likely to spend as much time erasing as he does writing or drawing.

SOCIAL SENSE OF A SEVEN-YEAR-OLD

When a group of second graders is released for recess, they may charge into the play yard like a herd of wild steers, but their anxiety to play is usually with two or three and not with the whole class. Under supervised game instruction the team spirit of a large group may be built up by praising each team for its performance, but the teacher must have the kind of games in which both sides have a turn at winning. Seven-year-olds are still poor losers and need the chance to win once in a while. They are also quick to blame the little fat boy or some other tiny timid soul for "making our Beaver team lose."

As a rule it is not difficult for an adult to build a good social relationship with a 7-year-old, he is so anxious to have people like him. When things go wrong he ordinarily responds to reason and praise better than punishment. Saving face is extremely important to a boy of this age, so an adult may express understanding and sympathy and still buck up his determination to do better. It will help if a parent remembers that Junior is balancing between the pull of wanting to be accepted and the tug of wanting to be somebody by asserting his independence. Therefore, if an argument arises, a 7-year-old will usually change his mind or shift his mental outlook if it can be done without deflating his ego by belittling him as a person.

A teacher notices that when a 7-year-old is working or playing with a group he is embarrassed to be singled out for either praise or blame. He is trying to establish himself with his own age group and therefore wants to be "just one of the crowd." A wise adult can exploit this factor by taking a lazy or uncooperative boy aside and gently prodding him with the suggestion, "Come on, Joey, let's show the other boys how well you can do." When a boy has excelled, the teacher also can take him aside and confidentially advise him that he is "doing swell." A 7-year-old glories in such a compliment when bestowed privately by a teacher he admires.

THE UPWARD REACH

Toward the latter part of the 7- to 8-year-old development period a boy will usually reflect an exceptionally strong ethical sense. It is as though a little motor inside of him were playing a continuous recording of "Don't do that!" Most of the things his parents have labeled as wrong will now be avoided with a studied determination bordering on monastic piety. As we have previously noticed, he not only sets up strict rules for himself, but he rather enjoys catching a playmate in a violation.

At this stage the ethical sense is mostly negative, that is, it tells him what *not* to do. The positive side of his ethical conscience takes several more years to develop. He may be a late teen-ager or young adult before he can force himself to do many of the positive things which common sense and his internal ethical sense tell him to do. Therefore, it is said, "The instinct to avoid evil comes early, the capacity to do good comes late." This latter part simply means that, while a young person will often do good for praise or reward, he is unlikely to do it "just for the principle of the thing" until nearly full maturity.

It is a sign of a strong and well-developed ethical sense when a person can play the role of the good Samaritan just because it is the right thing to do. Parents are less likely to get discouraged if they remember that it takes nearly half a lifetime to produce this positive quality in most human beings.

WHAT A SEVEN-YEAR-OLD DOES FOR FUN

A 7-year-old is no longer fascinated with fairies and fantasies as in the past. He now wants flesh-and-blood heroes. He plays at being a jet pilot, a policeman, fireman, cowboy, or some current TV personality. He wants realism in his toys, too—realistic guns, bullets, and belts, an electric train that smokes and toots, a fire engine with a siren, windup ladder, pump, and a spurt of real water.

He is no longer impressed with merely looking at toys. No matter how beautiful, he has to be able to do something with them. He may destroy an expensive train trying to discover "what makes it work." He loves to take apart clocks, radios, and mechanical gadgets. In self-defense some parents buy a boy a large, cheap alarm clock, give him a screwdriver, and tell him to enjoy it to his heart's content. When he takes off the back he spends hours watching the cogged wheels turning, the alarm device ringing, and the hands slowly moving.

The experts say a 7-year-old is a constructionist in spite of the impression he gives of being a *de*structionist. Even his tendency to take everything apart is believed to be part of his urge to build. Parents can capitalize on this. They will find that his building urge can make a medium-sized hammer, a sack of nails, and a few fruit crates far more exciting to a boy than most expensive toys. These can occupy him for hours. From such crude resources he can build planes, trains, and cars. His parents may not recognize the final product but they will be impressed with his pride of achievement as he displays it. Some fathers feel the need to get in and show Junior how to saw, hammer, and plane, but he will respond to such instruction a lot better later on. Right now he just wants to "build something" and "do it his own way."

This attribute of being a constructionist makes a 7-year-old a natural mud hog. He can spend his entire Saturday playing in mud and water. He builds mud roads, ditches, dams, and wading pools. He gets wet and dirty and loves it. It is less of a strain on a mother if she just accepts the fact that he is not trying to ruin himself and his clothes, but doing what comes naturally.

THE FAMILY LIFE OF A SEVEN-YEAR-OLD

The qualities of maturity in a 7-year-old make him a pleasant and responsive member of the family most of the time. He enjoys his younger brothers and sisters (unless they are interrupting him or taking his stuff). He likes to participate in short-term household chores. He is very excited about the prospective arrival of a new baby and takes great pride in reporting to the neighborhood all the latest developments. He is proud of his father and seeks his companionship. He longs for the love and approval of his mother. He talks about "our" house and begins asking for a room of his own so that part of "our house" is designated as his.

In spite of his leveling off since age 6, a 7-year-old is often a champion noisemaker. He does not usually go into frustrated tantrums as he did a year ago, but he will shriek back at a child or adult with whom he is having an argument. His fast-moving feet dart about the house, leaving behind a backwash of sound from slamming doors and noisy commentary. He and his little pals like to go racing in and out of the front or back door until the rest of the family think they are living in Grand Central Station.

A boy at this age can take care of himself fairly well, although he will have to be encouraged to hang up his clothes. He will also have to be encouraged to change his clothes. If permitted, he would wear a pair of jeans until they were so dirty they could be "stood up by themselves." He also has favorite shirts and sometimes resists changing.

At night when a 7-year-old is ruminating and meditating—especially when he is tired—he may bite his nails or wiggle one of his loose teeth. He will have worries and feelings of insecurity. He may call for his stuffed animals of bygone days or ask one of his parents to have a bedside chat with him before he goes to sleep.

Looking back on the 7- to 8-year-old period, parents cannot help feeling it has been a good year. Junior has been fun to have around, fun to talk with, fun to work with. He isn't a baby any more, he is a boy; and both mother and father get the signals from his growing brain and body that he's a fine little fellow in the making.

CHAPTER 10

EIGHT LIKES IT STRAIGHT

If Seven is symbolized by meditation and brooding, Eight is characterized by chest up and chin out. It is a combination of age 4 and age 6, but with enough common sense thrown in to make it more palatable to parents. In fact, parents usually remember a boy's development between 8 and 9 as rather pleasant. They see many encouraging signs of maturity which help them overlook some of his ripsnorting antics. An 8-year-old is far more sophisticated than he was a year ago. He is beginning to doubt the infallibility of his parents. On many subjects he would just as soon take the word of a playmate. He is developing a loyalty for the group his own age. A shadow of resentment toward the interference and domination of adults sneaks into the picture occasionally. "Why do I have to?" is his common retort to a parental request. His earlier resistance to authority was because it created a personal inconvenience. Now it is becoming a problem of personal status. "Who's boss around here, anyway?" he keeps saying to himself.

All in all an 8-year-old is a realist. He sees life bearing down upon him and accepts each new situation only after giving it a good shaking. He wants to know the what, why, and how of life. "What's inside the earth?" "Why do we have wars?" "How are babies made?" These are not idle questions. He really wants to know, and if he doesn't get satisfactory answers from his parents he starts looking elsewhere. This is why we say that when

Eight asks questions about things, "Eight likes it straight." In spite of this, however, parents must weigh their answers. An 8-year-old is not nearly as ready for many answers as he thinks he is.

PORTRAIT OF A BOY BETWEEN EIGHT AND NINE

Physically, an 8-year-old is much better built than he was at age 6. He has more stamina, is not so susceptible to colds or fatigue. He is filling out all over and can take on some physical tasks which would have stopped him cold a year ago. He likes a great deal of muscular activity and has to have something going on most of the time. At his school desk he wiggles, pushes his arms forward or outward, and stretches his body full length as though he needed to unleash some of the springs inside of him which shout, "Grow, boy, grow!"

This may be a year of accidents. He has lost much of the caution which characterized age 7, and the new physical powers within his wiry frame urge him to take daredevil chances. He tries to swim out too far; beat a car while crossing the street; climb a cliff too steep or slippery. He often overestimates his physical ability and responds to a dare whether spoken by a friend or conjured up in his own mind.

Age 8 is a liability at the family table. Unless the rest of the household are alert, they may find the main course disappearing in Gargantuan gulps. An 8-year-old eats each meal as though it were his last.

When the family goes out he may urge them to eat at a smörgåsbord "where we can go back and get more." Parents watch an 8-year-old devouring his third or fourth helping and reflect wistfully on his earlier days from 3 to 5 when they had to plead with him to eat. A father looks across the table and mumbles, "Is this the same boy?"

An 8-year-old will resist baths, haircuts, getting dressed, and going to bed on time. When he does get in the bath he wants it two feet deep and has to see how hot he can stand it. When he finally gets a haircut he expresses amazement at the improved appearance. When he finally gets dressed he may try to grab a sneak breakfast and take off without waiting for the rest of the family. As for sleep, he loves it, and that's why parents can't understand why he resists it. When he finally gets around to it, he sinks into such deep oblivion that he may not even dream.

A few boys will do a little thumbsucking at this late age even though they may have discontinued the practice earlier. This is probably the last time this phenomenon will occur, and it usually indicates the vestigial remnants of some childhood insecurity.

THE FADING WORLD OF CHILDHOOD

An 8-year-old is well aware that he is moving up into the world of adults. From here on his make-believe world of childhood fancy will gradually give way to the sterner realities of the grownup world. At certain stages he will fight it, but most of the time he exhibits an anxiety to enjoy the confidence of those who inhabit the upper regions. Thus, he hangs around his mother sometimes for two or three hours at a time. He wants to talk and play right beside her. It is briefly reminiscent of age 6 except that he wants more than his mother's physical presence; he demands the attention of her mind. He is seeking a psychological affinity with her. He wants her to explain things and share the secrets of her world with him. He is jealous of her as a person and seeks to sit beside her at the table or in the car. This inevitably causes a commotion with other children in the family. He may take his father's companionship as a substitute.

Because of his desire for adult recognition and status, he tends to resent being ordered or commanded to do things. He responds better to suggestions. Nevertheless, his ability to follow through is still pretty weak, and it may be necessary to use the direct approach if the suggestion or indirect approach doesn't work.

He does not like anyone from the adult world to josh him about his failures or inadequacies. He dislikes being kidded. He wants to feel that he is already "fairly grownup" and that adults accept him as such.

To gain reassurance, he will often beg for compliments. "This is pretty awful, isn't it?" is his 8-year-old way of saying, "Don't you think I'm doing rather well for my age?"

THE CLUBHOUSE KID

Because of his desire to mimic adults, an 8-year-old becomes a great clubber. He wants to hold meetings, raise money, have secret signs and signals, and perhaps wear badges and carry membership cards. These fraternal factions are usually short-lived. The embryonic gang can usually last only long enough to get organized. They set up headquarters in a garage, pup tent, basement, or oversized cardboard box. However, the slightest disagreement is likely to dismantle the entire organization. It often ends up with the original founders agreeing to loot the treasury and make a hurried excursion to the corner candy store.

This is the beginning of the "gang stage" which will become very pronounced during the next few years. It is an ideal time for parents to get Junior started in the Cub Scouts or some similar organization, where he satisfies that gregarious affinity for group activity without getting involved in some hooligan operations. It is preferable for the parents themselves to participate in the youth organization to which their boy belongs.

This is also a good time for parents to make up their mind that they will welcome Junior's noisy pals when they descend on the quiet home front demanding peanut-butter and jelly sandwiches or other ballast for their gnawing hunger pangs. 8- to 9-year-olds are quick to sense which homes welcome boys and which homes are hostile.

MONEY TROUBLES

When boys begin running in packs, they start comparing possessions. It isn't long before they all go home to their parents with the "gimmes." They each claim the other boys have ever so much more spending money and they assure their troubled parents that they feel like underprivileged orphans. Some parents fall for this line (which will be used repeatedly) and shell out enormous quantities of change just so their boy won't feel so cruelly neglected. Some parents do it just to prove to their own satisfaction that they are as good as the Joneses. However, the truth of the matter is that the 8-year-old money craze should be handled most judiciously. Overindulgence can lay a foundation for demands in later years which are out of all proportion to need or equity; it is part of a boy's training in property rights to learn the value of money. Value and scarcity are closely related. Therefore, he should be given money only as he can appreciate its value and demonstrate his ability (1) to earn it, and (2) to spend it prudently. This does not mean that a boy will spend it on things which his parents would choose. It does mean that he will consider his money sufficiently precious, so that he will think twice before spending it at all.

This is a good time to set up a regular earned allowance. Parents must be careful not to forget to pay when the work is done (which is a common fault and very discouraging to a boy). They must also dock Junior when he does unreasonably sloppy jobs or fails to get part of the work done. Out of such early lessons the future success of a man may have its roots and strength.

PETS, PLANTS, AND PROJECTS

An 8-year-old is interested in things—including all living things. This is about the time a horrified mother may find her boy showering affection and care upon some snake, frog, toad, lizard, or mouse. If she really objects, he can usually be induced to transfer his affections to a rabbit, dog, cat, or hamster.

At this age he may be neglectful and forget to care for his pet consistently. Nevertheless, he will love it as a creature because of the pleasure it gives him. Gradually he must be taught to express his affection in terms of care as well as admiration. It may help to require him to feed and water his pet each day in order to qualify for his weekly allowance.

This is also a time when a boy will frequently exhibit keen interest in a small garden or flower bed. He loves to watch seedlings and small plants grow, especially when they belong to him. It is helpful to suggest that he plant rather rugged representatives of the botanical world. He may treat his plants like he treats his pets. Cultivation and watering may become sporadic. Once again, it may be necessary to save them with the threats of a docked allowance.

Because this is a stage when a boy likes to collect things, his room may become a miniature museum. He may carry sample specimens of many of his treasures in his pocket. Parents can take advantage of this tendency by getting him started on some type of collection project. If possible, this hobby should be something useful and interesting which can continue up through the years.

THE THIRD GRADER

All of the factors we have itemized above combine to influence his behavior in school and his attitudes toward school experiences. The exception is his teacher. We would expect him to be moving closer to his teacher, the way he is seeking a closer psychological relationship with his mother, but the group pressure is so great at school that he tends to behave more formally toward her. He wants her to be fair and maintain order "like good teachers should," but he is not as likely to fall in love with her as he was last year. He doesn't depend upon her touch or the speaking of his name as he did at 7. He does not usually go up to her desk for help as much.

This does not mean that there is any inherent antagonism. It simply means that he likes to be able to take her more for granted. He may even become highly disturbed if for any reason he does not feel a warm confident relationship with her. A teacher of third graders finds that the boys in the class admire her and like to be sure she is around, but they don't want her to be too gushy or demonstrative in displaying friendship and kindness.

In the third grade, group control is becoming more apparent. An 8-year-old can be rather strongly influenced by the limitations or prejudices of his class. He feels a sense of loyalty toward them and tends to respect any opinions expressed by the whole group. Sometimes a third grader will express a deep conviction or display a spirit of independence and then let it quickly dissolve amid the jeerings and hoots of his critical classmates. Teachers can be quick to firm up an 8-year-old who prematurely collapses under one of these emotional avalanches.

Third graders generally pick up their attitudes, likes, and dislikes by copying what they see and feel rather than what they are told. They are beginning to sense that a lot of platitudes are mouthed by adults without having any application in real life. They therefore watch the members of the adult world to see what is fake and what is fact. From watching a teacher they gather her ideas of co-operation, fairness, loyalty, sportsmanship, and honesty.

Classroom participation is voluble and enthusiastic. Each one wants to answer every question. Third graders love to hear a classmate give a wrong answer so they can burst out with joyful objections and give the correct answer in a chorus.

Parents notice that their 8-year-old likes school. He is very seldom absent and will ask to go to school even when he isn't feeling up to par. Some of the mechanics of school are less painful than they were the first two years. A number of students will just now begin to enjoy their reading. The physical maturation of the eyes during the last few months will contribute to this improvement. In the third grade, writing is much less laborious and the student usually will try much harder to achieve neatness and good alignment.

THE AGE OF ACCOUNTABILITY

The growing ethical sense of an 8-year-old is rather obvious to his parents. They saw it sprouting last year, and they now observe that Junior expresses in both words and actions that he wants to be good. He responds favorably when praised for having made good choices and feels an inner glow for having "done it by myself."

An 8-year-old appreciates, almost for the first time, that "goodness" depends somewhat on intelligence and age. He gets the idea that a certain amount of "badness" must be expected in younger children "because they don't know any better." Often, he expresses more understanding and sympathy for a handicapped child.

He is also sensitive about his own failings and is quick to explain why he didn't measure up. These are more than alibis. They are genuine attempts to analyze why he flubbed when he knew better. By this means he gradually strengthens his ability to anticipate problems and surmount them.

Because of the appearance of a strong ethical sense in children at this stage of their development, we call it the "age of accountability." Both the common law and modern law give recognition to the early beginnings of legal responsibility for conduct when a child reaches this age.

SELF-JUDGMENT

Parents need to watch for the first signs of supersensitivity to unusual qualities or characteristics which a child of this age may feel for the first time. Because he is group conscious, an 8-year-old will be constantly comparing himself with his contemporaries and because he is so anxious to be accepted by the group he will be highly self-critical of anything which makes him different. This may be red hair, wearing glasses, being left-handed, or being of a different race.

As most children become conscious of these differences they will ask their parents or teacher about them. If they get satisfactory answers they are not likely to feel any further disturbance. The real problem arises when the immature members of the class begin poking fun at a boy because of some special factor.

"You're real poor. My dad said so."

"You ain't got no father."

"You're a carrot top."

"Hi, specs!"

"Your dad gets drunk."

"Does it hurt to be a cripple?"

These are common thoughtless gratuitous comments among some youngsters of this age. Adults need to be alert to such conversations. They can do immeasurable damage. At the time the remark must be passed off as casually as possible, but at the first opportunity the offender should be taken aside for a straight-from-the-shoulder talk. His ethical sense is strong enough to have it laid on the line.

PALS AND PASTIMES

An outstanding characteristic of age 8 is his desire to be with someone all the time. He thrives on companionship, either contemporary or adult. If it is an adult, he demands total attention. He wants to be treated as a companion, not a child. He wants continuous conversation concerning subjects which are cooking on the front burners of his 8-year-old mind. If he is talking with his mother, the conversation may expand into a rather stimulating argument. He likes this. He will deliberately promote it. He is often quick to point out her faults. He is very exacting and challenges things which she says and does. It helps if a mother realizes that this is just part of his apron-string cutting process.

When an 8-year-old seeks companionship among those his own age he shows strong preference for a certain pal. This is the beginning of highly selective friendships. Once he has picked out one or two bosom companions, he may deliberately avoid many opportunities for new friendships and go halfway across town just to be with one of his "old pals." Parents need to be alert to the uninhibited impoliteness of their 8-year-old when a non-pal contemporary drops by for a visit. "Why don't you go home?" they may hear him say.

The pastimes of 8-year-olds are dynamic and multiple. If possible they avoid playing alone. They like company. They like games where they can dramatize or act out the roles of robbers, policemen, Indians, and soldiers. Parents of a boy who started music lessons during 7 will notice a resistance to them during 8. He likes duets or music he can play with somebody but he hates practicing alone. He will do better on this next year.

RUDENESS AND CRUDENESS

As we have already hinted, there is a certain amount of rudeness and crudeness in an 8-year-old which may seem inconsistent with some of his other maturity traits. We mentioned his jealous and possessive feeling toward his mother and yet his tendency to challenge and argue with her. We noted his passions for having pals to play with, and yet he can be cruel and cutting to a boy who is not rated as a pal.

This same quality of rudeness sprouts up where grandmas are concerned. A younger boy tends to think of grandmas and grandpas as the greatest. At this age, however, he will turn on a grandma for the same reason he turns on his mother. A grandma who is living with the family must be extremely careful not to become involved if the mother or father are correcting the boy. There is nothing an 8-year-old would rather do than get his parents and his grandma in a hassle over him. He will even promote it. When he is alone with his grandmother he may tell her defiantly, "You aren't the boss around here!"

BOX SCORE OF AN EIGHT-YEAR-OLD

But in spite of his occasional problems, a boy's development between 8 and 9 generally leaves happy memories for his parents. They remember how he loved life, how he thrilled to each new experience, and how eager he was to try out almost everything and anything. They recall his animated conversations, his willingness to "work for a nickel," his affection for certain playmates, his numerous clubs.

An 8-year-old has laid the foundation for a very expansive and exciting development in the future. We would expect him to move into an ebb tide at 9, but he does not. He is simply going to build onto the foundation he laid while 8.

CHAPTER 11

NINE IS OUT OF TIME

According to our chart of ebb and flow, age 9 should be a quiet year, but it is not. Mother Nature pulls a switch on us. Up to now the even years have been aggressive, the odd years have been more level and calm. In many respects age 9 is a continuation of age 8, so that we do not hit our true leveling off until around 10. This is why we say, "Nine is out of time."

This is a stage in a boy's development when parents and teachers become more aware of the wide differences which are beginning to appear among boys of the same age. Some are falling considerably behind, others seem unusually advanced. Some are very shy while others are very cocky. The majority, however, continue to fall in the pattern we shall be describing as typical for this age.

It is during age 9 that many parents come up against some of their most difficult training problems. Many boys of this age have problems of lying, stealing, teasing, and fighting. It is a challenging year for both boys and parents.

PORTRAIT OF A BOY BETWEEN NINE AND TEN

While most of the thrust qualities of age 8 are perpetuated into age 9, he nevertheless exhibits greater maturity in dealing with them. He has increased self-reliance. He does not want to be babied. He is a self-starter and likes to put his mind to things.

He can work with an erector set or other constructive toys for several hours without becoming bored. He is a good reader, generally likes school, and wants to do new things like learning to swim, ice skate, or ski. He wants to be on a baseball team or learn how to play basketball. He is usually responsive to music lessons, and frequently he can be relied upon to practice without supervision for thirty minutes.

A 9-year-old has a tendency to carry things to extremes or overdo. If his parents will permit it, he will see the same show three times in one day.

At home he may challenge an opinion of one of his parents just as he did at 8, but, if a playmate challenges or ridicules one of his parents, a 9-year-old will go in swinging.

He seems to have a stronger sense of responsibility toward the rest of the family, but he is still sloppy about cleaning up after himself. His mother finds he is a clothes dumper, and his room usually looks like a cyclone recently passed through. Nevertheless, a 9-year-old may be very particular about a collection of stamps, butterflies, or birds' eggs. To him, these are important.

Emotionally, most 9-year-olds are fairly stable. They are not easily frightened and they seldom cry. They have a certain nonchalance and self-sufficiency as they sally forth from the home roost to circumnavigate the neighborhood. Underneath, however, a 9-year-old boy is a worry-wart. He has seen enough of life to appreciate many of its problems, therefore he does a lot of introspective fussing. He worries over school, whether or not he will make a good athlete, what he will do when he grows up, how will he be able to support a family. He also worries about his parents. He wonders if his father will keep his job, get a raise in pay, or do better in his sales. A casual conversation between Mother and Dad at the breakfast table can trigger a first-class worry session for their 9-year-old boy. Quarrels and arguments between parents are especially upsetting to a boy of this age. A divorce leaves a greater disruptive impact on a 9-year-old than almost any other age.

A boy has deep feelings of sympathy at this stage of development. When something is hurt, he hurts in the same place. If he sees a chicken killed for the first time, he cannot eat chicken for weeks. He is becoming conscious of the meaning of pain, injury, and death. He reacts to all of them with strong feelings of abhorrence.

NINE-YEAR-OLD MORALS AND ETHICS

A boy's sense of morals and ethics at 9 is as strong as at 8. However, obedience to his inner ethical sense may not *appear* very strong. This is because age 9 is a time of reconciliation. He knows he should not do a certain thing, but if he can think of a good excuse for doing it he may justify himself in going ahead. A statement typical of this age is reflected in the words of a 9-year-old boy who admitted stealing and said, "I knew I shouldn't do it, but I wondered what would happen if I did. I wanted those things real bad."

Youthful stealing is usually the result of one or more of these factors:

1. *Trying to satisfy a real or imaginary need.*
2. *Trying to prove to himself or his playmates how clever he is.*
3. *Trying to get even with somebody, usually some adult.*
4. *Trying to become popular by having something to give away.*

If a boy is stealing to satisfy some real or imaginary need, it is important to bring the problem out in the open and then give him a chance to earn money for the things he needs. If he has been stealing to show how clever he is, then it is almost certain that his pals and buddies have been stealing too. Any treatment should include the whole gang. If he is stealing "to get even," it is important to find the reason for wanting revenge. Sometimes the offense under which a boy may be smarting is very real. He will not respond to a lecture on honesty and property rights until he feels assured that the person who cheated or abused him also is going to get the straight-line treatment.

Finally, if a boy is stealing to give things away, it is generally because he is trying to buy friendship. Usually a boy who falls in this category is a lonely misfit. Solving his stealing problem will follow almost automatically if we can solve his more immediate problem of becoming accepted.

Telling falsehoods is usually motivated by these desires:

1. *To avoid punishment.*
2. *To get praise he does not deserve.*
3. *To protect a friend.*
4. *To impress people.*

When a boy lies, it is important to discover why. If it is for fear of punishment, then he must learn that his punishment will be less if he tells the truth (and parents must be certain that he gets proof of this). If he is seeking praise, it sometimes helps to wait until he does something genuinely praiseworthy before telling him that since he has *real* things to be proud of he won't have to use make-believe things any more. When he is telling a lie to protect a friend, it has to be worked out so that he can tell the truth without feeling guilty of disloyalty. It sometimes appeals to a 9-year-old to be told that if he will reveal the names of his co-conspirators, they can be kept from getting into future trouble or committing something far more serious than the current offense. If a boy tells lies just to impress people, he will usually respond to a rock-bottom discussion and discontinue the practice.

The main thing is to see that incidents of deliberate deceit are challenged and not allowed to pass unnoticed. Junior expects something to happen whenever he lies or steals and will be secretly disappointed if it doesn't.

THE TEASER

The dynamics of a 9-year-old frequently make him a good fight promoter both for himself and others. Even in the family he can drive younger brothers and sisters into a temper tirade with his continuous baiting and nagging. Much of it is done in fun, but if the opportunity is right he may provoke younger brothers or sisters to strike him just so he can really whop them back and then justify it to his parents.

For this reason, a 9-year-old may not be a good baby tender

in his own household. A boy who has previously been affectionate and paternal toward the smaller children can now become their top tantalizer. If parents are alert, they can keep an ear cocked for conversations between their 9-year-old and the younger children so as to intervene just before the baiting and teasing explode into a fracas.

The teasing tendency of a 9-year-old is evident at school and in the neighborhood. Quarrels and family feuds can develop between neighbors over the antics of youngsters this age. Adults need to be very careful not to allow the catcalls or shock words emanating from a neighbor boy to get their dander up. He may come back in a year or so and tell them he thinks they are great.

THE GANG AGE

During the past two years parents of a boy will have noticed a propensity for group action with other boys. By now, this gregarious instinct should have been channeled into some established boys' organization. It is helpful if parents keep in mind the numerous psychological factors which drive a boy to join forces with a group of other boys. These almost inevitably lead to trouble if the group does not have some adult supervision:

1. *He wants to enjoy the approval of those his own age and will sacrifice personal convictions as well as his reputation with adults to gain this objective.*
2. *He has a growing sense of loyalty toward those his own age or those just a little older, and will frequently accept their opinion in preference to adults'.*
3. *He has an inner urge to assert his own will in defiance of adults, including his parents and teachers.*
4. *He gains information on "secret subjects" from the gang, which he would be afraid to discuss with adults.*
5. *By observing clever members of the gang or older members of the gang he learns about pilfering, shoplifting, profanity, obscenity, and sex play.*
6. *The satisfaction of belonging to a secret society with its own code of courage, self-control, loyalty, obedience, and*

fair play within the group appeals to his better nature while allowing him to exploit his anti-social tendencies in group action against a rival gang, the school, parents, the playground instructor, or society in general.

Parents, teachers, and youth leaders should distinguish clearly between wholesome group activity and a genuine gang organization. Some adults have assumed that, since gang activity inspires group loyalty, obedience to a leader, a standard of behavior for members, and a few other positive qualities within the group, this type of organization should be encouraged. They overlook the fact that the in-group attitudes which spawn in youth gangs constitute the foundation for adult gangs. In-group snobbery, in-group loyalty, in-group secrecy, and in-group obedience by members of a youth gang are all liabilities where such a group is operating as an anti-social parasite in the community.

Some adults assume that boys will grow out of these negative aspects of gang activity, but the history of organized crime in the United States demonstrates that often boys grow into adult crime as a result of gang training in their youth. The exception is where a boy breaks loose from the influence of the gang.

For many years law-enforcement authorities have been urging that steps be taken to provide adequate police supervision, especially in the crowded, slum-ridden metropolitan centers of the nation, so that the youth are allowed to enjoy group play but not organized gang activity. The breaking up of gangs wherever they appear has been remarkably successful in curbing juvenile crime in those areas where it has been tried. Often such crime prevention service is ruled out as too expensive, but it is a drop in the ocean compared to the twenty billion dollars Americans pay each year for the consequences of crime.

THE MUTUAL PROTECTION GANG

Because of inadequate police supervision in most cities, the same thing happens on the youth level as that which occurs on the adult level. Youngsters band together in organized groups for mutual protection. They start carrying knives, blackjacks, brass knuckles, and homemade guns. Often the group then follows the history of the Black Hand Society or the Mafia. What started out to be a defensive, self-protection organization turns into a predatory shakedown operation, with violence and vengeance being heaped upon those who refuse to co-operate or to be intimidated.

This is precisely the pattern which many American youth are exposed to in large metropolitan centers. Younger children are shaken down for part of their lunch money, for sexual abuse, to carry out an assigned criminal act, or to provide answers on examinations to lazy or less intelligent gang members.

In many large cities a virtual jungle culture exists among the youth, and every so often it boils over into a scandalous rash of headline sensations. For some strange reason the whole matter is usually relegated to a study committee and then promptly forgotten. The submerging of such problems in a study committee solves nothing. The results of similar studies are voluminous and persuasive, but the recommended action is seldom taken.

The plain fact is that we are trying to force people to live together in crowded conditions without adequate police protection and supervision. This does not mean we need a police state but the security of an orderly society. England discovered this over a hundred years ago, and consequently invested in a crime prevention program of adequate coverage which reduced crimes of violence to a small percentage of what they are in the United States today.

Not only does the jungle culture scar the ideals and happiness of the boys and girls who are exposed to it, but it is perpetuated up into the adult world of commerce and industry. The frequent outbreak of scandals which are labeled the "moral breakdown of our culture" is merely a symptom of what is going on beneath the surface all the time. Such conditions definitely can be changed. Meanwhile, the youth of the land feel the impact of such cultural defects and bear the scars of their contact with them when they grow up.

A certain softness in the American culture is also contributing to the crime picture. Frequently youngsters are being allowed to get by with stealing, lying, and cheating for many years because "they are still too young to be punished for such things."

Even the juvenile laws tend to minimize the feeling of responsibility in youth, and society is paying a heavy toll wherever this is the case.

The United Nations world-wide survey of juvenile crime, under the direction of Dr. Manuel Lopez Rey, clearly demonstrated that, in those countries where parents and the law give children an early sense of responsibility for their acts, there is relatively little juvenile crime. On the other hand, in countries such as Sweden and the United States where youth are overprotected the highest crime rates for youth exist.

If conditions are normal, a 9-year-old enjoys school. However, in a jungle culture it is a nightmare. If parents, educators, and the police work closely together so that youngsters know they can get protection, they are more likely to report incidents of intimidation or abuse as they occur. It is then the responsibility of officials to see that the offenders are punished. The punishment need not be severe, but it must be certain.

THE FOURTH GRADER

Teachers generally rate this as a difficult year. A fourth grader will not be too easy to teach because he is such an individualist. He has strong likes and dislikes. He is beginning to become more subject centered and less teacher centered. His interests in the various subjects are giving him a thirst for knowledge, and he no longer feels the urgency for teacher motivation as he did in the first three grades. Fourth grade teachers usually watch their 9-year-olds from the corner of the eye and proffer help only as it is genuinely needed.

Once a student has become subject centered, he wants to plunge into the material. He resents being held back. He groans and moans about the students "who are so slow"—meaning, of course, those who are slower than he.

The fourth grade is a crucial year for many students because they reverse their comparative scholarship rating. Those who did so well in the first three grades sometimes have a lapse in the fourth. On the other hand, some of those who were slow the first three grades now become academic pace setters. Each student must be carefully analyzed to see that he adjusts to the challenge of the fourth grade.

A fourth grader is a competer. He likes to have his work graded. He gets dynamic motivation from each superior achievement and abject discouragement from each failure. His determination to rise and try again may have to be nurtured. In later years he will look upon his teacher as his competitive challenger. In the fourth grade he just "wants to do better than the other kids." He will, therefore, resent another 9-year-old trying to help him with his work. If he is really baffled, he prefers the help of the teacher. At the same time, he is not above sneaking a glance at a fellow student's papers "just to see how he's doing," or "just to get some ideas."

Because 9-year-olds are rather serious about schoolwork they tend to be more quiet than previously. They may get so interested in some subject that the whole class stays after the bell as though they were reluctant to leave. Even under normal circumstances some of the class will ignore the bell or casually clean up their desks and walk out after the rest of the class has rushed forth pell-mell.

PROBLEM OF THE SHY AND REJECTED BOY

Probably at this point we should pause for a moment to consider those parents who spend a great deal of energy worrying over a boy who appears to be shy or anti-social. These boys usually fall into three classifications. The first type is not really shy, he just ignores his own age group. After studying his behavior we find he is not anti-social but merely self-sufficient. He usually has advanced hobbies, mature intellectual interests, does a lot of reading, and seeks out the company of older children or adults. Boys his own age bore him, therefore he wanders away from them. Such a boy needs friends but he will accept only those who seem to have interests similar to his own.

This was the boyhood pattern of Thomas Edison, and it is typical of a great many boys who become outstanding leaders in adulthood. As long as a boy of this type maintains a wholesome attitude toward people in general, there is little cause to worry.

The second type is the overprotected boy. His problem is "Momism." He is usually the victim of a well-meaning but over-dominating mother. She lovingly hovers over him like a mother hen, constantly clucking at him: "Junior, leave immediately so you won't be late. Let me tie your shoes first. I'll comb your hair better, too. Did I get you your rubbers? Here is your lunch, and Mother piled your books together so you wouldn't forget them. Have a nice day, Junior, and be home exactly by three-forty-five, so Mama won't worry."

When Junior plays with the neighbor children, she is constantly interfering to make certain Junior is not imposed upon. During neighborhood quarrels Junior does not have to stick up for his rights. His mother does. When Junior is brought home by the police for some minor infraction or boyhood mischief, his mother defends him with heroic defiance. "I don't believe it! Junior just would not do such a thing. Imagine, grown men picking on a mere child!" As the officers go back down the walk Junior says to himself, "Boy, Ma sure pulled me out of that one! Now if I can just keep her convinced that I didn't do it."

Obviously, serious personality and character damage can result when a boy is the victim of overprotection. As early as possible a boy should learn to stand on his own feet, stick up for his own rights, and be accountable for his own acts. Parents can encourage this development by constantly keeping in mind the stage of growth Junior has reached. If they do this, they will not expect too much too soon, and, at the same time they can apply the appropriate amount of pressure on Junior so that the twig will be bent in the right direction.

The third type of anti-social personality is the classical problem of shyness which is characterized by an inferiority complex. This is the little fellow who is scared out of his wits by people. Because all children are sensitive to ridicule or excessive criticism, it is easy for them to get a feeling of inadequacy, inferiority, rejection, or failure. Many of them show evidence of more than an average amount of shyness at 2½ and again between 5 and 8. But there is no serious cause for worry unless there is marked anti-social behavior after 8. At 8 and 9 the normal youngster is usually capable of taking care of his interests and "getting in on the act." Failure to do so calls for special help from parents, teachers, the local Den Mother, or any other adult working with him. The task is to give him self-confidence and status with his own group. The attack is usually fourfold:

1. *Find out what he can do at least as well as others in the group.*
2. *Give him a chance to show it off when the group is together.*
3. *Try to find something in which he excels above the others.*
4. *Make this known to his own group in such a way that it will create group admiration. (If handled improperly it will create jealousy and resentment.)*

A shy child may take several years of careful supervision to bring him out of his social slump. Frequently, however, this type of boy possesses keen insights and is highly intelligent. He may become an outstanding adult.

Having considered most of the problems and highlights of the 9-year-olds, we are now ready for the golden age of 10.

CHAPTER 12

THE GOLDEN AGE OF TEN

Sometimes a grown man will look dreamily out into space and say, "You know, when I was a boy . . ." A man who speaks with such tender reflection of his boyhood days is usually thinking of the golden age of 10.

A 10-year-old has "arrived" as far as childhood is concerned. This is a plateau year. It has qualities that remind parents of ages 3, 5, and 7. This does not imply that it is a quiet year because it is characterized by much activity, but the activity is generally compatible with adult standards. A 10-year-old likes to get along with adults. He likes to get along with boys his own age. He wants to do well in school, he likes Cub Scouting better than ever, he enjoys YMCA camp. It is a year of positive living with enough salt and pepper thrown in to remind his parents that he is still a boy; in fact, a very live-wire boy.

Because age 10 combines exciting activity with "getting along," it is remembered as a happy golden year, a genuinely "good" year. And one psychologist quietly commented, "Yes, as a growing boy it is the last 'good' year he is likely to have!"

PORTRAIT OF A BOY BETWEEN TEN AND ELEVEN

Great forces of personality growth are piling up in a boy between 10 and 11, but only occasionally do they burst the dikes or flood over the walls of controlled conduct which a boy of

this age is trying to build for himself. He is learning to use his will power to set up a balance between "expression" and "suppression." It gives him a warm feeling of achievement to explain some of his more boisterous conduct to adults and have them smile back at him in sympathetic understanding. He says to himself, "Grownups understand boys better than I thought they did."

Parents are likewise getting a good impression. They observe that their 10-year-old is hearty, happy, and healthy. He is inclined to be athletic, a good sport, and a good student. He is generous, carefree, outgoing, and tolerant. He has all the gusto of 8 and 9 without the barbs and burrs. As in previous ebb-tide periods, he takes himself more for granted. His parents say he seems "much more grown up this year," and his teacher assures them that he is improving at school. They notice that he includes more youngsters his own age among his friends and doesn't depend on just one or two pals the way he used to do. They also notice an ever widening gang of new faces showing up at snack time for a round of peanut-butter sandwiches and a glass of milk!

In terms of growth graphs this is called a period of leisurely upward development, but in terms of energy output this is a year of all-out dynamics. He loves any kind of group play, he loves games, he takes dares. He is a fence-walking, wall-climbing, whoop-and-holler acrobat. He shows a lot of interest in the rough and tumble of touch football. He wants his own baseball mitt, bat, and ball. He loves to swim. Outdoor winter sports appeal to him. If he rides anything, whether a bicycle, skates, a scooter, or a "bug," he wants maximum speed. Power and speed are his favorite dish when it comes to anything on wheels. And parents must therefore take an equally *precautionary* interest so he doesn't break his neck. Many youngsters this age are involved in bike, coaster wagon, or sleigh accidents.

Finally, we should mention the superficial quality of a 10-year-old. He is more interested in conformity and doing the thing which will please people even if it isn't entirely right. If caught while doing something wrong, he may be quick to alibi or fib—especially on little things. He gets along well in school but tends to be a superficial student. He likes to assume an air of much worldy knowledge, and speaks of planes, cars, and rockets with an offhand sophistication which makes him sound much better informed than his parents. This desire to be glib and worldly-wise makes him spend a lot of time memorizing. He may memorize poems, songs, scientific facts, or baseball data. He may not understand all he is reciting but he proclaims it with eloquent conviction. He likes to see the surprised and admiring expression on the faces of adults. He responds quickly to commendation.

THE CLOUDS IN THE PORTRAIT OF THE TEN-YEAR-OLD

There are several things which come roaring out of the personality vents of a 10-year-old which surprise parents, particularly since the rest of his behavior pattern seems so well adjusted.

One of these thunder clouds shows up in his treatment of younger brothers and sisters. He reacts with particular vehemence toward those between 6 and 9. Part of this may be the factor of competition for attention, but more often it is simply an intolerance for qualities in these younger folks which he has so recently overcome himself. He hates to be reminded how silly, obnoxious, and unreasonable he used to be, and this is exactly what the behavior of younger brothers and sisters recalls to his mind. He therefore pounces on them with vitriolic vengeance as though he would suppress these unwanted qualities in them the same way he has suppressed them in himself.

If younger children are not to be abused, parents must intercede.

A similar storm cloud arises when Junior is playing with his neighborhood friends or schoolmates and something happens which triggers more anger than he can control. Anger is the one emotional quality which seems to evade the confining will power of a 10-year-old. Our pleasant, co-operative little fellow will suddenly explode with a passionate outburst that seems out of tune and out of time. It may be observed, however, that this is nearly always toward someone his own age or younger. It is very seldom exhibited toward adults. If asked about it, a 10-year-old will usually say, "Oh, if I get mad at grownups, I just go off by myself and let it boil without showing." He does seem anxious to get along with adults if he can, even when it involves swallowing his pride and passion.

GIRLS

An interesting attribute of a 10-year-old is his apparent indifference toward girls. This has been coming on for some time, but it becomes quite obvious during this period as he disclaims any interest in females whatever. He is really referring to girls his own age who seem to want to do "the dumbest things." Just as girls tend to group together to the exclusion of boys, so also the boys group together and exclude the girls. It is basically a problem of not having a common activity interest. Boys sneer at anything "sissified" and girls comment about "those crude, mean boys."

Latent physical attraction is nevertheless present, and occasionally youngsters require considerable supervision to prevent unfortunate boy-girl relations which may leave personality scars in later years.

As a matter of fact, this is the year that parents should be building a boy's respect for girls by finishing his general education on the basic facts of life.

ROUNDING OUT THE FACTS OF LIFE

Because age 10 to 11 is pleasant and generally a tractable year, it is considered the best time to have a rather comprehensive discussion with a boy about the facts of life. By this time he will know enough from his own emotions and personal feelings to accurately interpret what he is told. He is old enough to follow the entire miraculous process of procreation. He usually responds to a review of the diagrams in the family doctor book and likes to hear his father or mother discuss the processes of life in a scientific, matter-of-fact way.

A boy at this age may not voluntarily ask questions. It is therefore necessary for one of the parents to carefully introduce the subject. A father may take down the family doctor book, turn to the diagram of the human body, and say, "Come here, son. I think you will find this very interesting. Has anyone ever shown you the place in a mother's body where babies are made?" This brings back to a boy's mind the questions he asked in earlier years and the discussions he had with his parents. Immediately he is all ears.

Of course, by this time, a boy will have heard many sly and subtle insinuations about this subject from boys his own age. Older boys may have exposed him to a certain amount of vulgarity in discussing it. It is therefore highly important for a parent to establish a close, confidential, and trusting relationship during the discussion. He will not respond to the "birds and bees" approach. He is far too advanced for that. He wants to hear "just how it happens." However, it should be presented in such a way that he builds admiration and respect for the procreative powers. "Love" is not nearly as meaningless to a 10-year-old as many parents have presumed, and most boys are perfectly capable of developing a high idealism at this age with reference to their own personal relations.

This is also a good time to discuss with him the problem of "molesters" and the fact that older boys may attempt to introduce him into undesirable practices. Juvenile officers who interview moral delinquents find that more of them are subjected to degenerate influence at this early age than parents would ever suspect. It therefore warrants both the time and interest necessary to build up a warm confidence between a youngster and his parents, so that his problems can be anticipated and he will recognize certain pitfalls as they arise. Thousands of parents know that maintaining the ideal of complete moral integrity is entirely possible if parents enjoy the confidence of a boy and teach him how to understand and live intelligently with the powerful forces of life which are in him.

THE FIFTH GRADER

As a general rule, teaching the fifth grade is not nearly as strenuous as teaching the fourth grade. Most 10-year-olds like their teacher and depend on her more than they did last year. In spite of the desire of most fifth graders to get along with the teacher, there are usually two or three mavericks around to keep the class from getting dull. The teacher observes that the 10-year-olds are not afraid to ask questions on any subject. They like a lot of oral discussion. They are good at completing assigned tasks but will jolly well stop on the finish line without any particular curiosity to explore the subject further. The important thing to a 10-year-old is the here and now and the *status quo*. He doesn't worry like he did last year. "Everything is working out O.K.," he says. "I guess it will work out in the future."

The teacher notices that her 10-year-old boys are more solid in physical structure than a year ago. There isn't much increase in weight, but there is a filling out of the neck, chin, and chest. The health of the 10-year-olds seems good. There aren't as many complaints of dizziness, upset stomachs, and headaches as last year.

A boy's body is aching for activity at this age in spite of the equipoise of his mind. His interest span is short. While filling a reading assignment, he may look up between paragraphs and longingly scan the outside landscape. The out-of-doors is the first love of a 10-year-old.

This quality combines with others of this age to make him a superficial student. He willingly fulfills assignments but his mind plows a shallow furrow. He wants to know the answer without probing too deeply as to *why* it is the answer. He would rather learn things by rote or memorizing than by philosophical analysis.

He may resist wearing his glasses at this age even if the doctor has prescribed them. He may complain that only "sissies wear glasses" or that they are always falling off when he wrestles or slides into second base. Parents can help by getting glasses with sturdy frames and tight-fitting earpieces. Some who need glasses at this age can get along without them later on.

MONEY MADNESS

Often this is a stage when a boy has recurrence of his money madness. He does not want money for money's sake as he did at 8. He wants money to "buy stuff." Two things contribute to this trend. First, is a boy's ravenous appetite for candy. When his mother washes his jeans or cleans out his dresser drawer, she may find amazing quantities of used candy-bar wrappers. Second, there is the altruistic tendency of a 10-year-old to share everything he likes with all his pals. This takes money.

Ten-year-olds usually solve their problems by begging, bartering, or shoplifting. Most do it by begging. Their parents hear them plead their case of poverty almost every day. Many parents succumb to this pressure "just to get rid of the little beggar," but other parents hold out. This is where bartering comes in. The boy offers to run an errand or do his chores so he can get some money. The wise parent takes advantage of this offer; in fact, promotes it.

If neither of these approaches work, a boy may eventually fall into a pattern of thievery. Often a boy justifies it in the beginning with the excuse that the store owner is stingy or cheats his customers, and he deserves to have a few Robin Hood raids made on his candy bars. Other times a boy may shoplift candy and other articles on a dare. Parents need to be aware of these common practices so that they can watch for symptoms. They also need to set up a regular earned allowance so that a boy has less temptation to steal.

THE EARNED ALLOWANCE

Why do we have to have money? Eventually every boy asks this question. Only as Junior learns that money represents tangible chunks of somebody's sweat and labor will he appreciate the real meaning of this word. He gets the true meaning of money faster if it represents *his* work. This is not easy.

A child between 3 and 7 will seldom do more than play at doing work. The moment the work ceases to be play he abandons it with gusto and finality. That is why younger children usually work only when it is done along with one of the parents and is done "just for fun."

When parents set up earned allowances for younger children they usually make a list of tasks to be performed. The simple fact that such tasks seldom get performed by small boys is the reason why early allowances usually die abornin'. Resistance to work is normal from 3 to 7. Beginning around 8, however, most boys respond to simple duties. This is the year they also get their first major attack of money fever, so it is a good time to set up an earned allowance. By this time a boy is old enough to understand that cash is king. Not only must parents have this precious commodity to get the necessities of life, but even a small boy must have a few tokens of government specie.

We have mentioned in an earlier chapter that when a boy gets his earned allowance, it should be clearly understood that he will not be paid unless the work is done. He should also understand that he will be docked for a sloppy performance. Of course, parents must evaluate the performance in terms of children, not adults.

Should a boy be paid for everything he does? Experts say, "Definitely not." He should learn to do some things "just for love" or just to surprise his parents. A boy will bargain, however. "Don't I get paid for doing all these dishes?" A wise mother may reply, "No, son. You do the dishes while I fix the lunch for the picnic. Let's say that today we're both doing it just for love."

When should a boy be paid his allowance? The answer is, "Promptly." There is nothing more discouraging to a youngster who has excitedly announced that his task is all done than to have them say, "Oh, that's fine. I'll give you the money sometime when I have the right change." Most parents are guilty of this more often than is necessary.

THE TEN-YEAR-OLD AND HIS FAMILY

Except for the occasional temper tantrums which a 10-year-old has with his 6- to 9-year-old brothers and sisters, he feels closer to home and the family than he did last year. He loves to talk and work with his parents. He likes to take some of his pals and go places with his parents.

He even tries to share adult humor with the family, but this gets to be a bigger joke than his stories. Most 10-year-olds are kidded about their "corny jokes" and low-altitude puns. Usually they try so earnestly to be funny and cannot understand why adults don't laugh. After each story they look around wistfully and ask, "Do you get it?"

Parents sense that their 10-year-old is proud of his family and loyal to them. He spends a lot of time in boisterous outdoor play with his pals, but around supper time he comes tromping into the house as though he were a tired soldier back from the wars and happy to be home. When he has a ticklish problem at school or in the neighborhood, he seeks advice from his mother. He leans heavily on her for ethical decisions or social decorum. A father is a favorite, too. A boy of this age loves his companionship on hikes, hunts, fishing trips, picnics, or beach parties. He doesn't consider him the world's greatest in everything like he used to, but he rates him as the best father in town.

Around the house, Junior fits in fairly well. He gets up without too much coaxing, usually gets dressed in his favorite togs (no matter how dirty), and seldom has trouble getting to school on time. He can get clean in the shower, clean up his room occasionally (not daily), and run errands. He hates to go shopping for his own clothes unless it is to purchase shoes. He is very choosy about his own shoes.

A 10-year-old responds better to taking care of a pet than he did in earlier years. He bestows great quantities of affection on a puppy, kitten, guinea pig, hamster, or bird. This is the age when even a city boy thinks he would like to grow up and be a farmer.

When it comes to discipline, a boy at this stage usually responds to deprivation of some favorite item just so long as he isn't deprived of it too long. He is always judging teachers and parents in terms of "being fair." If a bike is taken away for a week he can usually accept it, but a month would be too long except in some extremely serious situation such as being accident prone or running away. Physical punishment is very rarely needed with a 10-year-old. Only in the most extreme cases should it be used. If he has been getting an occasional paddling when he deserved it down through the years, he is not likely to require this type of remedial action now. Postponing a trip or taking away a baseball glove or bike for a short time will usually pull a boy right back into line.

CONCLUSION

Age 10, then, is a period of live and let live. He likes people, places, and things to be friendly and informal. He seeks acceptance and contentment both from adults and contemporaries. He has an occasional temper outburst, but it is seldom serious. He still has to be coached occasionally to do what is right, but he has deep convictions about things that are wrong. He is nearly always truthful about important things. It is the little things that sometimes trip him up.

This is the year poise and lack of self-consciousness are fairly well achieved. Good manners, consideration for others, getting permission to do things, and generally fitting into adult requirements—all these seem to come quite naturally.

As long as parents are fairly flexible in their demands on a 10-year-old, they find it possible to make the golden age of 10 a wonderfully pleasant and satisfying interlude.

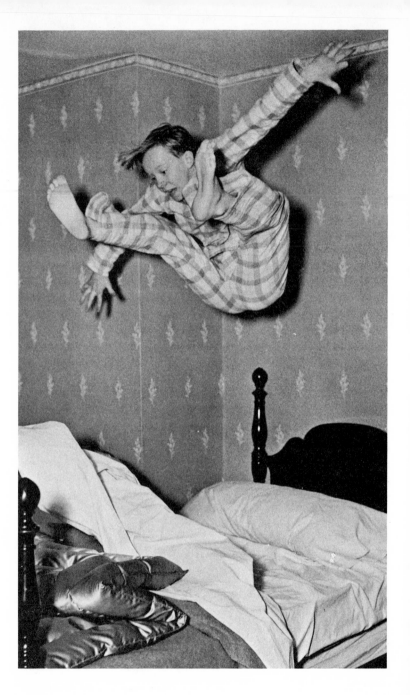

CHAPTER 13

ANARCHY AT ELEVEN

All the time a boy is enjoying his golden age between 10 and 11, he is stoking the furnace of his personality with some highly volatile stuff which eventually produces a roar of thundering dynamics, some time between 11 and 12. In some boys it may begin even before 11.

This period is characterized by a scratchy personality, open resistance to authority, indifference to parental standards, day-dreaming, independence, and sometimes downright defiance.

Parents tend to interpret this unexpected change as a total collapse in a boy's development. Here is what they may say to their family doctor:

"We just can't understand our boy. Here he was becoming such a fine, mature, responsible boy; good manners and every-thing. Now we don't know what to think. He is beginning to act as though he were raised in a jungle!"

"What does he do?" the doctor may ask.

"Well, he goes bellowing around the house. He has no manners at the table, shovels down his food like a starving tramp, quarrels with everybody, sulks when we correct him, throws his stuff around, won't tie his shoes, can't get himself clean in the shower, goes mooning around in a perpetual daydream, and acts as if he were the only atom in the entire universe!"

"I would conclude," says the doctor, "that as parents you feel like total failures."

"That's understating it," they assure him.

Then the doctor is likely to explain just what has been happening. Junior is in a new thrust period of development; furthermore, he is involved in the highly important process of proving to himself that all the things his parents have taught him are not mandatory after all. He has discovered that he is a free person in a free world and he doesn't really have to do *anything*. This is a great human discovery, and in process of time should mature into *self*-motivation and *self*-government. This is why an 11-year-old who has been told repeatedly to do something will sometimes snort, "Well, I don't see why I have to. . . . It's a free world, isn't it?"

The doctor may also explain that the recommended procedure is to keep a little pressure on him, but otherwise rock along and let him truly prove to himself that he is not a slave. He has to find out that he can be sloppy, grumpy, thoughtless and rude if he wants to. He also has to find out that people will not like him for it. It is this realization which usually brings Junior out of his revolutionary antics after a few months.

PORTRAIT OF A BOY BETWEEN ELEVEN AND TWELVE

From the doctor's point of view this latest outburst of anarchy is a normal personality thrust, which is scheduled by Mother Nature to arrive about this time. Our 11-year-old is no longer just a boy. His childhood is practically completed. He is now getting ready to ascend into the highlands of adolescence.

He weighs nearly eleven times more than he did at birth. He has acquired nearly half of his adult weight. His heart weighs seven times more than it did at birth, and his pulse rate has been dropping each year until now it is between eighty and ninety. He still burns up vast quantities of energy each day and needs around ten and a half hours of sleep.

As the new maturation forces within him come rumbling up through the vents of his personality, a boy certainly behaves differently than he did as a 10-year-old.

He is constantly challenging adults and contemporaries to prove he has increased status with them. He argues, resists suggestions, interrupts, gets on talking jags, slams doors, keeps the radio or TV at a blaring sound level. His physical wants are also extreme. His stomach is a bottomless pit. He raids the refrigerator, wants to drink malted milks by the barrel, and eat candy bars by the gross. Often he seems jumpy and nervous. At church or school he wriggles and squirms. At home he drapes himself on a chair like an octopus. His feelings constantly fluctuate. First he is too hot, then he is too cold. He claims to have the energy of a mountain climber, but whenever there is work to be done, he is permanently fatigued.

However, the one time when Junior scraps this whole catalogue of problems is when he happens to go visiting. Bewildered parents see him suddenly assume the mantle of little Lord Fauntleroy. He is polite and considerate, offers to run errands. He industriously helps a neighbor lady cut her lawn, while the grass at his own house is high enough to feed a herd of cows. All of this is encouraging, however, since it demonstrates potential qualities in Junior which are still alive and may some day embellish his home behavior instead of being reserved merely for neighbors and friends.

Of course, even at home Junior can be punished or disciplined into his old conformity, but the doctor suggests using vigorous discipline only when he becomes completely insufferable. It is highly desirable to let Junior get some of the vinegar and rebellion out of his system at this stage so that he can make a smoother adjustment during his teens. Often a youngster who has been forced to give up his program of independence at age 11 will explode at age 15 or 16. And a big husky 16-year-old in a wild state of anarchy is a much more formidable problem for his dad than a boy of 11.

THE FAMILY WRECKER

As one might suspect an 11-year-old can play havoc with a family unless the parents know what is happening. If they realize that his frequent binges of grumpy belligerence are merely manifestations of normal growth, they find it easier to take the obnoxious consequences in stride. It is also comforting to know his conduct is not a permanent fixture, but will ebb-tide back to more normal behavior after he reaches 12.

Meanwhile, the family watches the golden boy of 10 gyrate into what one mother called a "regular stinker." She said he demanded "equal rights with adults," wanted to challenge his parents with arguments and debates from morning till night. She said he handled situations with explosive rudeness; that he was "selfish, self-centered, self-assertive." Of course, she was assured that mothers of 11-year-olds were going through the same thing all over the city.

Even the most normal requirements of family life frequently send an 11-year-old into a pout. He resists going to bed, he spends volumes of energy trying to get out of work, he calls baths bothersome, compromises on a shower, and then daydreams under the spray until the hot water is all gone. His room is usually in a shambles, but it pays a mother to help him with a clean-up session occasionally because she may find all the things she's been missing. An 11-year-old is a pack rat. He hordes such things as pencils, pens, staplers, combs, punches, reference books, keys.

When a father chastises a boy at this age for his rudeness and unco-operative attitude, the father may be in for a surprise. His boy may retort, "Who's rude? Who's unco-operative? I'm no more rude than the rest of this family! A guy's got rights, hasn't he?" At this point the father may suddenly realize that his son is reacting to many situations in what he considers a normal, acceptable way. "I only do what I gotta do," he moans. This is a good time for a father to slap him on the back good-naturedly and say, "Well, just try to remember that the rest of us have rights, too." Actually, an 11-year-old has deep feelings of loyalty toward his family. He wants to be in the family circle. Seldom does he go to his room to mope. Around home he wants to be right in the middle of things.

THE ELEVEN-YEAR-OLD AND HIS GANG

Running in a pack is a prominent characteristic of 11-year-olds. Any such activity must be supervised by adults who possess a wholesome suspicion and a weather eye for trouble. Eleven-year-olds are chronic delinquents when they want to be. At this age boys are secretive. They like to get together and blast each other with shock words and dirty jokes. It makes them feel tough and grown-up. Half the time they barely realize what they are talking about. A favorite pastime is to pick up scraps of scandal from careless adults and pass these along to the gang with a smug air of worldly know-how.

They refer to the more immature and therefore more feminine boys their own age as fairies. They give the same label to the "fat boy" group. As time passes, some of these feminine boys may become more masculine than their name-callers. The 11-year-old understands homosexuality in a very obscure way but talks about it as though it were routine knowledge.

The group activity of boys this age is boisterous. The various members are constantly putting on an act of pretended hostility with a high-pitched volume of verbal violence, followed by solemn reconciliation. In between arguments there is a warm friendliness, and the observer gets the idea that these boys are merely playing at being grownups. They are trying to test each other for social or emotional reactions.

Boys this age like to stay overnight with a pal. This is good, providing it isn't a school night and providing the host parents are going to be home and on the job.

There is also a spirit of marked generosity among boys this age. They will sometimes "steal to share" with members of the group. When Christmas or a birthday gives them an excuse for sending a gift, they will usually want to buy something which is all out of proportion to their means. Their motto is "big gifts for pals."

Boys this age generally put the taboo on girls, but secretly they are beginning to notice the pretty ones. Some boys are extremely vulnerable to a flirtatious glance and try to cover up by saying, "I can't stand girls!" In their secret meetings they talk about some of the mysteries of life and make crude references to feminine charms. When they talk about girls they are thinking about older girls, or grown women, not girls their own age. At this age a boy can develop a real crush on his teacher at day school or Sunday school. He tells a pal, "She's the one I'm going to marry!"

It is common for boys at this stage of development to spend a lot of their spare time building tree houses or digging caves. They like to have a lock on the entrance and furnish the interior with everything from food to beds. They make elaborate plans to practically live in their new hideaway of 11-year-old security. Fortunately, such plans seldom work out because of their parents. Sleeping out may be satisfactory if the clubhouse is in the backyard of one of the families, but if it is over in a vacant field or patch of woods the chances for trouble run high. In such cloistered quarters the boy with the lowest moral standard or the most potent delinquency quotient often takes over.

THE SIXTH GRADER

There are some grades which demand the skills of a master teacher. The sixth grade is one of them. She must have an aggressive, affectionate, imaginative type of personality. She must be a good storyteller, appreciate sports and the out-of-doors. She must be capable of a warm affection for boys, even when they are 11-year-old stinkers.

The master teacher can actually develop warm enthusiasm for school among sixth graders, but, if she succeeds, it should be counted as a monumental achievement by her administrators. Eleven-year-olds are finicky, critical, restless, talkative. They want to move around the classroom, pass notes, play tricks, gossip. They often come to school upset, unfed, and itching for a fight. Parents report early morning quarrels with brothers and sisters, refusal to eat breakfast, reluctance to go to school. After they get to school teachers report teasing, grabbing, hitting, fighting, pushing.

To bring order out of chaos, the wise teacher finds it helpful to have regular opening exercises. This takes advantage of all the things 11-year-olds like to do—sing songs, present the colors, pledge allegiance, and listen to a short, exciting story with a patriotic or moral theme.

Because sixth graders feel the powers within them splitting the seams, they respond to the security of a well-run classroom. They like a teacher who is "fair, interesting, a good sport, and *makes us mind.*" Sixth graders cannot be indulged too much or they lose respect for the teacher and turn the classroom into a jungle. At the same time they can generate a hate-tinted passion of resistance toward a teacher whom they describe as "mean, selfish, unfair, too strict, and stupid." It is on this tightrope of narrow confinement between "too strict and too loose" that a sixth grade teacher must tread.

A good teacher challenges her sixth graders. She takes advantage of the urge in 11-year-olds to outdo their friends. She makes games wherever possible out of the learning process. She makes history come alive. She identifies great events of the past with current, familiar events. She makes heroes out of explorers as they trekked across oceans, deserts, and mountains to map the earth's geography. Quiz contests and blackboard speed exercises in arithmetic tingle the innards of a sixth grader. Story problems in mathematics are usually too complex for a sixth grader, but he loves a speed contest in adding, subtracting, or other basic skills.

When a teacher has a chance she can create a warm rapport with her 11-year-olds by getting them aside one at a time and developing a "touchstone of humor." A boy this age loves a teacher with whom he shares a little private joke. When she joshes him and winks at him over this little incident, he sparkles all over. It must be in private, however, or he is embarrassed.

As we have already mentioned, a young, successful sixth grade teacher is not surprised to find some of her students developing a crush on her. An 11-year-old boy has an eye for feminine charms and a very grownup appreciation of a congenial feminine personality. These can combine to stir his romantic emotions to an amazingly high pitch. He responds by bringing her gifts or trying to help her after school. He will not fall in love with more mature teachers but he will exhibit the same gift-bearing tendencies and the desire to be helpful. He says, "I like her. She's keen."

THE MULTI-PROBLEM BOY

Perhaps we should pause in our discussion of the normal 11-year-old to comment on that group of boys who have been in a state of rebellion ever since they were 6. This group does not follow the development program we have been discussing in the last few chapters. Instead, the boy from this group starts acting like a billy goat even in his middle childhood. His activity is characterized by chronic lying, stealing, truancy, quarreling, vandalism, burglary, sex play, resentment of church, and failure in school. This is the multi-problem boy and the solutions to his misbehavior require that we organize an attack on several fronts simultaneously.

First of all, the multi-problem boy usually lacks a warm, satisfying child-parent relationship. Sometimes this is solved by the simple expediency of having a working mother give up her job, if this is possible. Everything else being equal, a boy will respond to a woman better at 8 or 9 than he will to a man. From 10 on up the right kind of men can also help. This does not mean being a "buddy." A child resents an adult who comes completely down to his level. He wants companionship but he wants someone who is "just great," someone he admires and wants to grow up and be like. He wants counseling, not preaching, and he wants to get a look at the grownup things done by this person he admires so much. This is a perfect time to get this type of boy into competitive sports. Usually he prefers physical activities to academics, and this may be the reason for his difficulty at school. Baseball is usually a favorite, although he will respond to almost any type of sport with the right kind of leadership. An inspired leader of boys can often get him not only to excel in sports but often influence his behavior at home and at school. Once a boy gets a good dose of hero worship in his soul, it is good medicine for nearly all his ills.

A boy's school situation should be analyzed by a professional school counselor. Usually this type of boy will be a slow reader. This will handicap him the rest of his life unless it is conquered. Many parents have used exciting adventure books and reading out loud with a boy to get him going on his own steam. The school can suggest many additional techniques.

It is important also to have our multi-problem boy tested to make sure he has all his equipment, both physical and mental. Many a youngster has failed in school because no one realized he could only hear half of what was said, or could see only part of what was in front of him. Intelligence tests may also indicate that he will be a slow learner, and some things will be of no interest to him at all. Each human being must be dealt with in terms of his capabilities, not always in terms of his parents' ambitions.

And if a boy is found to have physical or mental limitations, this does not mean he cannot become a happy, well-adjusted adult. If handled properly he may far exceed everyone's expectations and completely overcome any evidence of his original limitation. To do this a boy must be loved for what he is.

A multi-problem boy is also going to require very close supervision, although most of this supervision need not be obvious. He must be recognized as a contagion, and other youngsters must be protected from unsupervised situations where their associations with him may result in their own delinquency. Unless this problem is recognized, our multi-problem boy will soon find himself without any playmates, for parents of other children will no longer tolerate him.

Finally, our multi-problem boy may be a victim of complexes and growing-up scars which his parents know nothing about. A few visits with a competent psychiatrist should disclose any problems in this area.

Parents whose boys are normal, average youngsters must be very patient in judging a neighbor with a multi-problem boy. Life being what it is, some boys are much more difficult to raise than others and excellent, conscientious parents may be wrestling with a maverick personality that even a professional institution would have difficulty handling.

In any event, a multi-problem boy in the neighborhood is really everybody's problem, and sometimes one of the neighbors can take an interest in a boy and do more to inspire and help him than even his own parents.

CHAPTER 14

AGE 12—THE BEGINNING OF ADOLESCENCE

As a boy moves out of his 11-year-old anarchy, he feels powerful forces within himself gradually receding. They do not disappear, they simply become more bearable. Having gained a new foothold on the ladder of maturation, a boy now takes it a little slower. Almost before he knows it, he is well within the precincts of adolescence.

In a sense, adolescence is like a ride on a roller coaster. It is a continuous pattern of ups and downs. Age 12 is the slow, easy climb that leads up to a high summit, only to be followed by a sudden plunge into the breathless depths of the "big dip" later on.

A 12-year-old knows he is climbing to new, exciting heights. He also knows that he doesn't understand many of the things which are happening to him. Nevertheless, because he temporarily feels a pleasant inner peace, he takes the climb in stride. Just as at 3, 5, 7, and 10, Junior senses that everything is going to work out all right.

He notes that he is not as rebellious, cantankerous, and saucy as he was last year during his "11-year-old thrust." He gets along with adults better, including his teachers and parents. He enjoys conforming more than last year. He hears his mother whisper to Dad, "I think Junior is over the hump." In response, Dad may merely mumble. He has seen Junior get over humps before. What he wants to know is when should the family expect the next *slump*. He remembers enough about his own adolescence to recall that it was one continuous round of humps and slumps.

PORTRAIT OF A TWELVE-YEAR-OLD

Physically, a 12-year-old starts out looking very much like his 11-year-old self. He is still a "little boy" in many ways. Parents can't understand what happens to all the bread, milk, meat, potatoes, and double desserts he has been wolfing down during the past year. Won't it ever show? It finally does. Frequently, during the latter part of age 12, there is a sudden splurge of growing and rounding out of bone and muscle which signal the physical transition from boyhood to youth. Nevertheless, there is great variation in the timetable of growth among boys this age, and some will postpone their growth splurge for as much as two years. If a large group of 12-year-olds is lined up together, they may appear anywhere from age 10 to age 14. Three years from now this group will have become much more uniform in appearance.

Parents need to watch a slow-growing boy to make sure he doesn't feel like a misfit. He is likely to be called "Shorty," a "little squirt," or other uncomplimentary names at school. It reassures him to hear an adult say, "He's little, but he's dynamite," or "His dad didn't start sprouting until around 14."

A number of boys will also pass through a "puberal fat period" at this time, and be called "Fatty," "Mr. Five by Five," "Paunchy," and so forth. He will feel reassured to know that generally this is a temporary condition and that he can expect to be much more athletic in appearance by the time he reaches 15.

This is also the age when a boy begins to discover that his sexual instincts are easily aroused. Glandular changes which are taking place create tensions and an awareness of sexual stimulation which will be new and troublesome. These forces of puberty also make him increasingly curious about sex. He becomes fascinated with obscene or pornographic pictures, which may be secretly passed around school. In his effort to appear matter-of-fact about sex he often picks up crude terms which he ties in with his earlier stock of shock words referring to the elimination processes as well as to sex.

Some boys this age become involved in sexual experimentation with older persons and may participate out of curiosity. When asked about it later, a boy may say, "I was just trying to find out what this is all about."

Most of these problems can be avoided if parents will stay close to a boy and make sure that he is made aware of the gradual changes which he should expect as he reaches puberty. It is especially helpful if a father points out to a boy that all of the problems which confront him are typical of the problems of all other boys, and that by developing the proper attitudes toward these new powers he can avoid the troubles and difficulties which will otherwise occur.

THE MIND AND EMOTIONS OF A TWELVE-YEAR-OLD

In other areas of mental and emotional development, a boy this age usually finds the things he was looking for a year ago. Last year he bullied his parents and pals to try to prove he had status. This year he finds he can take himself more for granted because he does have status. He feels more relaxed. His behavior becomes more generous, tolerant, and pliable. He finds it easier to talk with people. He does better in school.

In between these pleasant plateaus of leveling off, Junior will still exhibit an occasional flare-up of spunk and defiance, but these are generally shallow and short compared to last year. His main source of disturbance will be brothers and sisters close to his own age. Parents will be surprised at the explosions of anger which will occasionally arise in the midst of what appeared to be a congenial social setting. Fortunately, these are rare.

In a 12-year-old, parents observe an element of new sophistication. He likes to think of himself as having his emotions under control. He may complain that mystery stories don't scare him any more. He doesn't get the same hysterical chills and thrills out of *Dracula, The Batman, The Monster,* and *Frankenstein,* he did a few years ago. He also boasts that he doesn't "cry like the little kids." Parents note, however, that if the circumstances are right, a 12-year-old can still have a real good boo-hoo session occasionally.

The self-confidence of a 12-year-old makes him less inclined to brag. Even when some boy recounts a true but unusual achievement, his buddies are likely to get together later and assure each other that they bet "it was all a big lie."

However, when it comes to exciting stories and adventures of adults, boys this age are all ears. They are hero worshipers. Twelve-year-olds need to be surrounded with adults whom they can admire and emulate. These same adults may be lifesavers later on to help a boy get over some serious adolescent crisis.

THE SOCIAL TWELVE-YEAR-OLD

As far as sociability is concerned, Junior is far better adjusted at 12 than he was a year ago. It reminds his parents of qualities which were apparent around age 10. A 12-year-old wants lots of friends instead of just one or two. He has a propensity for being a laughing, noisy, pleasant frog in any pond in which he jumps.

The attitudes and traits of a 12-year-old make it a good time to work him hard in his favorite boys' organization. As a rule he develops a high-pitched enthusiasm for the Scouts, Boys' Club, YMCA, 4-H Club, or some similar program. However, supervisory adults need to make sure that meetings and activities are organized. Boys this age want a sharp outfit with precision leadership. They will gladly help with planning activities, but they are very insistent that the plans are carried out. If, for any reason, the plans fall through, a 12-year-old is very quick to criticize and get discouraged. A recent survey of drop-outs in a national youth organization indicated that the boys lost interest mainly because "we never did anything exciting," or "because nothing was organized."

It is common for boys this age to have an all-consuming enthusiasm for athletics. They enjoy all kinds of team play and exhibit a willingness to play in different positions. There is a certain group of perfectly normal boys, however, who will not respond to team sports. They tend to shy away from football, basketball, and baseball. Often they will participate if it is required at school, but they will not do it voluntarily for fun. The one sport which a boy from this particular group does enjoy is swimming. This seems to be a universal favorite, and many schools and colleges are enlarging their athletic programs to include swimming. This type of boy may also acquire a zest for some specialized sport involving only two or four players such as tennis, handball, wrestling, boxing, or golf.

TWELVE-YEAR-OLD ATTITUDES TOWARD RIGHT AND WRONG

By the time a boy is 12 he should have overcome most of his problems of lying, cheating, or stealing. Everything else being equal, parents should consider themselves running behind schedule if this is not accomplished by around 12. There will be relapses, of course, but they should be rare ones. Any *pattern* of lying, cheating, or stealing is what the law now calls "delinquency."

Authorities point out that, unless a boy has developed rather mature ethical values by age 12 he is likely to get into difficulty as he tries to cope with the many new insights and powerful motivations which come alive during adolescence.

For example, many things which he considered downright "bad" as a child will now receive far more sympathetic consideration. A case in point is the fact that he is likely to feel much more tolerant toward swearing, drinking, and smoking. During the next two or three years he is likely to experiment with all of them. He identifies these activities with being grown-up and being tough. Parents need to keep an eye to starboard for these explorations, because cussing, smoking, and drinking can become booby traps for a growing boy. Cussing and vulgarity will usually alienate him from adults and the "successful" group at school. Drinking among adolescents usually means "getting drunk." When this happens to adolescents it means doing crazy things—to people, cars, to themselves. A great many juvenile crimes result from what started out to be simply a "drinking party."

Smoking is something else again. Smoking is not as spectacular as drinking, and it is done for a different reason. Smoking is a symbol of independence, sometimes defiance. It is often done "just to show the principal" or parents. It becomes a badge. When a boy first starts smoking it is something to endure because he gets no pleasure from it. Only after the addiction has gradually taken hold does it evolve from a symbol to a necessity. Like other drugs, it sneaks up on the user until he finds it far more difficult to stop than he had thought. Thereafter, even widely publicized articles on lung cancer and heart disease carry little weight with him. He pretends he can stop but doesn't. As one teen-ager recently said, "I have to smoke so I won't get the shakes. But I can quit if I want to. I've done it lots of times."

Another activity which is prominent during early adolescence is the acceleration of a pattern which began during 11. This is a 12-year-old's proclivity for telling dirty stories. This is a further manifestation of a growing curiosity about sex, and this new, mysterious theme often becomes a tremendous source of humor at about this age. Even a poorly told or pointless story involving a sex angle will send a 12-year-old into gales of laughter. He doesn't understand all he talks about, but an eavesdropping parent can get quite a shock from hearing a weird tale being told by a pink-cheeked 12-year-old. If caught telling such a story, a youngster feels extremely guilty and it helps him get over the hurdle if the adult takes him aside to discuss it with him "man to man" without involving too much preaching or moralizing. Out of such conversations a boy can firm up his ethical girders without losing too much prestige and status.

THE TWELVE-YEAR-OLD ENTERS JUNIOR HIGH

When a 12-year-old graduates from grammar school and enters junior high school, it is one of life's epics. In grammar school, a sixth grader is a big frog. In junior high a seventh grader feels like a polliwog. Right away he senses the difference. Instead of a desk for his books, he gets a locker, together with a key that is easy to lose. Instead of a regular room, he goes to a different room for each class. And each class is taught by a different teacher. He has to pack books around, change classes quickly, do homework assignments.

All of this is pretty disturbing. Nobody "takes care of him" like his teachers did in grammar school. He has a home room, but that is mostly for reading bulletins and co-ordinating school administration. He is told about the boys' advisor but who wants advice? He wants to *belong* to somebody! When one boy was asked how he liked junior high he snorted, "Might as well live in a jungle." What he really wanted to say was that, for the first time in his life, he felt the need to somehow *survive*. Always there seemed to be somebody out to get him—the bigger kids, the bevy of demanding teachers, his ambitious parents, a couple of seductive older girls. He begins to feel the cross fire coming from all directions.

The seventh grader tends to search for a favorite teacher who can replace his "Miss Jones" from grammar school days. He wants *somebody* to please take a warm, intimate interest in him. At the same time he will avoid the title of "teacher's pet" like the bubonic plague. This is because he hungers for "total group integration" with his contemporaries. He definitely wants to be one of the gang. Therefore, when a teacher—even a favorite teacher—leaves the room, seventh graders are likely to burst forth in noisy antics to prove they are part of the group and "not under the teacher's thumb." They may indulge in throwing spit wads, chalk, erasers, in vandalizing the teacher's desk, and drawing weird pictures on the blackboard depicting unpopular teachers or pupils.

Academically, seventh graders have excellent potential. They can pursue factual or abstract knowledge with far greater facility than last year. They like to do research and hold debates. They like a teacher who commands respect because of superior knowledge. They also like to have classes which are well organized and firmly administered.

The seventh grade teacher finds that this age is remembered best for its enthusiasm. If she handles it right, she can direct this enthusiasm into very constructive channels. However, 12-year-olds resist homework. She can help out by making assignments exciting and adventuresome.

School officials have deliberately planned that this sudden shift from grammar school to junior high should occur during the ebb tide of 12 to 13. It does catch a growing youngster in one of his more favorable spells.

FAMILY LIFE OF THE TWELVE-YEAR-OLD

A boy responds much better to his mother this year than last, but he may still exhibit some independence toward her which is felt rather than seen.

At the same time, a 12-year-old may complain that his father is "too busy and ought to spend more time at home." This is a good time for a father to stop long enough to see whether this complaint has any merit. Too often, it might. He should make sure that there are regular opportunities to be together and talk together. But a father should not be disappointed if it turns out that his son does not need as much time and attention as he claims. In fact, many a conscience-stricken father has canceled important engagements to spend more time with his son, and then discovered that fifteen or twenty minutes of being together is about all his boy can stand. The interests of father and son are still too far apart. Unless they engage in common sport activities or work projects, the companionship quickly disintegrates and the boy wanders off to find one of his pals. Another couple of years and Junior will be ready for "long talks" or "just getting together."

A 12-year-old reacts in a variety of ways to the several age levels of his family. He resents the crowding of brothers and sisters just older or just younger. For several years he has shown this tendency. Now, however, if he has an older brother who is separated from him by 3 or more years, he starts admiring what he says and what he does. This puts a genuine responsibility on the older brother to try to set a good example for this 12-year-old hero-worshiper.

When it comes to the brothers and sisters who are still in early childhood, a 12-year-old can take a real paternal interest. He does not look upon them as competitors. It is the brother or sister near his own age who can goad him into a fit of temper without half trying.

Parents notice that their 12-year-old does not resist work quite as much as last year. However, he puts out so much energy in games and group play that he often arrives home in a state of exhaustion. During the latter part of age 12, he will have started his rapid growth pattern and consequently suffers from a shallow endurance quotient. He will resist work during this period more than he did earlier in the year. He frankly declares, "I'm just too tired!"

If something happens in the family to hurt his feelings, a 12-year-old tends to bury it within him rather than blow up the way he did at 11. This same reserve helps him bite his lip and hold back the tears when he's "mad enough to cry."

A mother notices that a 12-year-old is a kisser. He likes to kiss her good night and kiss her good-by. It is a sincere, genuine expression of affection. A little later on many boys have a period of several years when they are more restrained.

A 12-year-old is good company and a good conversationalist. His parents enjoy his budding sense of humor. He becomes quite a kidder. When his mother's high-fashion Easter hat is shown he doesn't gag and pretend to regurgitate the way he did last year. Instead, he says, "Boy, what a flower garden!" He also pulls puns on the family and loves "little moron" jokes, which he repeats over and over like a broken record.

A 12-year-old requires a lot of reminding. But he usually responds eventually. It is almost as though his mother were his alter ego and he expected her to remind him of almost everything he should do. Most mothers don't object to this. It is such a contrast with last year when he wouldn't accept suggestions or a reminder.

Between 12 and 13 is another period when parents can expect a boy to frequently bring home several friends as he did between 8 and 10. These friends will usually go with Junior to his room and stay pretty much out of the way. They respond heartily, however, if Junior's mother visits them with glasses of milk, slabs of peanut-butter and jelly sandwiches, or huge hunks of ice cream. Boys this age suffer from permanent starvation.

THE VARIABLES AT TWELVE

This is an age which impresses parents with the wide variations in sizes, shapes, and sentiments among 12-year-olds. A certain percentage of this group has not changed noticeably since 11. Even their attitudes are preadolescent. Another group is extremely advanced. They are large, sophisticated, and self-confident. The majority, however, fit the pattern we have described.

The variable factors in each boy are also impressive. He will work like a beaver fixing up his room, but fail to get around to cleaning it. He will not pay any attention to hanging up his clothes, and yet be extremely keen about picking out his clothes when they are being bought.

A 12-year-old is usually willing to go to bed if it doesn't interfere too much with his favorite TV diet. Once in bed, however, he often sleeps lightly. He may have bad dreams about his mother being kidnaped or his father being killed by a robber.

Altogether, age 12 is a year of modest contrasts. The variables are present, but the pleasant adjustment to life during this period makes it a happy interlude for both the parents and their boy.

CHAPTER 15

THE SILENT REBEL

Patterns and Problems of the 13-Year-Old

By the time a boy reaches 13 his adolescence is well on the way. Physically, emotionally, and intellectually, he may feel he has troubles. If so, he becomes very reflective and introverted. He is highly critical of himself. He has impulsive temper outbursts with occasional manifestations of actual or threatened physical violence. His 12-year-old enthusiasm for life is replaced by concentrated scrutiny of life. He tends to be on guard. He stumbles over words, trying to find precisely the right one. He hesitates to take action until he feels certain he is right. He is less of a gambler than last year, more of a student this year.

A 13-year-old often resists a warm relationship with his parents but turns around and criticizes them for not giving him more attention. He is often with the family but not part of it. He snaps at brothers and sisters between 6 and 12, but will often show affection for younger ones. He may be sitting with the family watching TV and get up in the middle of the program to wander off by himself. He seems to be thinking of faraway things. He has big conversations with himself: "I don't see why they make me do *that!* Don't they know a guy's got rights? Why do I have to do it just so? In fact, why do I have to do it at all?"

Parents are not part of such soliloquies. They see their 13-year-old more or less conforming and assume he must feel all right about things in spite of the silent treatment he gives them.

Often they would be amazed if they knew the high-powered stuff he is pouring into his personality furnace. He is building up some pressures which will erupt later on. Meanwhile, he is their silent rebel.

PORTRAIT OF A BOY BETWEEN THIRTEEN AND FOURTEEN

By age 13 most boys have started their splurge of growth. During the next two years many of them achieve four-fifths of their adult height. Some parts of the body get ahead of others. Arms and legs may elongate disproportionately and give a boy the feeling he is mostly elbows and knees. The nose may jut out prominently and make him feel he's another Jimmy Durante in the making. It sometimes takes three or four years for the face to fill out and catch up with the nose. The hair growth on the upper lip begins to darken, and the hairs at the corners lengthen noticeably. The Adam's apple begins to protrude as the larynx enlarges and the vocal chords lengthen in preparation for the coming voice change. For many boys the cracking of the voice comes during 13 or early 14.

Most 13-year-olds have universal tastes. They are not hard to feed, they are just difficult to keep full. Their stomachs are no longer tubular affairs but are taking on the proportions of a storage bin into which must be poured endless quantities of favorite foods. Tastes vary somewhat, but the craving for candy is not as pronounced as in earlier years. There is the usual gulping down of meat, vegetables, potatoes, and gravy, followed by large-quantity desserts. A mother notices that her boy is more responsive to fruits and salads than previously and that he also enjoys some experimental dishes occasionally. Table manners usually improve considerably during this year. He no longer tries to corner all the conversation the way he has done earlier. In fact, he may spend the entire meal buried in reflection, and while the family thinks he is enjoying the topics under discussion his mind may be a million miles away.

A 13-year-old notices that adults seldom compliment him the way they did last year. They always seem to be expecting something from him which doesn't quite come off. He does not articulate well. He eventually assumes people don't understand him, and for the rest of this year he may give up trying to be understood. When his highly critical analysis of his own inadequacies overwhelm him, he tends to move solemnly away to hibernate in his room. Occasionally parents may tiptoe to the door and hear muffled sobbing. It is mostly frustration crying. He is angry with himself.

MENTAL AND EMOTIONAL PATTERNS
OF A THIRTEEN-YEAR-OLD

This brings us to the mental and emotional patterns of our boy. The glorious enthusiasm of the 12-year-old is far less evident by 13. There is a quieting, a new subtle tenseness, a more serious approach to life. The bubbling happiness and sheer joy of living last year are replaced by constant introspection and calculating deduction. As we would suspect, this returns him to an earlier pattern of worry and wonderment. He even worries over how much he worries. This worry-wart trend inevitably leads to an increased irritability rate. He is easily annoyed, especially by younger children. He may snap back at his mother or mumble under his breath in response to an instruction from his father.

However, the mind of a 13-year-old tells him that life is wonderful and he shouldn't be in a hurry to grow up. He concentrates on the here-and-now more than the future as he did last year. He analyzes every passing situation and each new experience. He drains them of everything his faculties can absorb.

This tendency to deal with realities is the cause of some tender feelings and strong misgivings when he looks in the mirror. What he sees is far from what he imagines himself to be. Parents would be surprised to learn how much time a 13-year-old spends in front of a mirror examining his ears, nose, eyes, and mouth, his build, smile, frown, and grimaces. Out of such self-inspections come the motivation for his first primping. He experiments with his hair. He scrutinizes patches of freckles which may have become quite prominent during the past two years. He tries out various kinds of expressions and glances. He is glad this isn't his completed self. His hope is in the future.

THE THIRTEEN-YEAR-OLD AND HIS FAMILY

As we have already indicated, a boy at this age is with the family but not so much a part of it. He is independent, introspective, and individualistic. From here on his craving for privacy will be constantly emphasized to his parents. His younger brothers and sisters who find the greatest delight in snooping in his room will provoke him to outbursts of anguish which sound like the roar of a wounded bear. The same younger siblings discover how easy it is to get his goat and frequently take sadistic delight in goading him to fury.

However, anger with a 13-year-old is better controlled than at 11. The bursts are sharp and short. A mother notices that her boy tends to go off by himself when he's angry and stew in his own juice.

Because a boy this age is so critical of himself, his parents need to find excuses to encourage him. This will not come automatically because this age gives few occasions for it. Parents must be alert to his needs and compliment him whenever they have any reasonable excuse.

This is a good time for parents to give more attention to his clothes. His seances with the mirror will make him more sensitive to clothes than in earlier years. Some 13-year-olds are extremely particular about the variety and style of their clothes, not only for school but for dress.

A mother must not be alarmed if her 13-year-old seems suddenly distant and unapproachable. This will be the rule rather than the exception. The declaration of independence, which began at age 11, is suspended during age 12, but now the campaign is resumed at 13 with quiet determination. The mother image which a boy builds in his mind includes respect for her authority, and it is the instinctive urge to rebel against this authority that makes a boy withdraw. Some boys become quite vocal and sassy toward their mothers but most maintain the distant restraint of a silent rebel.

THE EIGHTH GRADER

The things about a 13-year-old which make it difficult for him at home often make it easier for him at school. He concentrates better. He takes the learning processes more seriously. His introversion gives him a stronger sense of personal responsibility, and therefore makes him more dependable. At home a 13-year-old secretly resents authority, but at school he wants an orderly world and, while he may vocally snort and buck at authority, he genuinely wants things "run according to the rules." This explains why a boy of this age will call his principal a "bantam rooster dictator," and then turn right around and criticize his teacher because "she isn't strict enough and the kids get away with murder." It is evident that two great forces are churning up a storm within him. One is for order, the other shrieks for independence.

Competent teachers assigned to the eighth grade generally describe it as a pleasant and satisfying grade to teach. They recognize the conflicts in their critical but studious wards, and capitalize on their pent-up energies to drive them hard scholastically. The 13-year-old has capacity for sustained attention. He has enough independent doubts to make him a challenging pupil. He has enough group identification to make him want to compete.

Up to now a boy's interest is usually in the things bigger than himself. He has liked astronomy and the related subjects of jets and space probes. Now his mind begins to turn to the tiny things of the universe. He gains interest in atoms, electrons, molecules, the elements of chemistry, and the principles of physics. A boy may suddenly disclose unexpected aptitudes in scientific subjects, particularly if it is being taught by a teacher whom he respects and admires. This is also a period when a boy may exhibit a new interest in world affairs, political history, and the cultural traditions which he formerly ignored.

Of course, 13-year-olds, being what they are, can easily repudiate their academic potential and go absolutely berserk if they sour on a teacher and decide to make her life miserable. Experts say this is one of the most critical school years insofar as relations between the teacher and her students are concerned. The temperaments of these 13-year-olds call for the touch of the master teacher.

BOY-GIRL RELATIONS AT THIRTEEN

To a 13-year-old boy, girls are very real but far away. They are "out there" somewhere. As we have already mentioned, a boy at this age will preen and primp to impress the girls, but if one should suddenly turn on him with a bright gleam of radiant romance he would spin like a whirligig. He wants girls to be coy and elusive. He wants to pursue them from a safe distance.

Some schools have experimented with dating in couples for special dances at this age and found it to be an administrative blunder. A 13-year-old does not want to be pushed into dating. He wants to attend mixed parties but have enough boys around to feel safe. Girls are still creatures rather than companions. Oddly enough, he will come out of his shell any time for a kissing game, but he usually moans boisterously if he gets "caught" and acts as though he hated to go through the routine. Secretly, however, he feels kissing is quite the thing as long as it is part of a game.

Girls this same age are often embarrassed for the boys in their own class because they seem so awkward. By the time these girls are ready for steady dating at 17 or 18, they will have set their sights on older boys. And by the time these present 13-year-old boys have come into their full romantic maturity, they will probably be looking to girls younger than themselves for dates. But this is something for the future. At the present moment the 13-year-old boys are most anxious to impress their female contemporaries and, as we mentioned before, "pursue them from a safe distance."

ETHICAL SENSE OF A THIRTEEN-YEAR-OLD

By this time a boy accepts the fact that doing wrong will make him worry and shroud him with regrets, so he makes up his mind in most cases not to get involved. However, in spite of himself, he does hit the skids every so often. The thing we notice on such occasions is his ability to take the blame for something he has done. He is sufficiently self-critical and humble about his inadequacies that he wistfully admits his shortcomings. His parents take pride in this new-found strength of character, but to their boy it is simply a matter of inner necessity. His ethical sense is alive and broadcasting!

But he does have a tolerance, as we noted in the last chapter, for some things which would have shocked him as a boy. Smoking, cussing, and drinking are among the grownup indulgences which he may secretly long to try. All during adolescence, he will wrestle with his urge to sample grownup vices, even though he knows they can bring him nothing but trouble. With a few boys, this urge will lead to experiments in narcotics, homosexuality, drunkenness, criminal assaults, or other acts of delinquency and crime.

None of this is necessary if a boy is trained to listen to his parents and the signal of his conscience. His ethical sense is perfectly capable of giving him the right promptings if he has the good common sense to listen.

REJECTED OR OVERPROTECTED?

Two types of boys often get into trouble during early adolescence. One is rejected, the other is overprotected. The rejected boy is the one who constantly comes home to a barrage of complaints:

"Shut the door!"

"Pipe down!"

"Don't track in that mud!"

"What? Those shoes worn out already?"

"Who's asking you?"

"Don't you do anything besides watch TV?"

"You're the laziest kid on the block."

"Don't bring that Jones brat around here again."

"Can't you sit up straight at the table?"

"You look like a tramp!"

"Turn down the radio!"

A boy can tell when he's in the way and a nuisance to his parents—especially around age 13. This is the beginning of the runaway period. Thousands of boys leave home each year because they feel unwanted. Even if a rejected boy does not run away physically, he may abandon his parents mentally and morally. He may do this by committing nighttime burglaries, stealing cars, committing vandalism, playing hooky from school, or indulging in some of the local adult vices. He knows this will alienate him from his parents, but he deliberately lunges into it with a defiant shout of retaliatory vengeance. He is out to show his parents he can hurt them.

Strangely enough, an overprotected boy may do exactly the same thing.

Overprotection is another form of rejection. "Momism," as we have previously mentioned, can be lavished upon a boy to the point where the love she showers upon him becomes a symbol of destruction. The boy feels her flood of love is drowning him. He can never be himself, stick up for himself, or find out for himself. Always Mother is right there to take over. A boy ultimately comes to feel that the mother does not really love him but is merely trying to satiate her maternal instinct. He feels like a moth in a cocoon—ready to burst forth to freedom. Crime sometimes becomes the symbol of that freedom.

WHY THE INCREASE IN ADOLESCENT CRIME?

The pressures of modern living plus the explosive powers of early adolescence frequently combine to create criminal thrusts on the part of the multi-problem boy. Experts are beginning to feel that society itself is contributing to the problem by setting up values which are proving fallacious. This is particularly evident in some of the more progressive nations such as Sweden, the United Kingdom, and the United States. These countries have the highest sociological development, but often 13- and 14-year-olds are committing the crimes of violence ordinarily expected of adults.

Many experts feel that in our anxiety to share the new levels of prosperity and free, comfortable living with everyone, we have taken a lot of the discipline out of human relations. Not only have we softened our behavior restrictions for adults, but we have sometimes battered down practically all of the important restrictions for youth. A skyrocketing crime count has been the result.

Rebuilding the "barriers of security" in society can be done in a very short time. It simply requires the elimination of some false values and the popularizing of some true ones.

What are some of the false values?

1. *The idea that children can be raised as well by nursery schools or some welfare agency as they can by their mothers.*
2. *That delinquency usually thrives only in big cities and poor neighborhoods.*
3. *That our youth are not responsible for their criminal conduct until they have passed the age of a juvenile.*
4. *That delinquent youths are simply "maladjusted."*
5. *That children develop best when parents give them everything they want.*
6. *That it is all right to keep children in one world and adults in another.*
7. *That it is all right for adults to indulge themselves in poor practices so long as they do not allow their children to do so "until they grow up."*

In contrast to these false values, what are some of the true ones?

1. *Society has never worked out a satisfactory substitute for a good mother. It should therefore become part of our cultural framework to encourage mothers to remain at home with their children if at all possible.*
2. *Delinquency can be expected to strike in either city or countryside, in rich homes as well as poor homes.*
3. *Youth must learn that there is no such thing as "freedom from consequences." Youth must expect to be held responsible for criminal acts which are deliberately planned and calculatingly executed.*
4. *Every human being is maladjusted most of the time. This is*

what gives zest to life and a reason for solving problems. Therefore, a certain amount of maladjustment is perfectly normal. We must teach our children how to adjust to changing circumstances from day to day. We should refuse to make special concessions to a youth who pleads "maladjustment" unless clinical studies show him to be physically or mentally handicapped to a significant degree.

5. *After a child has been provided with his essential needs the parent should not try to spend every waking moment attempting to keep Junior from feeling frustrated or developing "tensions." Children should be taught to try to work out their tensions and satisfy their own needs insofar as possible. Studies of American boys who were captured in Korea showed that we had raised a soft, pampered generation. Many were easily discouraged and easily brain-washed.*

6. *There is only one word for both children and adults, and the sooner children acquire the ambition to meet the demands and responsibilities of the adult world of reality, the sooner the child is likely to taste the fruits of happy, well-adjusted living.*

7. *Parents should decide what they want their children to be like and then strive to lead them by example; otherwise many children will strike out at their parents. They resent double standards by parents who force them to do what the parents will not do themselves. They prefer parents who say, "Follow me."*

When a 13-year-old has been raised in a home where these seven rules prevail, he has a good chance of making his adolescence a blessing instead of a booby trap.

lots of stamina and seldom misses school because of illness. His measured strength is more than twice what it was at 10. He likes to roust about, enjoys playful wrestling, and usually wants to participate in physical impact sports.

Junior's sprouting beard may create a problem. He is likely to lock himself in the bathroom once or twice a week and skim off the fuzz. Most boys resent being kidded about their shaving at this early stage. Furthermore, shaving may irritate the skin and help promote a good case of acne. Acne adds to an already well-developed sense of self-consciousness and may impair the normal maturity of a boy's personality. If acne becomes serious, a doctor should be consulted. Improper diet or some other contributing cause may need to be identified.

During this period the skin is also very susceptible to blackheads and large pores. Somehow a boy cannot remember to wash regularly, and when he does the water on his face usually covers no more than six square inches. A quick lesson about "the regular scrubbing of the face with soap and water on a washcloth" is likely to help as much as anything. The use of witch hazel or an astringent will also help keep the skin pores, particularly around the nose, from becoming distorted or enlarged.

THE FOURTEEN-YEAR-OLD AROUND THE HOUSE

If a 14-year-old blows up from the pressures of adolescent life, he is likely to take his spite out on his home. This we will discuss in a moment. But the average youngster who is generally well adjusted will get along better around home than almost anywhere. At first he may try his social wings abroad and express a desire to be "independent of the family," but when he finds that for the moment he seems to be a social misfit he is likely to retreat to the family fireside.

Parents can do many things to help Junior maintain his moorings during this difficult period. For example, they will find that he generally responds to praise better than criticism. He needs encouragement at frequent intervals because he is still suffering from a heavy dose of self-criticism which he gulped down during age 13. He can also be helped in his social adjustment. He should feel free to invite his friends over to the house. These friends will be wild, woolly, and noisy, but they can be kept under control without embarrassing Junior if the parents keep their sense of humor. Two things, however, can be fatal.

One is to impose oppressive discipline on the group or talk to them as though they were "little kids." Junior may never forgive his parents for this kind of breach, and he may be too embarrassed to invite any of his friends back. The other parental booby trap is turning the house over to 14-year-old Junior and his gang with the admonition, "Now be good boys while we're gone!" The only thing they will want to know is "how long" the parents will be gone. The pandemonium which will then break loose is likely to make some rather lurid history for these half-baked cakes.

About this age a boy may express a desire to get better acquainted with a certain girl at school who is "real cute." Parents can make it easier by encouraging Junior to invite her to go with the family to the show on Saturday night or go on a picnic or a beach party. In fact, "family" dating under these circumstances should be encouraged by the parents of both the boy and the girl.

Parents will notice that Junior is capable, during his better moments, of being more adult around the house than when he was 13. He takes responsibility a little better and will generally do his share of the chores around home. However, he will resent having disagreeable jobs unloaded on him, especially if it looks like Mom and Dad are "just trying to get out from under." Doing dishes and other routine household duties are just as much a bore to a teen-ager as they are to parents. And as for the yard— its appearance is a lot more important to Junior's folks than it is to him.

Parents may find themselves jawing at Junior because he seems to be involved in far too many things. If he is a normal, outgoing boy, he is likely to have his mind loaded with such miscellaneous items as astronomy, electronics, ham radio contacts, model planes, science fiction, 4-H Club, Scouts, building a motor scooter, getting a job, getting good grades at school, and trying to be more popular.

The breathless excitement of all this mental rushing about is probably going to make him a little forgetful about such irrelevant things as washing the car, doing dishes, running an errand, or going to bed.

All of these interests plus a growing passion for privacy also make Junior begin pressing the folks for his own room. If feasible, this is desirable. However, if it cannot be arranged conveniently, it will help to give Junior a dresser or at least a drawer which can be locked. Nothing plagues a 14-year-old as much as having the little kids get into his things. And nothing is more fascinating to small fry than Junior's stuff. A lock and key seem to be the only known solution.

THE FOURTEEN-YEAR-OLD AT SCHOOL

A few boys this age will suddenly come into full bloom academically and begin their careers as honor scholars. For most boys, however, 14 is a rough year. They claim they would like to get good grades but just don't have time. The mad scramble of many competing interests as well as the strong inward anxiety to be accepted socially combine to make school just a phase or a minor part of life's big pattern. Both parents and teachers have to concentrate to keep Junior's eye on the ball. Teachers can help by making classes as stimulating as possible, and parents can help by making Junior's outside activities dependent on whether or not he gets his homework done or keeps up in school.

At school the teacher finds her class of 14-year-olds very group conscious and therefore easily distracted from the lesson. The challenge is to keep the lesson so constantly interesting that the group stays on it. Group focus can be shattered by one or two in the class showing off, whispering, giggling, or acting up. The average 14-year-old is far more hungry for group identification than teacher identification. Therefore, his mental radar is always tuned in on the class. If they are interested in the lesson, then he wants to be. If the class is distracted by something, then he prefers to focus on the distraction.

Noise and buffoonery characterize the normal inclinations of boys this age. In between classes they play around like overgrown puppies. They grab each other, push, wrestle, and punch. They do the same thing with their voices. Their bellowing back and forth down the hall is to get attention and appear blasé. To them loudness is not noise—at least it doesn't bother them. The main thing is to communicate sound and fury, and if the whole world can hear it, so much the better.

Teachers find their 14-year-olds anxious to test life by trial and error. They want to find out about many things which are far too complicated for them. It is "just to see if I can handle it." A wise teacher tries to keep the fundamentals of learning sufficiently interesting so that her students don't wander away into the nether world of space travel and rocket making. This tendency to wander away from a good preparation in fundamentals will likely remain a problem all through the next three or four years. Sometimes it even extends into the first two years of college.

At school 14-year-olds are often greatly disturbing to the meditative 13-year-olds and the easygoing, inoffensive 12-year-olds. Originally, the junior high setup was designed to accommodate the group which was considered too old for grade school and too young for high school. This was thought to be the seventh, eighth, and ninth graders. Some authorities are now beginning to wonder if there isn't a better arrangement. They point out that seventh graders are often confused when uprooted from the grade school pattern. They also point out that the meditative 13-year-olds (meaning, of course, those who are 13 by the development clock) are more easily accommodated in a school covering grades one to eight than in a junior high. The real problem group, they believe, is the 14-year-old ninth graders who are at loose ends and, while not ready for high school, create chaos if left with younger students.

These authorities suggest that junior high might be restricted just to this one troublesome age group in the ninth grade. Where this has been tried experimentally, it has proven impressively successful. Perhaps this portends a development in education for the future.

THE MAVERICK FOURTEEN-YEAR-OLD

There are many facets in the personality thrust of the normal 14-year-old boy which may tend to make him blow up:

1. *This particular stage of development is painful to him. He may be heard to say, "I hate this age. I'll be glad when I'm more grown up!"*
2. *He tends to be extremely critical of his parents, especially his mother. This is because he is trying to justify his inward anxiety to be independent of his parents and resents the fact that every time he tries his wings he seems to fall flat on his face. Furthermore, up to now the mother may have provided most of the discipline for Junior, but a 14-year-old is a man's chore. It is time Father took over.*
3. *Junior ventures into so many new things at the same time that he tends to be a frustrated failure more often than he is a howling success. Particularly at this age he needs to be guided into the areas of accomplishment where he seems most likely to succeed.*
4. *He now has practically all of the grownup desires of an adult, and yet must be constantly told that "it isn't time yet." In spite of Junior's complaining and grumbling, his parents must resist the temptation of abandoning Junior to his own devices. He never needed the closeness of his parents more than right now.*
5. *He often gets punished for the extremely harsh language which he uses on his younger brothers and sisters. Parents will observe that frequently their teen-ager has a good reason for feeling imposed upon by "the little kids." The small fry learn how to get his goat and may ride him unmercifully. It reassures Junior if his parents side in with his point of view once in a while (and that, of course, when he's right).*
6. *A 14-year-old is stubborn. He resists being corrected and may argue vehemently, especially with his parents. At 12 he*

*liked to have an occasional discussion about his faults. At
13 he listened carefully to each biting word of criticism and
took them to heart. But at 14, he has suddenly become
impervious. Either he will argue noisily or become like a
turtle in a shell. In the latter case, when the storm comes up,
he just pulls in his neck and says, "Let her pour." Nevertheless, Junior needs to hear how his parents and teachers
think he is doing. The main problem is to be sure there is
plenty of praise. mixed in with the criticism and that the
criticism does not degenerate into nagging.*

POTENTIAL DELINQUENCY AT FOURTEEN

From our discussion thus far it will be seen how easy it is
for a boy of this age to slip across the boundaries of good citizenship and develop an acute case of juvenile delinquency. This will
be particularly true with the boy who is either rejected or overprotected, but it can happen to any boy. Resentments may have
been building up in him since age 5 or 6. He may have tried to
do something about it during his 11-year-old thrust, but found
himself promptly suppressed. After sliding across the 12-year-old
stage he may have found himself at 13 bitterly cogitating on his
feelings of retaliation and breaking loose. Age 14 then becomes
the boy's mobilization date. His sudden change from 13-year-old
meditation to 14-year-old activation makes him easily triggered
into an explosion by the normal restraints which his parents may
need to put on him. As a result, crime rates for youth begin
climbing rapidly at 14 and will continue skyrocketing through
15, which is another troublesome year. Every so often newspapers carry the shocking story of a boy of this age committing a
murder or being guilty of some other serious crime of violence.
It is easy to criticize on such occasions by blaming the parents
and so forth, but the police who investigate these cases learn
that a 14-year-old who has curdled and turned maverick can be
dynamite regardless of who is raising him. Even state institutions
with highly skilled professional psychologists and youth workers

have difficulty untangling many of these youngsters. Sometimes parents are to blame, either because of their ignorance or neglect, but other times it appears to have been more a problem of the boy's personality collapsing under the pressures of life.

The important thing to keep in mind is that age 14 is a time when a boy's cake is "only two-thirds baked." He has lived fourteen years and has seven years to go to reach his majority. He needs careful, watchful supervision. He needs affection, praise, and guidance. He needs patience and discipline. He is wrestling with one of the most difficult periods of his entire life.

CHAPTER 17

FREE WHEELING AT FIFTEEN

When the normal boy reaches 15 he has a tendency to go out of control temporarily. There were symptoms of this thrust much earlier, but the forces of adolescent rebellion now acquire a full head of steam. Junior may ask himself, "What has come over me lately?" His parents may be wondering the same thing.

Looking back over the past five years, it is interesting to see what has been happening to Junior. At 10 he reached his golden hour of happy contentment as a fully developed "boy." At 11 he suddenly came out into the arena of life with a chip on his shoulder and his chin jutting out. At 12 he leveled off into a pleasant interlude of "live and let live." At 13 he turned philosopher and submerged himself in deep, sullen moods of wishful thinking—mostly for independence and total self-sufficiency. At 14 he came out of his shell to enjoy life, but found himself stumbling over his own feet and behaving with pathetic inadequacy. Now he is 15. He no longer feels pathetic, and he doesn't particularly care whether or not people think he's inadequate. His whole attitude and bearing seem to send out one single, sizzling message: "Clear the decks, I'm coming through!"

PORTRAIT OF A FIFTEEN-YEAR-OLD

By the time a boy completes his fifteenth year he probably will have attained 95 per cent of his full growth. Junior likes his new physical status. He often mows the lawn or works in the yard stripped to the waist. This is so the neighbors can see he isn't "a scrawny little kid any more." If he is athletically inclined, he starts eating, drinking, and sleeping in terms of football, basketball, or baseball.

But Junior is not his handsome self yet. His features are strengthening, but his face still looks too small for his developing torso. There is also some of his 14-year-old awkwardness in his limbs and gait. His good looks may still be impaired by a continuing problem with acne. Furthermore, he will still be having difficulty making his hair behave and probably ends up telling the barber to "butch it." By this time the novelty of shaving will be gone, and often he has to be reminded that his "peach fuzz is showing."

As for his disposition, this is the year he may display the mulelike manners of a Brahma bull. At this stage of adolescent rebellion a boy tends to resist all forms of authority, particularly where parents have not taken the time to establish respect for authority during his earlier years. Resistance to authority will show up at home, at school, at church, on the playground, and in the neighborhood. The best cure for a boy's declaration of civil war is a father with the intestinal fortitude to "labor" with his son. This labor includes a lot of "man-to-man" talks, taking trips together, creating opportunities for rewards, and sometimes taking away rewards. During this period a boy has to learn some of the most fundamental lessons of life.

Father-son relations are often strained and sometimes broken during this stage because of a boy's abuse of his mother. For a couple of years he may have been "talking back" to her. Now he may become downright defiant. He may even resort to strong language, including profanity, if he thinks he can get away with it. The father, of course, should see that he does not get away with it, but at the same time the father should not look upon his son as though he were an outsider who has deliberately insulted his wife. The boy is very much an insider who feels the mother of the family is the symbol of restraint—that is why he strikes out at her. In later years he will recall his angry words and harsh behavior with bitter regret and probably tell his mother that he loved her all the time. At this particular moment his love seldom shows.

It will be helpful to the 15-year-old boy if the father began laboring with him long before now. As early as age 11 a boy begins weaning away from his mother and starts looking to his father for attention and leadership. If the father is careful, he can develop love and discipline side by side. Fortunate indeed is the boy who has a father who recognizes the need to develop this balance in his boy's life. In fact, this kind of father sometimes finds his boy going through the difficulties of age 15 at a rather easy gallop and wonders why other fathers are having so much trouble.

Perhaps this is the explanation for an interesting verse in the Bible. It says that eventually the earth will enjoy a thousand years of peace called "the millennium," and that during this period children will "grow up as calves in a stall." This may have been the scriptural way of describing children who receive a happy combination of love and discipline in their upbringing. Some parents have already achieved the peace in their homes which the Bible is talking about by applying this formula.

A MOTHER'S VIEW OF HER FIFTEEN-YEAR-OLD BOY

There are many things about a 15-year-old boy that are sometimes difficult for a mother to understand. Take, for example, her attempt to draw out the most casual kind of conversation.

"Hello, son."

"Hi."

"Have a nice day at school?"

"Yep."

"Anything exciting happen?"

"Nope."

"Get any homework you have to do tonight?"

"Uh-huh."

"Get any of it done at school?"

"Nope."

"Where are you going now?"

"Joe's."

"Will you be sure and be back in time for supper at six?"

"Uh-huh."

Junior straggles out the door, giving the impression that he wanted to say more but thought it might provoke a quarrel and therefore condescended to restrain himself.

This is a year of moody, sometimes surly and irritable, personality development. Even the most normal boy will tend to be dreamy, apathetic, preoccupied, and introverted. He is likely to speak in a soft, smothered tone and mumble in gutteral monosyllables. It is no wonder many mothers end up on the brink of distraction. In fact, if a boy sees he is irritating his mother beyond her capacity for self-control, he counts a victory. Somehow it makes him feel big. It is easy to understand why the relation between a mother and son is never more likely to be weaker than at mid-adolescence.

At school, teachers often view their classes of 15-year-old tenth graders and woefully shake their heads as they talk about the "15-year-old slump." Poor grades may result from too many interests, unsettled pattern of living, too much TV, too much running around at nights. Since this is an age of resistance to authority and discipline, the 15-year-old may be very resentful of school just for what it represents. Students will describe teachers as "hating" them, being sarcastic, giving unfair grades, or otherwise giving them cause for much self-pity. Most parents simply keep the pressure at a healthy level and ride out the storm.

IMPORTANCE OF ADULT ATTITUDES

In spite of his strange behavior, a 15-year-old is genuinely concerned about what people may think of him. He is ego-hungry and tends to play whatever role his parents, teachers, and society pin on him. Thus, a delinquent adolescent may wear his badge of delinquency with as much pride as the boy who makes the high school honor society. For this reason parental attitudes need to be as positive and hopeful as circumstances will permit. The same thing is needed at school. The experts say it is best to "talk up" a boy's good points even when he is being punished for some delinquency. If the newspapers or the student body start publicizing a boy's mistakes, he will find it getting him a lot of special attention which he never had before and which may give him a sense of overinflated importance. Of course if a young teen-ager has been given numerous opportunities to straighten out but remains completely defiant, a good warm exposure to community indignation through the press has been known to help. However, in the run-of-the-mill situations, the less publicity the better.

But not only is Junior likely to absorb his parents' and teachers' estimate of himself—he is also likely to absorb their estimate of life. For example, a father who has his children watching out the back window for a motorcycle officer can scarcely complain a few years later when his son is picked up for speeding and whines, "I was watching for cops but don't know where this one came from." The father might recall saying almost the same words because the boy learned to cheat on the law from his father.

Boys also frequently pick up their parents' attitudes of tolerance toward other things—immorality, drinking, smoking, gambling, or chiseling on a business deal. And they are also likely to reflect their negative attitudes toward the armed services, demanding a soft job, evading income taxes, or belittling a neighbor.

A boy may also learn from his mother how to use sly, deceitful alibis to avoid distasteful situations. This may have happened when his mother took him on a quick trip, to a show, or for a visit with Grandma, and then gave him a written excuse for his teacher saying, "Junior has been sick."

Indeed, parental attitudes *are* important.

WHAT ABOUT A CAR?

Many parents have their greatest arguments with their 15-year-olds because of demands for a car. In many states, if Junior takes his driver training at school, he can receive his driving test and license as early as age 15½.

Parents will probably save themselves a lot of trouble if they will make several rules very clear to Junior:

1. *Under no circumstances is he to drive a car until he has qualified for a learner's permit.*
2. *He will be given formal driving lessons from someone other than a member of the family. (This is to keep him from picking up Mom's and Dad's bad driving habits.)*
3. *If he gets a driver's license, he can use it only so long as he is able to drive a car without violating the law.*

Because of the independence which a car gives a boy it sometimes interferes with school, keeps him out after curfew, and exposes him to the wrong kind of associates. Therefore parents should make their son's driver's license contingent upon his willingness to exercise good judgment in matters of behavior and academic effort.

The next question which naturally arises in this motor age is: "Should Junior have a car of his own?" The experts say "No!" There are a number of good reasons:

1. *It tends to further weaken the control which parents have over a boy during this particularly difficult bronco age. It is one thing for a boy to have a license and occasionally drive the family car, and it is quite a different matter when a boy can go when he wants, where he wants, with whom he wants without having to hurdle any parental control barriers.*
2. *It often gives a boy a sense of smart-alecky superiority which gets him into trouble. He feels he can do about anything he wants with "his" car, including rodding, bumper-kissing, road racing, and fender-skimming.*
3. *A mid-teen-ager with his own car seldom has the judgment that goes with ownership. He therefore goes to one of two extremes. Either he lets the brakes, lights, windshield wipers, and other equipment get dangerously out of repair or he goes to the other extreme and loads his car with expensive extras, including race-car carburetors, and then can't resist the temptation to try them out.*

Because we have had a whole generation of relative prosperity, some fathers have made the mistake of buying a car for a boy just to show off their own financial superiority. This makes it very difficult for other fathers whose sons feel they are being discriminated against. Nevertheless, the wise father will hold the line regardless of his neighbor's foolishness.

Sometime during the late teen-age period it may be justifiable to let a boy have a car of his own, but if this is done several factors may prove beneficial if kept in mind. First of all, a boy should not have his thrill of owning a car drowned by the over-indulgence of a loving but unthinking father. The preferred procedure is to start out with a safe, older model rather than smother the boy's sense of appreciation by presenting him with a fancy souped-up foreign sports car or some gadget-glamorous domestic model. When the boy gets out on his own with a wife and a few youngsters, he may find himself completely spoiled with exotic tastes he cannot afford. A boy needs to be psychologically conditioned for the battle of life, and many an over-indulgent father has lived to regret the extravagant tastes he built into a weakling son.

This is also a good reason for having a boy pay at least half of the cost of a car before he is allowed to own one. Usually when this is the case a boy will see the desirability of riding the bus a few more years or be willing to go in for a cheaper, older model rather than wait until he can earn the twenty-five hundred dollars necessary to pay for his half of that exotic sports car he has been dreaming about.

PASSION FOR PRIVACY

Not only does a 15-year-old begin demanding his own private car, but he may assert passionate pleas for a private bedroom, private TV, private bathroom, private refrigerator (full of food, of course), private library, private tennis court, private swimming pool, and almost anything else he can think of. In fact, he secretly tells himself it would be a lot better if the rest of the family moved out!

All of this erupts from the caldron of bubbling growth boiling within him, which says, "Boy, you're getting to be a man!" He longs for manly possessions, manly independence, manly powers. Ten years from now he will have made the shocking discovery that the role of manhood is mostly learning to share things—

with a wife, with children, with friends. At 15, this is the last thing he wants to consider.

As in earlier years, the 15-year-old finds his privacy seriously invaded by younger siblings. He hates it. They wander through his room, check dresser drawers, read his mail, read his diary, borrow fishing equipment, baseball gear, pens, pencils, books, and clothes. The tiny small fry are especially fascinated by a big brother's room. It is a great place to play. They spread debris all over the room and have such a wonderful time they can't understand why he gets in such an uproar when he comes home.

Another way in which younger brothers and sisters get the goat and invade the privacy of a 15-year-old is teasing him about his current crush. Romance often comes into the life of a boy about this age, and he wants it to be strictly a private affair. He hears people calling it "puppy-dog love," but for him it is very serious and very sincere. That's why he so deeply resents freckled-faced siblings tantalizing and teasing him. They are treading on sacred ground.

"Puppy-dog love" seldom lasts more than a few months. It is mostly a case of being in love with love. It seems so wonderful to have a private girl, to whom he can write notes, with whom he can have serious talks, and upon whom he can shower such gifts as his weekly allowance will afford. However, a 15-year-old falls out of love as neatly as he fell in. Sometimes it comes from the boy and girl taking each other too much for granted, sometimes it comes from jealousy or a routine lover's quarrel. In any event, it demonstrates that it was a shallow affair, not likely to leave scars.

MONEY, MOODS, AND MORALS

Finally, let us consider three remaining qualities of the free-wheeling 15-year-old.

Parents may become conscious of a new money mania. He demands it in quantities to spend when he wants and on what he wants. Parents observe that he is very fad conscious. He is controlled by group loyalties. He wants to keep up with the crowd in clothes and customs. He likes to show off by treating the whole crowd to eats or a show.

Unfortunately, however, this mania for money is seldom related to any passion for a job whereby these increased quantities of money can be earned. He prefers to have it directly from Dad without the taint of work. A father needs to recognize the forces and pressures operating within a boy, but still keep up a goodly supply of persuasion to see that Junior earns his allowance. If he wants more, he works more. This the rule of life.

Parents notice that a 15-year-old has moods. He takes himself rather seriously. Sometimes an emotional tide of self-pity will engulf him. It is good to be understanding but not pamper him with sentimentality. Life is a tough game with rich rewards. Its rewards do not go to the man who sits around feeling sorry for himself. A boy needs to learn this lesson, too.

Of course, there are other kinds of moods. One is the speculative mood in which a 15-year-old dreams of science fiction, of building robots, ray guns, and flying saucers. He imagines the heights of life he will scale. He visualizes the vistas of the dark unknown he will explore. This is a profitable mood. Another good mood is the reflective mood of introspection and self-evaluation. So long as this does not degenerate into worry or clabbered self-condemnation, it is helpful in building stable character and healthy ambition.

This brings us to the last word on our 15-year-old—his attitude toward morals. Parents should know that the average 15-year-old really prefers to tell the truth and respond to most basic moral values. He also hates cheaters and has a sense of chivalry and service which can be cultivated. But his moral sense is a delicate blossom. It can wither under the blast of adult abuse or loss of confidence in adult leadership. Parents, teachers, and other adults must be careful not to berate a noisy, mischievous 15-year-old as though he were only a 3-year-old. He doesn't mind being challenged for misconduct, but he counts belittling and browbeating an unforgivable sin.

From all we have said, it will be appreciated that age 15 to 16 is an epic in human development. It is speedy, spicy, and spunky, but it produces the fuel and thrust which are needed to propel a half-grown human being into orbit.

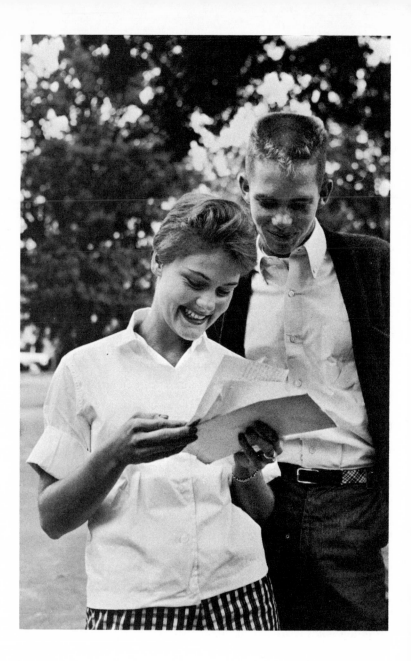

CHAPTER 18

SWEET SIXTEEN

In terms of adolescent semantics age 16 means "B.T.O.—Big Time Operator," but in spite of these pleasant prospects age 16 sweeps down upon the average boy unexpectedly and far too soon. It finds him suffering an emotional hangover from the year before. For several months he will continue to feel the heady intoxication of those former 15-year-old explosions.

Looking back over the past year, Junior recalls how he told everybody off, made everybody mad, broke all the rules at home and school, and did a lot of crazy things "just for fun," "just to get even," or "just to show people." He was like an unhappy octopus, threshing his tentacles out in all directions, trying to smash down the barriers of home and society at every point of the compass. "How did people put up with me?" His father says that's a good question.

Nevertheless, when his sixteenth birthday arrives, Junior believes things should improve. He feels confident they will. No more loggerheads with the family, no more sassing Mom, no more flunking at school, and no more scandalism or vandalism in the neighborhood. After all, isn't this the fabulous stage of mid-adolescence called "Sweet Sixteen"?

The answer is, "Yes, but unfortunately Mother Nature is behind in her homework. She is rarely ready for the big change exactly at age 16. Nevertheless, the change will come sometime during 16, and what a sweet contrast it turns out to be!"

PORTRAIT OF A SIXTEEN-YEAR-OLD
(AFTER THE CHANGE)

In the normal course of events, age 16 will be remembered as soothing and satisfying by both Junior and his parents. Physically, Junior will have attained 98 per cent of his growth. His muscle co-ordination will be free-swinging and pulsating with rhythm and vibrancy. He will be hearty, robust, and radiant with good health. His complexion will be noticeably better and he will be shaving every other day. Mom will notice that he is much easier to lure to the dinner table than last year. He won't be so finicky with his food and will even venture into some highly seasoned Italian casserole or untried Chinese dishes.

His sense of humor will be coming around. He will begin enjoying loud guffaws accompanied by knee-slapping and shoulder-swaying demonstrations of boisterous mirth. Sometimes he will unload a pressure pocket of pent-up emotions with a hearty belly laugh.

When he talks to people he will have a natural, matter-of-fact "eye to eye" contact with them. He will purposely keep the conversation light and fluffy, and there will be little or no desire to build issues into crises like he did last year. He will avoid deeply serious subjects, unless, of course, he has the science fiction bug. In that case he will break into a rash of "outer space" vernacular and will amaze his parents with intense and authoritative discussions of "intergalactic exploration," "extrasensory perception," "neucleonic quadridimensional phase inverters," and "B.E.M. monsters from the Id."

For a 16-year-old a bed will be hard to get into and nearly impossible to get out of. He will resist retiring until after midnight, but once he is in the sack it will take the Jericho Marchers to blow down the walls of Morpheus and get him up. He will be a sound sleeper, undisturbed by nightmares, fears, or frustrations. He can scarcely believe his parents who talk about his childhood days when he used to get up and restlessly wander around the house during the night.

A 16-year-old will show surprising skill in managing his temper. He will not only struggle to control it but will try to cover up most of his feelings. He does not like to blow up like he used to, and he will shower his humble head with vats of brimstone if he does. He feels a temper outburst is kid stuff, and kid stuff is a label he despises. Fortunately, his feelings are not easily ruffled on most subjects, at least not like they were a year ago. He isn't as defensive as he was at 15.

A 16-year-old will have a low "hate" quotient. A year ago he hated a hatful of subjects, but this year he says, "I guess they weren't so important." He has a number of dislikes and will express them frankly but these usually pertain to specific problem areas like "Bull Sneeder's Gang," "that lousy class during fifth period," or "doing gymnastics instead of playing ball." But even where he expresses dislikes he somehow manages to get along fairly well.

Altogether, Junior will now appear to have in his possession a nice new package of power and charms to add to his personality. It portends well for the future.

THE MIRACLE OF SIXTEEN-YEAR-OLD ADJUSTMENT

Perhaps the miracle of human maturation is nowhere better illustrated than in the 16-year-old as he passes through the "big change." To appreciate what happens, we need to remind ourselves that very often a maladjusted personality will have all the qualities of a normal person with the exception of just one or two factors—and it is the absence of these important bolts and burrs which puts a knock in his motor.

This was the situation last year when Junior was 15. For the most part he had the ingredients of a successful adult, the independence of a Missouri mule, the courage of a rodeo cowboy, and the emotional dynamics of a Western movie hero. But somehow, at 15, these ingredients all added up to sour pickles. They did not spell success but "psychological maladjustment."

The experts say it was simply a problem of missing bolts and burrs. This becomes apparent when Junior finally slips across into his 16-year-old development pattern. We are inclined to say he has "changed," but on close analysis we discover that everything we used to object to is *still there!* Nevertheless, these qualities have suddenly lost their barbs. They don't seem objectionable any more. When we ask the experts what has happened they tell us Mother Nature has just added a new ingredient to lubricate the others. She has given Junior the wonderful new capacity to *take himself for granted.*

This is what a 15-year-old lacks. At 15, when a boy feels his surging hunger for independence, he cannot take it for granted, he has to prove it to everybody. The proof usually comes in some kind of a crash program. He is also putting on the same kind of act when he grunts and talks in monosyllables to his mother. In his anxiety to be equal with her, he overcompensates and treats her as an *inferior.* He also thinks it gives him status to smoke, stay out late, drive a car before he has a license, and otherwise show defiance toward his father, the school, the neighbors, and the police.

Of course, as we have mentioned in the last chapter, the wise father of a stampeding 15-year-old makes up for Junior's missing bolts and burrs by mixing in some counseling, discipline, and comradery. This usually creates enough balance in Junior to get him over the hump. At 16, however, after the big change, Junior doesn't feel the same strong need to prove his independence, his status of equality, or his right to a place in the sun. He still wants to feel independent but says, "So what?" As long as he stays within reasonable bounds everybody apparently wants him to be independent. And if someone asks him if he still feels equal to his mother or father, he says, "Sure, so why fight about it?"

He has found he can choose his own friends, earn his own money, drive a car, run for a student body office—what is there to get so excited about? He can take it all for granted and says, "Live and let live." This is the maturation miracle of a 16-year-old.

FAMILY AND FRIENDS OF THE SIXTEEN-YEAR-OLD

It would be a mistake, however, to assume that a 16-year-old will revert back to his former warm and intimate relationship with the family which he exhibited up to about age 13. On the contrary, he is with the members of the family but seldom of them. He does not resist the family, he simply takes them for granted. The family is like a row of trees in the middle of the highway. He drives around them. If the folks have something clever or particularly entertaining to say, he responds cordially just as he would if they were a group of total strangers he had just met at the dog races. But if things around home are *status quo*, he simply passes in and around his relatives as a necessary part of getting his board and room.

By the same token, Junior assumes that the family is also taking him pretty much for granted. He no longer demands as much as he used to. He is fairly successful in managing his own clothes, keeping himself clean, maintaining his own room, and doing his homework. He has the feeling that he has attained semi-adult status in the household and conducts himself accordingly.

Junior may still be the cause of some intramural disputation when it comes to using the family car. Now that Junior has a license, he may take the car for granted. This must be straightened out quickly and firmly. He must understand that the use of the family car is strictly a luxury and can be achieved only through careful preplanning and prearrangement with the boss man. A 16-year-old can usually absorb the disappointment of not getting the car as long as there is a reasonable basis for the refusal. What sends him into a jive-by-five tantrum is the father who says, "You can't because I say you can't!"

As for his friends, Junior tends to take his contemporaries for granted just as he does his family. He likes everybody to be his friends. If he selects a pal, it is generally because of mutual interest in certain studies, sports, hobbies, or extracurricular activities.

A similar attitude usually reflects itself in Junior's feelings about girls. He likes to be around them in a cautious, non-specific sort of way. He fears overspecialization, but can be lured into going steady if some particular girl gives him the casual treatment on a somewhat non-romantic basis. "We're just pals," he says. However, this same casual attitude can get them both into unforeseen difficulties if their going steady gets serious. The more wholesome arrangement is socializing by mixing it up in group activities and restricting solo dating to very special occasions such as the Class Dance, the Junior Prom, or other activities which may be several months apart.

This problem is solved for most boys by the simple fact that the attractive 16-year-old girls are usually attracting handsome older boys, and this leaves Junior in a seething fit of gloom because he says, "None of the other girls mean much to me." This is mostly play acting. He would have been too scared to give any of the popular girls much of a campaign anyway, but it does give him an excuse to say, "I wish those cotton-picking Seniors would leave the girls in the Junior class alone!"

THE SIXTEEN-YEAR-OLD AT SCHOOL

Being a Junior in high school can be the "beginning of living" for lots of boys. Many a boy who stumbled and struggled through junior high and the tenth grade suddenly finds himself coming alive as he moves into the eleventh grade as a Junior. Should such a spark appear, parents and teachers can immediately rally round and apply some tinder. Often the tiny light of hope can be whipped into a conflagration of intellectual and extracurricular development by the time Junior is ready to graduate.

One of the greatest appeals to a 16-year-old is the chance to be somebody on campus. He feels so grown up in so many ways, but he needs a chance to shine in at least one thing. Therefore he should be encouraged in whatever talent he appears to possess—sports, music, drama, radio, TV, debating student programs, student government, school clubs, and so forth. Frequently grades will improve with student activity, and that is not all. Sometimes parents are shocked to suddenly hear their son and heir say, "Gee, I like school. I almost hate to think of graduating!"

JUNIOR GETS A JOB

Just about the time a set of parents become accustomed to Junior's new role as a 16-year-old, they discover that he wants to fly the coop and get a job. If this happens it is a good sign, but should he do it? There are several important things to consider:

1. *Will it seriously affect his studies?*
2. *What kind of associates will he have?*
3. *Will it seriously interfere with his getting enough sleep?*
4. *Is it likely to impair his health?*

At this particular stage, Junior's studies are mighty important. More than likely he just "got the hang of it." However, if he takes the job knowing he will have to quit if he doesn't keep up his grades, it may help. In fact, surveys show that students who work a moderate amount of time before or after school usually get better grades than the average student.

As for associates, Junior is highly impressionable at this age. It is most important that he get started in business with people who want to build men, not bend them. The important thing is not the kind of job, but who runs the job. I know a father who felt his son should be a newsboy, because he had heard that many newsboys grow up and become corporation presidents. This is true, but some newsboys also grow up and go to Sing Sing. If Junior wants a job it is his father's task to find out what kind of people Junior will have as his associates.

Sleep is also important to Junior but not as important as it was between 12 and 15 while he was growing so fast. A 16-year-old is usually tough and robust. As a rule, he can get along on a little less sleep than before, but he can't sacrifice sleep to the point where it affects his school or his health. Parents can usually tell after a few days whether Junior is going to be able to stand the gaff.

Some jobs are too rugged for a 16-year-old and he can hurt his health. This may be due to the hours, the working conditions, or the pressure of other commitments which he already had. It is up to the parents to watch Junior carefully and, if he begins caving in, pull him off the job.

DOES A WORKING BOY MISS TOO MUCH FUN?

Some parents feel that a boy should not work because he will miss some of the fun other boys will be enjoying. Such parents have the wrong slant on "work." A job can be fun, too. In fact, a wage-earning boy has a much better chance of getting in rhythm with the melody of a happy living than a pampered playboy who has a car, an allowance, and his dad's credit card.

The real test is in the attitude of the boy himself. Up to now most boys will have resisted getting a job unless the family suffered some kind of economic crisis. During 16, however, Mother Nature usually whispers to Junior that it's about time he "got started in life" and began earning part of his own living. If Junior expresses a desire to do this, it is a signal that he is becoming a man and it should be as welcome to parents as tulips in spring.

If parents have a question in their minds about the merit of encouraging Junior's work sense, they should recall the lives of men like Washington, Franklin, or Thomas A. Edison.

George Washington's father died when he was 11. He had only three years of schooling; but he had to get out and work. By the time he was 14 he had become a good "rule-of-thumb" surveyor. He continued working and finally joined the armed services to help protect Virginia against the Indians. By the time he was 20 he had been made an adjutant, by 21 a major, by 22 a lieutenant colonel, and when he was 23 they made him the Commander in Chief of the entire Virginia Militia.

Then consider Benjamin Franklin. He was a tallowmaker's fifteenth child. By the time he was 12, people in Boston were reading his published poetry. By the time he was 16 he had become famous as the secret author of the "Do-Good" papers in a local newspaper. He was a full-fledged publisher at 17 and had a flourishing business of his own in Philadelphia by the time he was 22.

Our last success story belongs to Thomas A. Edison. He set up his first chemistry laboratory in the basement of the family home when he was 11. The next year he obtained a job as a newsboy on the Grand Trunk Railway and set up the world's first mobile chemical laboratory in the baggage car. He also got permission to buy vegetables in the country, store them in the baggage car, and sell them at premium prices when the train passed through a city. This got to be such a thriving business the vegetables practically monopolized the baggage car, and Tom had half a dozen boys working for him in several of the towns. Describing how he got started, he says: "At the stations along the line I bought butter from the farms and was quite a dealer in blackberries during the season. My purchases were made at a low wholesale price, and I gave the wives of the trainmen and engineers the benefit of a discount. This may partially explain why no complaint ever came from the railroad."

When he was 14 Edison decided it would be cheaper if he sold a paper he printed himself, so he set up a small print shop in the baggage car and brought forth the *Weekly Herald.* The circulation got up to four hundred copies a month which he described to his customers as "the largest circulation of any newspaper in the world printed on a train"—his being the only one!

After that Edison became interested in telegraphy, but got fired from his first job for inventing an automatic device which would send a certain "check-in" signal while he was asleep. By the time he was 22 he had made his first great invention—the Universal Printer—which was an automatic telegraph printer that brought him a fortune of forty thousand dollars. By the time he was 24 Edison was world famous.

So much for success stories. What if the mother of Washington, Franklin, or Edison had said, "My boy, I don't want you to work, you might miss some fun!"

CHAPTER 19

"LOOK, MOM, I'M A SENIOR!"

Patterns and Problems of the 17-Year-Old

Mom can hardly believe it, but it's true. After all these years Junior finally made it. He's a Senior.

Secretly, Mom is pretty proud of him. She notices how casual he is about his growing strength and increasing good looks. He uses an amazing vocabulary—sounds like a college student already. He is intelligent, too. She notices that he often discusses things with his friends which are completely over her head. He is interested in science, politics, crime, war, thermonuclear developments, local government, world affairs.

Age 17 is a year of *status* for a boy. It is fortunate that he is also in his final phase of a twelve-year battle to graduate from high school. The qualities of a 17-year-old and the demands of his final year of high school fit well together.

Mom notices that her boy is proud, sensitive, ambitious, friendly. Most of the time he likes to treat her as a woman now instead of merely the family housekeeper. May even ask her for a dance some time—perhaps at school or at a church party. She knows that underneath he is still a little scared about life, but he would rather be boiled in oil than show it.

PORTRAIT OF A SEVENTEEN-YEAR-OLD

Age 17 is a good year, but it is also a year of thrust. Junior has only had part of one good year to build upon, and he can still recall with a shudder the haunting void of age 15 and early 16. His positive qualities are like delicate blossoms in a summer sun. They can be carefully nurtured to strength and permanence or be shriveled and wilted by a single exposure to a blistering heat treatment. The task of parenthood is to see that every positive trait is enthusiastically cultivated and every negative trait is gently but firmly suppressed.

Because status is so important to a 17-year-old, success is likewise important. Too much success can make him smug and egotistical, but too little success or an avalanche of embarrassing failure can make him feel like "$-X^2$." When you ask him what that means he says, "Lower than a worm—worse than nothing." The genius is to find the happy medium where he is thrilled with the discovery that he can succeed in most things, but is occasionally humbled by the unpleasant reality that sometimes he can fail.

A 17-year-old boy still has a lot of the "Old Nick" in him. He loves to play jokes on people. He also likes to impress them with his reckless bravado. Last year he wasn't so sure of his judgment and sometimes he slowed to a snail's pace to avoid making a boo-boo. This year he doesn't worry too much about his judgment—he feels an occasional boo-boo is elevating elixir for a man's soul. It is easy to see how these two competing qualities—hunger for success and reckless irresponsibility—frequently combine to put him squarely behind the proverbial eight ball.

However, Junior isn't likely to be malicious about it. In fact, he seems to lack the ability or insight to sometimes realize just how serious his senseless pranks can be. This characteristic is also apparent in crimes at this age level. Recently a 17-year-old boy with no previous criminal pattern decided to snatch a purse from an elderly woman. To him it was just a prank, but in the scuffle he knocked her down and serious injuries resulted. Later the boy read in the paper that the woman was in the hospital and immediately turned himself in. "I didn't mean to hurt her! Honest, I didn't!" He repeated it over and over.

LEARNING RIGHT BY RESISTING RIGHT

This brings us to one of the strange paradoxes in a typical 17-year-old personality: *learning things by fighting them.*

He knows, for example, that he shouldn't steal because his parents always told him so. But WHY shouldn't he steal? "Maybe it's a good idea." The next thing parents know, the family pride and joy has tried it out and gotten himself in a whopper of a jam. He is embarrassed, the family is embarrassed. Parents cannot understand why the juvenile officers treat the whole thing so matter-of-factly. "They act like they were expecting Junior to do it all the time!" a father complains. "No," the officers may reply, "not exactly, but this is the age when lots of young folks test the barriers of society just to make sure they will hold."

"But Junior is just not that kind of a boy!" his mother explains.

The officers agree that no doubt he is a very fine young man, but at the moment he *was* that kind of a boy and he did test the barriers and that is why he needs to get the usual "character improvement treatment."

This is Junior's opportunity to learn for himself that stealing is for the birds. Sometimes parents will argue with the officers (who are sincerely trying to be helpful) that Junior is being abused, being misunderstood, being blackened for life. If this continues Junior soon starts singing the same tune. As a result, he not only fails to get his personal lesson on stealing but he gets inoculated with a particularly potent shot of personality poison and soon starts wailing, "They're picking on me!"

Recently, a boy was picked up with a juvenile gang who were in serious trouble. At headquarters the parents of this boy were urged by other parents to sue the police because this particular boy was not involved in any crime. He just happened to be along with the crowd. The father of the boy realized this, but knew he might never have a better opportunity to teach his boy one of the big lessons of life. Therefore, he turned to his son who had been listening to the conversation and said:

"My boy, I'm not going to sue the police, I'm going to thank them. I have told you all your life, when you see a crowd headed for trouble, break away and leave. Tonight I hope you learned your lesson."

Later this same boy told the juvenile officers, "Dad was right. Ten minutes more, and I would have been as guilty as the other kids. It was beginning to look like fun and I was going to help pull the next job."

When parents understand the psychology of the mid-adolescent they can be very helpful to themselves as well as their boy. If the police pick up "a real fine boy"—which most of them are— who has been fooling around, the boy's father can add a building block to Junior's personality by saying, "My boy, you know better. Now take your medicine like a man and we'll just call it one of life's lessons."

Junior may try not only stealing but also drinking, smoking, gambling, perhaps even some narcotics. A wise parent will move in on these problems with a boy and try to remove the mysterious glamour which surrounds them. All Junior wants to know for sure is whether or not the things his parents have said were "bad" are *really* bad. "Parents might be wrong," he keeps telling himself.

The same doubts and suspicions arise in connection with religious teachings and developing a mature philosophy of life. Junior will manifest a new desire to get to original sources. He is no longer satisfied with merely being told. He wants to be shown. Patient handling of each problem by a well-informed parent or other adult will usually keep his faith alive and his convictions open to the evidence.

GIRLS

At 17 a boy can go in and out of love like a beaver diving in and out of a pond. There is a reason. Girls in the Junior and Senior class with whom he associates are mature enough to be attractive, sympathetic, and radiant with the possibilities of adult life. He senses that they see in him all the full possibilities of a man. They reflect it in their speech, in their coy flirtations, in subtle gestures which are felt but not spoken.

A 17-year-old boy interprets all of this as a wonderful compliment to his "adequacy" and his "competence." It satisfies a gnawing hunger. He wants so much to "arrive." In the companionship of certain girls he gets the feeling that they think he has arrived already. They talk to him about grownup subjects —even delicate subjects—in a casual, sophisticated way. He likes it. It is as easy to fall in love with one of these girls as falling off a log.

But he falls out of love just as easily as he falls in. He finds some girls seem to be feeding him a line and putting on an act with him. They seem extremely fickle, and he is sure they are trying to wrap him around their finger just for the thrill of a conquest. In fact, the first time he gets let down by a girl his ego collapses like a deflated balloon.

"Think of all the weekly allowances I wasted on that girl," he moans. To himself he secretly admits that he thought she was his predestined soul partner. Now he is convinced she has no soul. He decides she is a professional heartbreaker, a gold digger, truly a colossal disappointment. His emotional disturbance is no illusion but raw and real. He may try to cover it up by bragging that from now on he is going to be a confirmed woman hater. "Women just can't be trusted," he says, "I never expect to marry." This firm resolution may last two or three weeks.

In later years he can look back on these experiences and realize that the trial and error method of finding a mate is Mother Nature's most preferred way. He may even realize that the girl he thought was so fickle and heartless was actually a very sweet and sensible creature who knew she would be getting married before he even reached his second year in college and her intuitive wisdom therefore whispered, "Better cut the boy loose before he goes into a spin."

Because this is not the marriageable age for a boy, it is a good time for him to begin polishing up on the things which a girl will be looking for later on when he really decides to campaign for a certain "one and only."

The girls themselves have described the things they like in a boy:

1. *Good manners*
2. *Friendliness*
3. *Good sense of humor*
4. *Being a good sport*
5. *Nice looking (manly, not "pretty")*
6. *Good talker*
7. *Popular with other boys*
8. *Popular with other girls*
9. *A "fun" dancer (not just a "mugger")*
10. *Belongs to a friendly and interesting crowd.*

NEW MOTORS, NEW TALENTS

By the time a boy is 17, he is beginning to feel powerful new motors operating within him. His intellectual powers are increasing. His physical skills have acquired strength and improved precision.

What surprises Junior the most is his unexpected success in a lot of new endeavors. He finds he can excel in any one of a number of things—acting, debating, journalism, student government, telling jokes, singing, dancing, athletics, playing an instrument, even getting good grades in school. Sometimes he excels in several of these. A couple of years ago he would have hooted at the idea that he had such talents. Nevertheless, he likes the new role.

And one of these fine days he wakes up to see his name in print for the first time. "This is very significant," he thinks. And it is, even if his name happens to be in a six-line article buried in the real estate section. Sometimes he hears people refer to him in conversation and people speak to him at the grocery store, the five-and-dime, on the street. Some of these people he can't even remember meeting before.

THE GLORY OF GRADUATION

For a lot of boys, graduation from high school marks the end of formal education. Many more will struggle on through one or two years of college and some will graduate, but for a great many boys the high school cap and gown remain the crowning memory of academic achievement.

The high school graduation represents a lot of things.

First of all, it means that Junior is not a quitter. He is not one of the hundred who dropped out of school. Modern life is a continuous obstacle course for the boy who has not completed high school. Junior can always feel proud that he struggled through and graduated.

Secondly, it means that Junior knows quite a lot about many things. He has been exposed to a little history, a little science, a little law, some phases of government, the basic elements of mechanical arts; he knows a lot about his own language and some things about a foreign language; he knows more mathematics than many of the best scholars in Colonial times and he has probed the mysteries of a chemical, physics, or biology lab; he has improved his writing technique, his ability to speak, his athletic skill; he has learned a great deal about citizenship, something about working through group dynamics in committees and on teams; he knows the rudiments of intellectual research and feels at home in the archives of a library. Yes sir, Junior has come a long way!

Third, graduation from high school means basic preparation for a happy and profitable life. He is now equipped so that he can continue improving himself through self-education; twelve years of schooling will have triggered interests in many fields. It has also prepared him to become an apprentice in nearly any occupation except those requiring very advanced or highly technical skills. Probably 80 per cent of the jobs in the country demand high school graduation as a basic requirement for employment.

Fourth, he has struck a level of educational preparation which makes him equal to the vast majority of the citizens of our country. One of the most important aspects of education is getting a feeling of confidence—not a feeling of superiority over other people, but a feeling of being equal. He learns that nobody knows everything about anything. He has learned to approach even the so-called experts with caution. He learns to think for himself, to ask to see the evidence, to weigh, ponder, and decide. To the extent that he does this he reduces the "margin of risk" in life. It helps him take the gamble out of new business ventures, the mystery out of new acquaintances, the gullibility out of everyday affairs.

Fifth, graduation from high school fulfills the dreams of a boy's best friends—his mom and dad. At 17 Junior represents an investment in cold cash of around thirty-five thousand dollars. His parents don't think about that, however. They leave it to the Children's Bureau in Washington, D.C., to figure out. All they know is that Junior has been the object of vast quantities of love, devotion, care, teaching—and a certain amount of fret and worry. No matter what happens they will never regret a single moment of what they have done to help him, but it is such a tremendous reward to a mother and father to see Junior turn out to be the wonderful fellow they knew he could become. That is why moms and dads get sort of sentimental at a graduation exercise. As Junior walks across the stage in his cap and gown, it does something deep down inside. To hear his name called out and see him accept his diploma in front of a crowded auditorium of admiring townspeople just cannot help but open up the floodgates of a happy parent's heart.

CHAPTER 20

THE GENTLEMAN BRONCO

Patterns and Problems Between 18 and 19

"Smooth" is the word for age 18. Smooth like a slumbering volcano! There are two sides to this boy of 18.

Junior's parents have noticed that, since he graduated from high school, he seems so much more like an adult. He seems to recognize that he is building a world of his own—and that his planet is about to sweep out into orbit. Junior feels his parents already know "it's about time." He observes how they talk to him as though he were an equal. They discuss serious family problems in front of him; even ask for his suggestions, sometimes. They seem to take for granted that from now on he will be working out his own ideas most of the time, earning his own money, planning his own time, and setting up a variety of social projects with one or more close friends. Somehow or other they don't seem to worry as much about him as they used to.

This, of course, is the picture of a "gentleman" 18-year-old. However, a few boys will still be manifesting more of the bronco side. The bronco 18-year-old sometimes acts as though the rules of life were a saddle that somebody threw on his back when he wasn't looking and then cinched it up quickly before he recovered from the shock. To show his resentment he bucks, squeals, shouts, and pouts. His mother and dad will have to do a little corral work with Junior to get him accustomed to the fact that he is a little behind in his personality development. But we will say more about this in a moment.

In most cases parents can start taking off a little pressure now that Junior is 18. First, however, it is good for the parents to remember that this age involves the tides of life which churn up a lot of big breakers to bowl a boy over. From Junior's point of view, the future prospect is disquieting. People are beginning to expect an awful lot of him. He has to make so many decisions. Like choosing friends, for example. Without even trying he can get messed up with the wrong gang. Girls are a problem, too. Then there's his job—shall he give up his part-time job of his high school days and look for a man's job, or shall he go to college or enlist in the Service. And what about a car?

Junior can literally feel himself slipping away from the moorings of home, and he can also feel himself losing the old sense of security when he was "just one of the family." Mother Nature whispers to him that everything is going to work out all right, but in the dark hours of the night Junior sometimes gets a sinking feeling in his solar plexus. "Gee, life is tough!" he hears himself saying.

PORTRAIT OF AN EIGHTEEN-YEAR-OLD

On the surface an 18-year-old is the epitome of independence and self-confidence. His physical bearing is impressive—strong, co-ordinated, muscular. Although his endurance quotient is shallow, time will take care of that as it takes care of so many things.

Mentally, he is alert, analytical, and capable of many of the subtle insights which characterize mature adults. He is fairly shrewd and isn't easily fooled. Whether he takes a job, enrolls in college, or enters the Service, he becomes aware of new intellectual powers which are often surprising, even to him. Occasionally, he finds himself saying some rather clever things, and quite often he is greatly impressed by his obvious ability to do many things "as well as a grown man."

The special genius of the average 18-year-old is his remarkable capacity to take pressure. At least, it seems remarkable compared to his past behavior pattern when he sometimes blew up at the slightest nudge. This capacity for "taking it" is often evident in

the military service, where a boy can go from a raw recruit to a
fairly seasoned soldier in a short period of intensive training. It
may also be reflected in his ability to leave home and sink new
roots on a college campus, where he must acquire new friends,
create a completely new niche of existence for himself, and
learn how to study under a schedule of pressure that he thinks
would have killed him a year ago.

Altogether, an 18-year-old reflects a marvelous constellation of
positive traits which generally make him delightful company, a
good worker, and a good student.

THE EIGHTEEN-YEAR-OLD BRONCO

However, underneath the positive traits of this rapidly maturing human personality is a strata of molten lava. It is the furnace
of human drives which make him courageous, adventurous, independent, and self-sufficient. If these powers have already been
disciplined and domesticated during their normal maturation
between 11 and 17, then we should see the results in a "gentleman" 18-year-old. On the other hand, if these explosive forces
have not been sublimated and compressed into socially acceptable channels of conduct, then we are in for at least two years of
ripsnorting, wild and woolly bronco busting. For some reason or
other a boy of this age who gets off the beam of normal development has a slow recovery rate.

Because an 18-year-old feels so independent he is likely to
continue his 17-year-old tendency to shoulder-test every fence
or barrier society has set up for him. Whenever there is a break
in the barrier or it gives way to Junior's pushing, he is likely to
charge through the breach and sprint away like a wild colt. It is
the job of parents to see that the barriers hold. Barriers may
lean a little here and there as part of the give-and-take between
parents and their son, but they must never be allowed to collapse.

If the parents cannot do the job, the community should have
adequate resources to quickly shore up the line of defense.
Junior needs to learn early that he belongs to an orderly society
and that he not only has some *rights*—he also has some *duties!*

Perhaps the same thing could be said another way. The training of a thoroughbred requires that he learn respect for a rope, then for a halter, and finally a bridle. Without this respect, not even a thoroughbred can win races. It is the same way with a boy.

Nevertheless, it is easy to see how an 18-year-old boy can get to "roaming the range" if his parents do not counsel with him frequently. His instinct says, "See if you can stay out late and get away with it." When he comes in at 2 A.M. something should be said. If not, he will try 3, then 4, and finally he may stay out all night.

THE FIRST STEP IN A CAREER OF CRIME

And what is the fun of staying out all night unless he does something? Whenever the parental barrier has collapsed, the boy is likely to test the police barrier. He finds millions of dollars' worth of property in the downtown area which has only thin protection while the city sleeps. He therefore lets his sense of adventure justify him in playing Robin Hood—"stealing from the rich," he says "to help the poor"—meaning himself!

If he succeeds once, he tries it again. Then he finally runs into the police barrier. If it holds, he is apprehended. All of a sudden Junior's "stealing for fun" becomes a monumental personal problem with unexpected consequences.

He can't understand why people pick on him. "Can't they take a joke?" He didn't mean anything serious. "People act like I'm a criminal!" he protests.

As we pointed out in the previous chapter, what happens to Junior when these criminal patterns appear is extremely important. Police, parents, judges, and probation officers must take a firm, fixed position on a solid, united front to let Junior learn once and for all that this is no joke. He is caught in the cross fire of his own foolishness. He will watch his parents hungrily for the first signs of sympathy and a willingness to use their influence to get him out of this jam. The parents actually have only one question for Junior: "Did you do it?" If he denies it, they can go to the police and get the full particulars.

Once parents are assured that Junior is in the wrong, it will be helpful if they will take the attitude that they love him and want to help but they will have to let the demands of the law run their course. This may come as a shock to Junior, but learning to take his medicine is a most important part of growing up.

WHAT ABOUT MILITARY SERVICE?

Some 18-year-olds who get in a jam decide to ask the judge to let them enlist in the Service so that they can finish growing up under military discipline. And for some boys this works. Not because the military has any magic tricks for changing boys, but mostly because the boy enters the Service with a *change in attitude*. This is the only thing which counts. If a boy uses the armed services merely as an excuse for getting out of a jam, he is headed for double trouble and so is the Army. There are more rules to break, more situations to foul up, more temptations to fall for, and more supervisory officers to catch him if he does.

On the other hand, military service can be very profitable for a boy with the right attitude. For the "gentleman" 18-year-old military service may come in any one of three ways: he can wait until he is drafted, he can enlist in the Service of his choice, or he can sign up for one of the Reserves. Each of these has advantages for certain boys. The important thing is to avoid regrets by finding out about all of them before making a final decision. Here are a few suggestions to consider:

1. *This is an age of technical warfare, therefore most draft boards will postpone drafting a boy if he will go to college. In fact, military leaders urge all qualified boys to attend college.*

2. *Even if a boy enlists in one of the Services, he can receive vocational, technical, or academic training while getting regular service pay.*

3. *Most of the Reserve programs permit a boy to take a short period of camp training and then go on to college for technical training as an active Reserve.*

The reason military men are deeply anxious to have college-trained personnel available in case of an emergency is reflected in these words of Colonel Barnett S. Allen of the U. S. Air Force: "Today we must think in terms of minutes of warning and speeds of 18,000 miles per hour. Along with these seemingly fantastic speeds we must consider the destructive capability of modern missiles. One such weapon will carry a destructive load equivalent to that carried by thousands of B-29s during World War II. Can we afford *not* to have capable, intelligent men directing such operations?"

Regardless of the branch of military service which a boy chooses, his success or failure is almost completely dependent upon his feelings. The public schools may or may not have taught him why military service is important. Parents must be alert to the possibility that Junior may not really know for himself whether this country or any other free country is worth fighting for. He may have deducted this from the desperate way his father tried to get him out of the draft or the comment of his mother that "military service is simply a waste of time in a young life!" Such a boy can go through military training hating every minute of it.

On the other hand, a boy who enters the Service with a great sense of loyalty toward his country and a feeling that wearing the uniform is an honor—this is the boy who will make every minute of his military service count. He becomes a great soldier and in the process becomes a great citizen. An American boy, for example, should know that:

1. *The people of the United States were among the first free people in modern times.*
2. *The Communists have set up a timetable of conquest which contemplates destroying American freedom by 1973.*
3. *The course of freedom and self-determination chartered by the American founding fathers has been a blessing to every nation which has copied or shared these principles.*
4. *Modern free government is the nearest thing the human race has ever discovered for the spreading of universal peace and universal prosperity around the world.*

A British boy, a Canadian boy, a boy living under any flag of freedom, can feel the same kind of pride in making himself prepared for the defense of that freedom which took centuries to carve out of human despotism. No man is worthy of freedom who is not willing to protect it, and no man may expect to live in peace if he is not ready to defend the sanctity of home and loved ones against those who would destroy them.

Once a boy gets a sincere understanding of these principles he can find an urgent and meaningful purpose in his military service.

WHAT ABOUT COLLEGE?

As we have mentioned, the problem of military service and going to college can be solved simultaneously if a boy wants college. Unfortunately, however, many capable boys reject this opportunity. Going to college is a subject which needs a lot of "talking up" with Junior prior to his reaching 18. His decision is most often influenced by the attitudes of his parents, his teachers, and his pals. Things which usually get in the way are:

1. An interesting and well-paying job.
2. Prospects of an early marriage.
3. Necessity of keeping up large payments on a car.
4. Feelings of perplexity and insecurity about leaving home.

Nevertheless, there are many dynamic and persuasive reasons why a capable boy should go ahead and plan for college even though the entire family may have to rally round him and help him work out individual problems.

A nation-wide survey of college graduates was published under the title "They Went to College," by Ernest Havenann and Patricia West. This report should make every 18-year-old think twice before rejecting a college career:

1. The average college graduate STARTS at a salary far above the average wage earner's TOP salary.
2. His earning power increases with age. (He usually makes his highest salary after 50, whereas the non-graduate usually reaches his highest salary at 40 and then begins falling off sharply.)
3. College graduates are more likely to become their own

bosses. (84 per cent of male college graduates become pro-
prietors, managers, or executives, whereas only 16 per cent
of the non-graduate men in America attain such positions.)

4. *Even students with average mentality can double their*
potential earning power with college training. ("A" students
get the highest salaries, but even "C" and "D" students do
well—in fact, 80 per cent as well!)

Of course, earning a good living is only one reason for getting
a good education. The founder of one of America's great uni-
versities said the purpose of education is to gain three kinds of
power:

The POWER to think clearly.
The POWER to do well in the world's work.
The POWER to appreciate life.

Finally, what about finances? This is a universal problem, but
more easily solved than many boys think. One out of every
four male college students is able to put himself through college
with practically no help. In fact, 71 per cent of the male students
earn their way in whole or in part. The main thing is to *want*
to go to college.

If at all possible, it is best for Junior to save enough so that
he can get through his first year without having to hold down a
job. That is because the Freshman year is the toughest. It is the
year he discovers that, while he is in the classroom only sixteen
hours a week, he has to discipline himself to study two hours
for every one hour in class. Until he gets this routine established
it is sometimes difficult for him to take on the distraction of a job.
Nevertheless, it can be done if necessary—and many students do.
The key to success is the passion to get an education. In the
presence of a "fever for learning," almost any problem can be
solved somehow.

CHAPTER 21

ROMANTIC AND RECKLESS

Patterns and Problems of the 19-Year-Old

Age 19 is called the natural age for romance—at least, parents are warned to expect it around about this time. Junior has become a gay blade now. He feels it inside and shows it outside. He is handsome, self-confident, adventurous. In spite of his former years of awkward growing up, he finds that he is now attractive to a great many girls. Even glances from feminine strangers sweep his way. He senses, somehow, that they are sizing him up and most of the time they approve. "Wow!" Mother Nature whispers to him. "You are the greatest!"

But Mother Nature has added something to Junior besides the aromatic spirits of *romance*. The recipe for age 19 also calls for a liberal dash of *recklessness*. Perhaps this is to keep parents on their toes. In any event, just as we had the paradox last year of a gentleman and a bronco, this year we have the sweetness and light of Renaissance romance combined with the blind and crazy recklessness of Russian roulette.

PORTRAIT OF A NINETEEN-YEAR-OLD

Now that Junior is 19, he is almost like another adult around the house. He is developing strong personality traits—likes and dislikes—which occasionally put a strain on the rest of the family. He is instinctively aware that he is outgrowing the family, but he still feels strong ties to the home base.

"Home" is something Junior would like to take for granted—like a hotel or boardinghouse. He is inclined to resist the routine requirements of farm chores, yard work, doing dishes, or even picking up after himself. Occasionally, he exhibits a burst of ambition and shocks the family with his secret talent for getting things done in a rush. But this is probably just before a planned house party "for the gang" or because of the prospective visit of some sweet young thing he is trying to impress.

Junior at 19 is a primper. He is also a regular clothes horse. If he has a car, he primps that too. He seems to exist in a theatrical world of bright lights and brilliant costumes. Appearances are of paramount importance. His hair must have the latest cut, his slacks and sport jacket must have the latest drape. Everything about him seems to shout, "Come alive, man, come alive!"

All of this is part of Junior's driving ambition to become *somebody*. He is not only sensitive about himself but also about his family. He may worry just a little about the impression his parents make on people—feelings he used to get when he was a Junior in high school. He secretly criticizes them. Mother is so engrossed in the home, Dad in his business.

"They should be more progressive," he tells himself. Now that Junior is a Sophomore in college (or a young man about town with a fairly good job), he feels he is learning so much. He wishes his parents would do a little more reading, try to keep up. Of course, in two or three years Junior will discover that his parents were smarter than he thought, but at 19—"Well, I just feel like the folks ought to be boning up on a lot of these new things, like me!"

He is also allergic to the prehistoric barbarism of his younger brothers and sisters. "Crude!" he mumbles as they go through their normal childish antics. He is definitely sure he was never like *that*. When important visitors come to dinner he secretly wishes Dad would take "us grownups" to a restaurant and leave the jabbering little kids at home.

Finally, we should comment on 19-year-old self-sufficiency. "There is absolutely no question whatever about the future. I can handle it."

He feels immortal. He is radiant with health. He possesses

optimism to an incredible degree and refuses to believe that he lives in anything but the best of all possible worlds. He cannot understand why people worry so much. He thrusts out his chin and says, "All I need is an opportunity!"

The people who have to live with this personality sometimes feel that he is a little too cocksure for comfort. They occasionally spill out with, "Boy, have you got some surprises coming!" But as they meditate about it they have to admit that life demands a lot of zip and vinegar from a boy. Perhaps this overabundance of super-self-sufficiency is simply Mother Nature's ammunition for future survival.

NEW PLACES, NEW THINGS

Junior's spirit of adventure at 19 is something to behold. He makes a good river rat, bronco buster, or fighter pilot. He climbs mountains like a billy goat and makes jokes as they pack him down from the ski run with a broken leg.

This very same spirit demands other outlets, too. His entertainment appetites and sight-seeing adventures become much more sophisticated. Parents recall how he used to have his favorite resort, his favorite malt shop, favorite park, and favorite beach. Now the familiar things seem to lack luster. All of a sudden he wants to explore a weird assortment of strange new places.

If he can afford it, he likes to strut a tux once in a while, go to hotel dances, to supper clubs, or places with a big name band. Parents need to remind themselves that the dynamic urge to "go to high-powered places" and "do big-time things" is almost universal for this age group. They say they want to see "life." The ideal arrangement is for Mom and Dad to introduce Junior to a few supper club experiences and realistically interpret for him what is going on. This helps Junior get a proper perspective and take such things in his stride without being bowled over.

Parents who are too tired or too busy for such family excursions might remember that, if Junior has to do his own private exploring, there is a psychology of "going out on the town" that can spin a 19-year-old boy right off his chassis. For him it is a dizzy new world where he is anxious to fit in. And far too often there will be some smart aleck around who is anxious to make a fool out of Junior by slyly offering him his first drink.

Some boys can decline a drink without any embarrassment whatever. They have learned how to say "no thanks" or "I'll take a ginger ale *straight*." Everybody laughs and that is the end of the matter. Others feel compelled to conform to the crowd pattern, even though it may mean overriding a lifetime of training. If this happens to Junior he may gag at the first sip. "Tastes like a barrel of mildewed excelsior!" he sputters. This may cure him.

On the other hand, if he decides to drink it "even if it kills me," then he has another, and, for him, unexpected experience. He feels the warm glow in his stomach, then in his head. The gang watches curiously to detect the first signs of this new drinker getting high. It doesn't take long. Even an experienced drinker can digest only approximately half an ounce of alcohol per hour. All the rest flows directly into the blood stream. This raw alcohol bathes the brain with its narcotic depressant effect. Junior feels his thinking motor slowing down. He can't say words very plainly. When he does say something everybody roars with gales of laughter. For the first time in his life he thinks he's a comedian. He doesn't realize they are laughing at him rather than at his jokes. They urge him to drink more. Perhaps he does. He squints his eyes as tunnel vision closes in on him, and he reels unsteadily when he tries to stand up.

Suddenly he has a feeling he needs fresh air. He is seized with a spasm of whimwhams. His stomach region threatens at any moment to do a convulsive flip-flop. He rushes to the nearest exit.

The following day, Junior may think a long time about this crazy new experience. He may tell his folks about it and promise to lay off from here on. Or he may secretly lavish his ego with the memory of being the life of the party. This may trigger his eagerness to be a big shot via this route. In fact, such eagerness can be set on fire by an empty-headed female from the next older set telling him coyly, "Junior, when you're drunk you are *so* cute!" If this happens Junior may be a gone goose. He can hardly wait for the next party. This is particularly true if he is emotionally immature and has a gnawing feeling of being inadequate, dull, and inhibited.

"Somehow," he reflects, "that nasty [and expensive] stuff lubricates my personality." What he probably doesn't realize is the fact that if he starts relying on alcohol to lubricate his personality he is headed for the skids. It may take a few years to get there, but psychologists predict habitual alcoholism for those who pursue this course.

WHAT PRICE PROGRESS

However, at 19 it is sometimes impossible to convince a boy. He may think that for the time being, at least, this is progress. He has made what appears at the moment to be a sensational new discovery. Worried and heartsick parents cannot help but become alarmed as they watch the gyrations of confused disintegration appearing in the personality of their boy, who was once solid, natural, and normal. They cannot help but agree with the youth leaders who said, "Liquor and a little wild life can produce a flash explosion in a teen-ager's personality that wreaks havoc!"

Police officers who may be called by the parents will recognize some familiar symptoms as Junior exhibits a mockish independence, a defiance of authority and law, a reckless indifference toward the welfare of himself or anyone around him. In time, drinking is the prelude to senseless crimes or roaring down quiet avenues in the middle of the night with throttles open and tires screaming. There are also screams after the crash, but these usually come from the more sober passengers who went along for the ride. The drunken driver often goes out without ever knowing what hit him.

When a young life suddenly terminates in a police station, a penitentiary, or a morgue, thoughtful people cannot help wondering how a youngster could have jammed up his life so completely. It isn't hard to trace the pattern. It all began with "little things."

One final thought about another type of 19-year-old who reaches the same terminal but follows a different route. He may have been a drop-out during high school or may have gone to seed after graduation. In any event, he is the boy who decides to become a "peon," a "slum bum," or a juke-joint rock 'n roll artist who requires all-night sessions and a "barby" to keep the gang awake. These are symptoms of personality perversion and, while not hopeless, they certainly spell doomsday if not corrected.

A boy of 19 is moving out across the horizon of life with limitless possibilities before him—adventures in glorious achievement or expeditions in human negation. It is worth the time of a mother and dad and all the resources of a community to see that a boy gets a lift in the right direction when he needs it.

THE AGE OF COURTSHIP

Now we hasten to return to the more pleasant part of being 19. Let's talk about courtship.

No 19-year-old is likely to admit he's courting. He will tell you how he enjoys dating. He might even admit he's campaigning. But not "courting." For him courting is too fancy, formal, and old-fashioned.

However, when Mom and Dad get down to cases, they find love-making hasn't really changed much. A few new words maybe, to describe some routine and well-known adventures in billing and cooing, but, as a grandfather recently said, "It's still the same old go-round of boy meets girl, girl likes boy, girl plays hard-to-get, and boy pursues her until she catches him."

For Junior, however, it isn't quite that simple. Even getting to meet girls, at least the right kind, may be a barrier. This is particularly true in a large city or in a family where there are few social ties. Such a boy may wander around "just hunting." Likely as not he will eventually find a girl, but a pick-up may turn out to be a girl with more experience than Junior knows how to cope with. A girl on the hunt (with happenstance morals) can send a boy reeling. In fact, a chance meeting with the wrong girl can derail a very promising boy's career.

It is the task of parents, teachers, and youth leaders to give young people frequent opportunities for well-supervised recreation where there is a common meeting ground on the "crowd" level and dates can be made under wholesome conditions.

PROBLEMS OF MATCHMAKING

As it finally turns out, most boys have very little trouble getting dates once they reconcile themselves to a few fundamental rules for dating:

1. *Date for fun—to go to a show, a dance, a party, a sports event, or to church.*
2. *Date someone you know—perhaps someone close to home. (Some boys get the idea they have to date a girl way off yonder, who doesn't know them as well as the local girls.)*
3. *Make it a simple date—pick the girl up, go to the party, have fun, take her home, thank her for the grand evening, and tell her good night.*
4. *Avoid the reputation of being a "smooching Casanova." If that's all a boy sees in his date, the word soon passes round and he starts getting the go-by from the more desirable girls.*

It helps if a date can be as casual and natural as possible. That's the reason for suggesting that a boy look around his own circle of neighborhood or school friends before canvassing the next township. A date with a stranger depends for its success on strained and breathless efforts to somehow make an impression. Such desperate dating usually discredits both parties.

There is a special problem of dating for the boy who is looking for his one and only soul mate, and will not date until he finds her. Such a boy lives in a dream world. He needs to learn that he is far more likely to find his dream girl if he circulates around in a constellation of dating experiences rather than roaming about like a lonely star broadcasting for his space mate to come orbiting around. Such a boy is also usually bashful and sensitive. Double-dating may help break the ice.

At the other extreme is the boy who has an enterprising mother, aunt, schoolteacher, or any one of a dozen ambitious "mothers with daughters" who are always trying to set him up. He finds himself being invited unexpectedly to parties, trips, games, or school socials and then finds that a certain girl is always there.

Gradually Junior gets the feeling of smothering. Like a drowning man he feels himself being engulfed. He strikes out to resist the tidal wave of pressures. He may leave a broken heart in the scramble but he makes no bones about the battle: "My single object was to escape!"

Adults who truly wish to help young people get together can be more successful by simply telling a boy what nice things they heard a certain girl say about him (or vice versa—whichever said the nice things first). A young person goes forward with quickened stride if there is assurance of affinity or reciprocal feelings in the one to be pursued.

Most young people get so much coaching before they go on a date that they find themselves trying to be a dozen other people instead of their natural selves. This is all the result of insecurity or of acting like dating was "old stuff." The idea is to make a date feel that Junior has really been around. If the date has really been around, she will see through Junior's act in a second. On the other hand, if she is as new at dating as Junior she will resent his act. He is better off following a few fundamental rules and putting his own best foot forward without trying to copy someone else. The suggested rules are as follows:

1. *When you pick up your date, don't sit out in front of her house honking your shiny jalopy. Go in the house, say hello to her folks, and tell them what you plan to do for the evening. This gives the family confidence that you have a worthwhile project for the evening and won't be "just rodding around." It helps them feel they can expect you to bring their daughter home at some kind of a reasonable hour because you operate "according to a plan." Nothing worries the father of a beautiful daughter more than some gay blade who is asked where they are going and replies, "Out, just out."*

2. *Show a girl that you are not unfamiliar with the common courtesies which every girl appreciates and most girls expect. Help her with her coat, anticipate opening doors, allow her*

*to proceed ahead of you down the aisle or through door-
ways, be quick to introduce her to people you meet.*

3. *Help her have a good time. Most girls will indicate what
they like to do and what they would rather not do. A smart
young fellow will keep an eye and ear to starboard and
constantly check the changing climate. Once a boy gets a
reputation for being a "swell date," he can pick his company
almost at will and mow down the competition.*

4. *Don't rush the romance. A girl worth dating is particular.
When she goes for romancing it's because she really likes
a boy. She doesn't do it just to be good company. A boy
should follow the same rules if he wants this happy get-
together to continue.*

5. *Save your kisses for that someone special. Some boys think
they should start smooching and wooing as soon as they get
out of sight of a girl's house. A girl appreciates a boy whose
kisses are saved for someone special. It makes her want to
qualify.*

6. *Respect the biological barriers. Expressions of affection between a boy and a girl come as naturally as blossoms in
spring. But it is one thing to express playful affection and
quite another thing to start a pattern of intimate love-
making which belongs to marriage and the building of a
family and a home. Every boy learns early how impulsive
these powerful feelings can become. If he is smart, he will
recognize the biological barriers and respect them. A successful young bridegroom recently confided, "The best advice
my dad ever gave me was when he told me about the stop
signs on a date."*

It is a genuine mark of human achievement when a 19-year-old
can go through the jungle of late adolescence without getting
caught in the many marsh traps which are out there to snare
him. If he is willing to listen to a little common-sense advice
from his parents, and then keep his wits about him, he can
make it. One boy who recently emerged from his teens philo-
sophically commented, "Toward the last I got scared and a little
scarred, but I made it!"

CHAPTER 22

IN SIGHT OF THE SUMMIT

Patterns and Problems of the 20-Year-Old

By the time a boy has climbed up the trail of life and reached the ripe old age of 20, his parents can usually see that he finally has his sights on the summit.

In fact, about the time Junior slips across the threshold of 20, Mother Nature seems to sprinkle his brow with a sparkling ingredient called "serious ambition." This replaces the adventurous recklessness of age 19. Most parents are gratified and relieved to see the change. It comes at a time when they know their boy needs to be just a little more serious about playing the role of a man. They want to see his "capacities" begin to show—capacities for hard work, for concentrated study, responsibilities, emotional maturity, and good social adjustment.

But whether or not they are going to be pleased with Junior at this stage of his life will depend largely upon the qualities which they helped their son build into himself through the passing years.

"HAVE WE RAISED OUR BOY RIGHT?"

It is around 20 when most parents realize that they are about to lose their son. College, a career, or marriage, is about to take him away. And in most cases he will be away almost continuously from here on. Suddenly parents ask themselves, "Have we raised our boy right?" If they admit that he is a victim of some degree of neglect and is not really ready for adult life, they may say excitedly, "Well, we had better get busy and build Junior into a man!" Unfortunately, by the time a boy is 20 the "building" is practically over.

I once heard a famous psychologist say that the greatest lesson parents have to learn is that human nature is similar in many ways to concrete. Every parent is working against the day when their child's personality will begin to "set up" or become fixed. Once this has occurred, it literally requires a miracle to alter its basic structure. That is why the growth period is so important. The point which the psychologist was trying to emphasize is demonstrated in studies of adult criminals. The rehabilitation rate of adult criminals is only a small fraction of the success which can be achieved with youthful offenders. As long as a boy is still maturing, he seems to find it easy to shift or even reverse his direction of personality development. Once the growing season is over, however, his willingness or ability to adjust narrows sharply. Of course, this fixation process is all to the good for the boy who has developed positive, wholesome traits. It makes him a solid citizen, capable of weathering the storms of life without collapsing. But if a personality has been developed with many negative attributes, that individual finds it next to impossible to change his basic pattern unless he is willing to undergo a major revolution.

Psychologists tell us why this is true. It is because the growing individual learns to do things by chain reaction. In other words, he builds circuits in his brain which permit a whole series of activities to be triggered by a single mental signal. Take writing, for example. In the beginning a child goes through seven intellectual steps to make a capital "A" in script. He says to himself, "Up, over, down, over, up, down, and up." After doing this a few dozen times a child can finally write an "A" in two phases: around and down. Eventually it will become a single phase. In fact, after "A" has been put with words like "Art," "Act," "Aid," etc., it becomes possible for a person to write a whole word by pulling a single mental trigger. The individual no longer stops to think how to write each letter but simply writes "Art" as a single impulse of intellectual activity.

Now this is not only true of writing, but of all other aspects of living—eating, getting dressed, taking a shower, carrying on a conversation, meeting new people, playing a piano, or telling the truth when it hurts. We develop literally thousands of behavior patterns which were originally very complex but have been learned through constant repetition until they can be performed almost automatically whenever the signal is given by the mind or "will" of the individual. It is easy to see why we sometimes refer to ourselves as "creatures of habit." It is also obvious why habits are so difficult to break. Once a pattern of circuits has been set up, most people find it far too painful and frustrating to dismantle them. By the same token, a person with good habits can also resist terrific pressures to make him change. The "fixation" process was intended as a providential blessing. It is a curse only to that person who did not prepare for it.

Psychologists tell us that by the time a boy is 20 the fixation process is in its advanced stages. The concrete, so to speak, has been poured. The mixture ratio of sand and cement has already been determined. The internal structural reinforcement has been laid and cannot be materially increased without the greatest imaginable difficulty. So, this is our boy. From here on there can be shaping, refining, polishing, and pushing, but the basic ingredients for this particular human being are now in the package and the sealing of that package is taking place.

What he does in the future will be conditioned to a remarkable degree by the strength of the equipment (motives, habits, disciplines, and ideals) which he and his parents have already built into him during the earlier years. As time passes, parents learn to agree with the psychologist who said, "Verily, the child is the father of the man!"

PORTRAIT OF A TWENTY-YEAR-OLD

As a result of the fixation of personality traits which have been growing more and more evident, the parent finds it possible to predict Junior's general reaction to a multitude of different situations. Tastes in music, reading material, food, friends, entertainment, recreation, and a host of other things are now so marked that we can expect them to be developed to their logical conclusion during the remainder of his life.

As we would suspect from the above discussion, Junior's personal habits are now becoming quite stable. Eating, going to bed, taking care of his personal hygiene, keeping appointments—all of these seem to fall into a more routine pattern than last year. He can assume many adult responsibilities and likes to do things without too much "snoopervision." He resents too many suggestions and may grimly comment, "They still think they have to treat me like a kid!"

He responds favorably to compliments where he knows they are deserved and tends to cultivate those talents which bring the most immediate rewards. He is hungry to succeed at something, and is quite deeply impressed with the comments or commendations of those he respects.

He has greater personal insight now. He does a lot of self-evaluating and self-criticizing. His general reaction to others is also far more tolerant this year than during the past three years. He wants adults to accept him on *their* level. He likes to have them ask him his opinion and responds to adult conversation far better than he did last year. At a job he will often go far beyond the call of duty just to prove he is a man. If he had trouble as a teen-ager, he is likely to refer to it with the greatest disdain. He will call it "kid stuff" as though it were now totally alien to the very nature of his being. Although he will have spurts of youthful exuberance from time to time, it will be impressive to see how quickly he can humble himself in the face of an honest and forthright criticism from a friendly adult.

He still resents the interruptions and confusion of younger brothers and sisters, but he seems more resigned to it.

Capacity for planning is a quality of a 20-year-old. The flea-hopping antics which typified his behavior almost from the time he was 14 are now being replaced by premeditated study of nearly everything he does. It is a sign that Junior is feeling the impact of life. It is gradually making him a liberal conservative.

All of this "settling down" by a 20-year-old should help him make the right decisions as he approaches the unlimited opportunities of adulthood. During the next four years he will feel the need to make decisions in many areas which will affect the rest of his life.

CHOOSING A CAREER

One of the most important decisions he will make is choosing a career. There are, in fact, many things he can do or learn to do. The question is primarily, "What does he want to do?" The next question is, "Can he make a living at it?" At this point it is good to remember the advice of the economist who said, "A career is trying to make a living at one of the things you enjoy doing most." This is achieved by investing several years in education, by taking advantage of opportunities as they arise, by working as an apprentice or being willing to work up from the bottom of the ladder in a chosen profession. An ideal career provides two things, "work satisfaction" and "good compensation."

Sometimes, however, circumstances force a young man to make other choices. He may need considerable flexibility to fit the labor market of his particular community. Or he may decide to leave his home town to seek the kind of career he wants in some other area. Before going too far, however, he should make arrangements to take a battery of aptitude tests, which are now accessible to almost everyone. Through these tests he can rather accurately determine the fields in which he is most likely to succeed. These tests are available in many colleges, in various industries, and in some special guidance clinics. It is amazing how many people are fighting the current of life by trying to row their boat upstream. They find that by turning their boat around and going in the direction of their natural aptitudes their journey through life can be smoother, faster, and far more enjoyable. These tests will usually show that a person has abilities in far more career fields than he had ever dreamed. The thing to do is choose one of these fields and then try to get "a" job in it. In order to make a breakthrough it may be necessary to accept a very modest and humble position at first. This has many advantages later on when a person goes up through the ranks. It makes the people under him respect him because he has followed the traditional American formula for success by following the course which ascends "from office boy to president." They also have confidence in his judgment because he once worked "in the ranks."

Today, many jobs are obtained by filling out an application, taking a series of tests, and undergoing a personal interview. The experts on job counseling have a few suggestions concerning each of these stages:

FILLING OUT THE APPLICATION:
1. *Study the job requirements to make sure you can qualify.*
2. *Print or type out the information requested.*
3. *Be sure the application is complete before you sign it.*

TAKING EXAMINATIONS:
1. *Read each question slowly and analytically before trying to answer it.*
2. *Briefly map out the highlights of your answer before writing anything on the exam paper.*
3. *Write legibly.*
4. *Make your answers as pointed as possible.*
5. *Review all your answers before turning in your paper.*

BEING INTERVIEWED:
1. *Advertise your best self in your appearance—clothes, grooming, etc.*
2. *Avoid negative advertising—chewing gum, appearing nervous and fidgety, bluffing.*
3. *Make up your mind you want the job and then let the employment officer see your enthusiasm for it.*
4. *Tell the interviewer as much as you can to help him get an honest appraisal of your experience and ability.*
5. *Have a brief summary already typed up for him, describing your experience, education, training, and personal background.*

After this processing has been completed the final step is follow-up. Go back frequently to ask the personnel officer how your application is coming. Many good jobs are lost just because of an applicant's failure to express a continuing interest in getting the job.

"DID I CHOOSE THE RIGHT GIRL?"

Assuming that Junior does get his job, it is possible he may soon start talking about getting married.

Between 20 and 24 the vast majority of young men choose a mate and get married. Just prior to getting married both the boy and girl suffer serious doubts. The boy says to himself over and over again, "Did I choose the right girl?" The marriage counselor will answer, "Measure your choice."

He will go on to explain that when a boy first decides to court a girl, it is usually more by instinct than reason. The providential design is to try and get the right combination together. If Junior makes himself circulate around in order to become acquainted with many different girls, his intuition tries to lead him to the girl who most nearly provides the things which his own personality requires. Parents and close friends may not always agree with the choice and will counsel accordingly. Junior himself may have difficulty justifying it and may prolong the courtship just to make sure. But experience demonstrates that often when a strong, extroverted, boisterous boy chooses a sweet little specimen of intelligent, quiet, patient, madonna-like qualities, there may be far more merit to the combination than various onlookers may perceive. From these two Providence intends to make one complete, totally integrated personality. Literally, "these two shall be one." It is toward such a goal of oneness that intuition draws them together, each contributing qualities in which the other feels strength. This is the role of instinct. Next comes the role of reason.

There are several helpful ways Junior can test his choice of a mate to reassure himself he is right.

First, does he really know her? She must be appealing to him both in person and personality. It is easy to become infatuated with her physical charms, but after the "I do's," he will have to live with her total behavior pattern, her personality. He must not only see her in the beauty of the moonlight at the Junior Prom where there is the exciting attraction of heady perfume, soft music, the gentle rustle of her chiffon formal, the modeled perfection of her hair and face, or the romantic closeness of her embrace during the dance; he must also watch her on a hike, see what happens when she is hungry, disheveled, tired, and irritated; what kind of a person she is in blue jeans, with a bucket and scrub brush, washing windows. This, too, he will be marrying.

Second, does she really know him? Has he been honest with her in his days of courtship or did he give her a fast, smooth line? Has he been his natural self or has he been putting on an act? Has he promised things he knows down deep he will never really fulfill? Has he told her that after they are married he will do the things he is unwilling to do for her now? If Junior has charmed his lady fair with feverish falsehoods and phoney pretensions, he may be laying a trap that will doom them both to years of violent quarrels, riotous antagonism, and eventually, perhaps, divorce. Nothing is more important to a happy marriage than an honest relationship between a boy and girl during their days of courtship.

Third, how much do they have in common? Love can overcome many differences between two people, but the storms of life are too great to risk the shipwreck of a marriage on the ragged edges of several submerged icebergs. Differences between a boy and girl are not nearly so apparent during the intoxicating rapture of romantic days and nights when a boy and girl feel like they are on an island and that nothing else in the world really matters. One day, however, they will awaken to find that not only everything in the world matters but that the whole world has moved in on them. The more they have in common the easier it will be. Common factors of race, nationality, education, social patterns, personal ideals, intellectual attitudes, and ultimate goals in life can play a most important part in solidly cementing the oneness of a boy and girl together and sealing out the howling blizzards of life that will eventually sweep down upon them.

Fourth, do they have the same religious advantages? This does not mean merely belonging to the same religious faith. A mutually serious attitude toward that faith is the vital key. Marriage is basically a religious institution and is intended to survive through the construction of spiritual bonds that will unite them whether in sickness or health, in poverty or wealth, in old age or in youth. These bonds may forever remain weak if religious differences divide a couple. At first it may not seem important, but with the coming of children it can be the point upon which the marriage itself can split asunder. When a boy marries a girl he should honestly ask himself, "Is the spiritual foundation for our marriage a sound one?" If not, he should proceed slowly. Sometimes one of the parties may be capable of deep religious feelings but will not have been given the opportunity to explore them. Where this is the case the marriage should be postponed until there is ample opportunity to see if this spiritual insight can be achieved. We have learned from experience that the durability of the marriage may very well depend on it.

Fifth, what about children? This should be seriously discussed by a boy and girl to make sure that they share common feelings about the raising of a family. This is not so much a problem today when substantial families are more in style than they were a generation ago; nevertheless, the matter should not be taken for granted. If a boy plans on a large family, only to find that his bride is antagonistic toward having children, this marriage will cease to have meaning almost from the beginning. The same holds true, of course, for a girl whose strong maternal instinct longs for a brood of little people in the home and her husband insists that there be no children or at least no more than one or two. Out of such explosive differences a volcanic eruption can wipe out the whole foundation for a marriage and leave nothing in its wake but bitter fumes of seething frustration and cold dead ashes of parental dreams.

A generation ago a "planned family" usually meant planning not to have any, or at least planning to limit any children to one or two. Fortunately a new trend has arisen where many parents "plan" for a big family. When such plans or hopes are discussed before marriage, it avoids the likelihood of a quarrel over the subject later on.

SHOULD A BOY IN COLLEGE MARRY?

A college student may feel very certain he is not ready for marriage. It may even worry him to go out with a girl more than once or twice for fear she might take him too seriously. Mother Nature is whispering to Junior that it would be mighty nice to have a certain girl for his very own—to love, honor, and cherish—but, "the obligations that go with marriage make it impossible," he says. He would want her to have a nice place and beautiful things, and he knows it is going to be two or three years before he can get through school and support a wife. He keeps saying, "I'd like to, but I can't afford it."

However, in spite of this philosophical soliloquy, Junior often finds himself campaigning as though he were ready for marriage now. He finds himself seriously courting a very special girl and waging a gentle war of wooing as though the whole matter were already settled for next June. Only in his more sober moments does he suddenly stop short and wonder what in the world he will do if she interprets all this activity as evidence of his ability to ring bells come June. He decides to evade the evil prospect of facing such an issue by simply avoiding the delicate subject of marriage.

But a smart girl usually sees Junior's dilemma and comes to his rescue by reminding him that she is an excellent typist and can make enough to support two. She tells Junior what a terrific future he has and says she would love to work a couple of years to help him through school. She explains how fair this is, since he will be supporting her the rest of the time. And anyway, look at all the other couples who are doing this very thing!

Almost before Junior can figure out what has happened he may have consented to her proposal and wired home triumphantly: "Asked Jane to marry me. She accepted!" He then writes a lengthy letter of explanation to the folks, telling them how he and Jane have it all planned out—finances and everything.

COLLEGE HONEYMOONERS

Since more and more young people are getting married during college, nearly every campus has a village for them with extremely modest rents. College counselors are usually very emphatic, however, that marriage will be rough unless the boy has reached at least his Junior year. Both boy and girl must be reconciled to the fact that it will be easier if a few rules are kept in mind:

1. *Everything must be geared to the immediate object—getting a college education. Social life, buying fancy things, entertainment, and travel must be sublimated to "the cause."*
2. *Don't even pretend to be prosperous. Make your frugality fastidious. Take pride in it. Dress neatly, simply, properly, but make no bones about the fact that your food and clothing are on a "bare subsistence" allowance.*
3. *Learn to enjoy doing everything you can yourselves. Pay out money only for necessities, rarely or never for luxuries or conveniences. This discipline is an education in itself.*
4. *If possible live on or near the campus so you can get along without a car. A car can cost as much as college itself. It is surprising how much less complicated life can be if your friends know you just don't have a car.*
5. *Entertain simply. No expensive beverages, food, or treats. Get your friends accustomed to entertainment with a purpose—to meet some new friends, hear some unusual experience of a special guest, or participate in a discussion of a subject which someone present in the group has mastered. Evenings spent at a "party with a purpose" are often the most popular and best remembered at college.*

In later years a married couple may count these days of college honeymooning among their choicest moments. Warm friendships with many other young couples are usually developed. The dedication and sacrifice are rewarding, the prospect of growing careers is satisfying.

If both husband and wife are able to continue school together, it is fortunate. Often, however, the welcomed arrival of a new personality on the scene or the necessity of having the wife work at least part time may interrupt her schooling. If this happens, Junior has an obligation to keep his wife close to all the happenings at school, reading choice passages to her, reciting difficult problems he has solved. In this way his newly wedded sweetheart gets the continuous reminder that she is part of the great preparation which Junior is receiving for their future mutual welfare.

As many as 25 per cent of the students at Junior's university may be married couples. This makes more sense than some conservative souls might suppose. Sociologists have found that a boy makes a mistake to sweat through four years of college and probably several years of graduate work with the thought that only then will he be justified in asking a girl to marry him. If this happens he frequently chooses a person much younger than himself who has no opportunity to appreciate what his profession and the newly acquired comforts of life have cost him. As a result misunderstandings easily arise. The girl may feel jealous of the demands in time and energy which her husband's profession make of him. She may become restless with the leisure that her husband's professional success has won for her.

All this gives substance to the recommendation of marriage counselors, psychologists, and sociologists that a boy should marry before he hits the high income brackets. It is far better if a young couple "earn" their way to independence and abundant living together. The struggle and mutual sacrifice during the lean years form the foundation for the warm appreciation and companionship which bless the golden years that follow.

MAKING MARRIAGE LAST

In many primitive societies marriage is a very temporary and unstable institution of whim or convenience. In advanced civilizations a solid family life is the very foundation of the higher

culture. Rising divorce rates signal the erosion of a nation's un-
derpinnings and the presence of a creeping dry rot in the rafters.
It is the task of every young couple to marry wisely and plan to
be married for keeps. Marriage counselors have a few suggestions for things that might help. For example:

1. *What about inlaws? A boy not only marries a girl but also
her family. He should do everything possible to make himself not only acceptable, but a source of pride to his adopted
family. The girl should do likewise with her husband's family.
But this does not mean they should live with either family!
There is profound wisdom in the sayings of the Good Book
which declares: "For this cause shall a man leave his father
and mother, and cleave to his wife; and they twain shall
be one flesh" (Mark 10:7–8). The girl should also leave her
mother and father. When a couple are isolated from their
respective homesteads, they are far more likely to work out
differences and make the continuous adjustments which
marriage calls for. If they are too close to the folks, it is so
easy to run home to Mama with wailing woes. And who can
blame an outraged parent for rearing up in righteous indignation when she hears the sad recital? The husband's
mother demands, "What are you doing to my boy?" And the
wife's mother sweeps up like a whirlwind. "What wretched
things are you doing to my sweet innocent little girl!" Few
parents can muster up the courage to shrug off complaints
and tell their children to go on back home and make their
marriage work.*

2. *What about money? Who can count the marriages that are
wrecked on a dollar sign? Money problems are worked out
most successfully where there is an early agreement on finances. By mutual consent, either the husband or wife
should have the specific responsibility for keeping the bud-
get in balance. Any special expenses should be approved by
both parties. Because one will be inclined to be more extravagant than the other, the bookkeeping might best be
left to the mate whom nature has made the most frugal.
In passing we should mention that a joint bank account is a*

convenience for some people but a nest of serpents for others. Only a well-disciplined couple should risk having one.

3. *What about compatible marital life? This need not be any problem at all. There are a few basic biological facts which every pair of newlyweds should get from a competent family doctor. From there on they can depend upon their mutual love and confidence to carry them through. These associations are the highest expression of affection and can always bring happiness when accompanied by mutual thoughtfulness and consideration.*

4. *What are the pitfalls to watch for? First of all, the problem of "growing apart." A wife can run a home too strictly for happy living, so that a husband goes elsewhere to read his paper and relax. Or she can run it so sloppily that he seeks out some old cronies at the club as preferable companions. By the same token a husband can get so involved in business, civic affairs, a hobby, or a sport that he shuts his wife almost completely out of his life without realizing it. Another pitfall for parents is arguing over the management of children. A little study of child psychology will give them both a basis for management and discipline and then, when one of the parents gives an instruction, the other parent can give running field support whenever necessary. There is also a related problem of using children for crying towels. This is where one parent tries to win the sympathy of the children by complaining against the other parent. Ultimately this may not only break up a family but drive the children toward the parent who is the alleged offender. Being crybabies themselves, children have little trouble seeing through a grownup crybaby. If they don't catch on as children they will in later years and what was once sympathy for the complaining parent often curdles into disgust.*

Last of all, there is the pitfall of falling in love with somebody else. This is usually inexcusable but is terribly real when it happens. It comes from deliberately flirting around, fooling around, or just simply playing with fire. A young married couple needs to realize that physical infatuation (as distinguished from genuine love) is mostly proximity, and if they allow themselves to neglect their own love, it leaves a vacuum which nature may fill with some fetching creature whose proximity is dynamite. Almost before anyone quite realizes it, there is a triangle. In time, bleeding hearts and wilted flowers become the mournful theme of life. Likely as not things will never be the same again. A beautiful dream has died.

Love and fidelity are twin sisters. Happiness is their goal. To make any marriage last the boy and girl must be zealously jealous of the castle they are building. Their slogan might well be, "No intruders allowed!" Both must nurture the tender roots of happy living in their own special garden. Out of a lifetime of such efforts the subtle perfumes of ten thousand glorious memories blossom forth.

In a home of dedication and affection, God seems to have little difficulty diffusing his choicest blessings, bounties, and beneficence.

CONCLUSION

As we conclude this brief résumé of the patterns and problems confronting the average 20-year-old, we cannot help but acknowledge the maze of vital decisions which he must begin making. The next four years are all "years of decision." Never in his life has it been so important for Junior to be right. It is a task for a boy and his parents which calls for sympathy, understanding, and a united front!

CHAPTER 23

"TODAY, TODAY I AM A MAN!"

Patterns and Problems of a 21-Year-Old

When a boy stretches himself to full height, takes a deep breath, and says, "Mom, today, today I am a man!" it sounds like a Tarzan call coming from the topmost timbers of a very tall tree. However, Junior is broadcasting a very special kind of call on this, his twenty-first birthday. He is trumpeting for destiny to meet him any time, any place, and preferably in the next twenty minutes!

Age 21 is a year of thrust, a year of arriving, a year of budding adulthood. It normally radiates confidence, exuberance, poise, spunk, and big dreams. Psychologically, it is a great year.

PORTRAIT OF A TWENTY-ONE-YEAR-OLD

Although traditionally age 21 is the threshold of manhood, Mother Nature knows the job is not quite done. Junior is simultaneously both a boy and a man. In swimming trunks, slacks, or work clothes, he can pass for a well-developed 17-year-old. In his Sunday go-to-meeting clothes he can pass for 24.

Last year Junior was always very anxious to impress people with his being a man. This year he occasionally likes to slip back briefly into his old teen-age ways of being an irresponsible gay blade. It may happen only two or three times during the year, but when it does happen it will seem so out of character it may shock the whole family. For Junior it is simply a nostalgic backward glance over his maturation shoulder to taste for the last time the carefree ways of "the good old days." Like a grown colt, he instinctively feels that this is perhaps his last opportunity to kick up his heels before settling down to the daily chore of pulling his share of life's load.

Essentially, however, Junior is remarkably well equipped to play the role of a full-grown man if circumstances require it. In pioneer days early maturity was one of the demands. A 21-year-old was frequently the owner of a farm, father of a young family, and already attracting attention as a force for good in the bustling frontier community. This shows the potential of a 21-year-old. However, modern life tends to postpone these demands. Therefore, some 21-year-olds will still be marching up and down the earth acting like uninhibited teen-agers.

BIRTH OF A CITIZEN

Nevertheless, as far as the law is concerned, Junior has now arrived. All the laws which formerly protected him as a "minor" are now inapplicable. No longer does his mom or dad have the responsibility of providing his board and room. They may help out once in a while just because they love him, but, legally speaking, Junior is paddling his own canoe. Many a night he will lie awake thinking how nice it used to be when Dad was at the oars.

No longer can he buy an expensive sports car and then get out from under the payments by turning it back and claiming he was under age when he signed the contract. From here on his contracts can be enforced with a vengeance, even to the extent of garnisheeing his wages if he gets in arrears.

Junior is on his own in other ways. If he successfully avoids the nicotine habit with its risks of cancer, it will be to his own credit. The tobacco laws stopped protecting him the day he became 21—in some states even earlier. If he avoids becoming an alcoholic, it likewise will have to be a credit to his own judgment. The "Minors Not Allowed" signs no longer keep him out. Likewise, if he visits Las Vegas or Reno, he will learn that the law assumes that by this time he will have acquired enough sense not to gamble. Therefore, he will find there is no law to keep him out of the casinos and no law to help him get his money back after he has dumped it down the hungry gullet of a slot machine or into the trapdoor lap of a dice table.

It is important for Junior to catch a whole new perspective of life. As a full-fledged citizen he is expected to be a patron of law and order, good government, and intelligent, happy living. Society no longer feels either the desire or the necessity of treating him like a baby. From here on he will be honored as a man; a man of judgment, controlled appetites, tempered emotions, and restrained conduct; a man of skill and ambition with a warm social sense and a genuine sense of service. Some 21-year-olds, of course, do not measure up. Some act at least part of the time like little boys indulging in emotional immaturity, explosive tempers, impulsive decisions, and childish antics. Some even go snorting across the fenceline of the law. When this happens the fence-riding forces of law and order move into the gap like a charging bull-dozer.

Society is far less patient with a 21-year-old who assaults, robs, cheats, or steals than with a growing boy. A 21-year-old hears the terms "adult criminal" applied to him, and he doesn't like it. It is the community's way of saying, "Stand up, Junior. Be a man!"

Fortunately, however, the vast majority of the nation's new citizens are ready for their responsibilities and can say with the Apostle Paul: "When I was a child, I spake as a child, I understood as a child; but when I became a man, I put away childish things" (I Corinthians, 13:11).

"MY VOTE IS AS GOOD AS THE PRESIDENT'S!"

As a full-fledged citizen, Junior can now vote. When he was 18 he may have wondered why the voting privilege had to wait until 21. Now he may be able to see the reason. Junior has certainly changed his thinking since 18. For some reason, 18 and 19 were revolutionary years. They were years of doubt and challenge. This was all to the good and an important part of growing up, but probably it was far from being a period of reflected wisdom.

In fact, dictators and imperialists nearly always try to capitalize on the reckless, revolutionary spirit of 18- and 19-year-olds. Hitler surveyed the youth of his own day and said: "Look at these young men and boys! What material! I shall eradicate the thousands of years of human domestication. Brutal youth—that is what I am after. . . . I want to see once more in its eyes the gleam . . . of the beast of prey. With these I can make a new world . . . and create a new order!"

Often, even at 21, we find there is still some of the revolutionary spirit smoldering beneath the surface, but, for the most part, it will have been sublimated by maturity and experience. Everything else being equal, a citizen of 21 will make a far more intelligent voter than he would have at 18. Recently, a 21-year-old reflected some of that intelligence when he commented, "Say, my vote is as good as the President's!"

INCREASED CAPACITY FOR WORRY

Psychologists tell us why a 21-year-old makes a more responsible citizen. It is because of his increased capacity for worry. Not that Junior couldn't worry in his teens; he did. But his worries in those days were mostly about himself. Now he has developed a capacity to worry about things like the high cost of living, the international situation, inflation, civil liberties, the rising crime rate, union-management problems, juvenile delinquency, and the national debt.

A wholesome amount of worry is not only a necessary ingredient for good citizenship but the mainspring of action in getting community problems solved. Junior ought to be fully aware of what would happen if all of us refused to be bothered with unpleasant things like crime, inflation, and the boast of the Communists that they will soon conquer the world. Obviously, if we refused to be bothered, this would be the last generation to live in freedom. That is why political scientists say an alert, worry-motivated citizenry is the kind which solves problems and therefore continually improves civilization.

We also want Junior to recognize the kind of worry that digs graves. Worry is a perishable commodity and must not be stored. It should be promptly turned into constructive action and thereby disposed of. Stored-up worries tend to turn into pickles and vinegar and consequently endanger sound mental health. This is the kind of worry most people have heard about, and therefore conclude that all kinds of worry should be avoided. This, of course, is not true. We want Junior to recognize worry for what it is—*fuel*. When put to work it makes him a success, makes him a better citizen, a better parent, a better career man. On the other hand, it is volatile stuff. If stored, it explodes.

"MOM, HOW'S MY SCORE CARD?"

When parents see a boy reach 21 they always hope they have helped him acquire the habits, attitudes, skills, and social amenities necessary to become a successful adult. It is a time of unspoken evaluation, and, for some parents as well as boys, a time of regret. But for most parents and boys it will be a time of great hope and great pride. A boy may even respond to a sudden urge and say, "Mom, how's my score card?"

There are a number of things we certainly hope our boy has achieved by 21:

First, by this time we hope Junior has learned the difference between *being* a character and *having* a character. Character is like a personality. It involves the sum total of a man. Character is the development of a human being's best self; Lincoln called it "the better angel" in each of us. When we say a young man has character we mean he stands for something. He is not a sniveling, servile, spineless parasite, but a hearty, friendly, honest, outgoing sort of person who makes good company, a good employee, a good husband, a pleasant neighbor, and a good soldier. Perhaps we would say that character is simply a good balance in life:

> Bold, but not overbearing.
> Honest, but not blunt.
> Adventurous, but not reckless.

Frugal, but not miserly.
Considerate, but not fawning.
Generous, but not gullible.
Self-confident, but not proud.
Independent, but not defiant.
Religious, but not pious.
Loyal, but not blind.

Second, we hope our boy has acquired a tremendous capacity for good hard work. In certain circles this may not be in style, but it is a popular commodity on the labor market. Those of us who have had to hire and train many hundreds of young men during our professional careers count capacity for hard work among the prime virtues of a 21-year-old who wants to go places. It is not merely that he will produce more and help the company stay in business. Equally important is the fact that a man with a good "work quotient" is a pleasure to have around. His will to work shows in his voice, in his handshake, in his stride, and in his pay envelope. He is available for an emergency, volunteers suggestions, carries the ball during his regular shift, and, where necessary, after his shift. His enthusiasm changes work into pleasure and a "job" into a "position." It is a great achievement to build a boy into this kind of a man.

Third, we want our boy to be honest. He wasn't born honest. Nor was he born dishonest. Both are learned. Almost any normal person is honest when it is convenient or self-serving to be honest. The test comes when it is embarrassing or a temporary disadvantage to be honest. A boy learns from his parents whether or not to hold the line. If they avoid social pressures both in and out of the family by telling "little white lies," then Junior does the same. If they face up to each situation without garbling the truth, Junior has a better target to shoot for.

The boy who is honest has a high survival rating. He may not be as flashy as the boy with a quick line and the ready lie, but he wears better. We want our boy to wear well. We want him to know that honesty is an attitude and it should have become a habit. In the final analysis it simple means he can be trusted;

trusted in what he says and what he does. Employers pay premium wages to employees they can trust.

Fourth, we want our boy to be morally strong. This may seem a little old-fashioned, but it is still civilization's best foundation for a happy home and a solid family life. Mutual trust is built before marriage when a girl finds that a boy is morally disciplined and can keep his emotions under control. It helps her have implicit faith in him after marriage. Morality is therefore a special kind of honesty which permits a young husband to be trusted by the most important people in his life. Almost everyone admires moral integrity, even the less moral.

Fifth, we want our boy to have become a good student. He should have cultivated a sharp appetite for good books. We live in a technical world of extremely advanced cultural complexity. The boy who has not acquired a thirst for knowledge is likely to get left behind. There are thousands of bright youthful personalities in our land who appear overwhelmed by the world they live in. Actually, this is the most favored generation of the race. But only the good student will know about it. We want our boy to have a dynamic part in the throbbing heartbeat of modern history as mankind prepares to launch into the great new space age.

Sixth, Junior should have become a skillful problem solver. A young child attacks a problem by pulling a tantrum. Some grownups do the same thing. We want our boy to have acquired a sound sense of human engineering. We want him to have learned to attack a problem by (1) clearly defining it, (2) probing and studying until he has selected the most practical solution, and (3) generating the necessary steam to carry it out. We also want him to have learned the prayer of the ancient philosopher who said, "God give me strength to change what should be changed and the patience to endure what must remain."

Seventh, we would not want our boy to have attained 21 without acquiring a sense of belonging in the universe. This means a strong religious faith built on truth. A generation ago it was popular to say that a religious faith was for the weak. Time is proving that an enlightened religious faith is the supreme virtue of the strong. A boy of 21 should already have learned that he is part of a carefully designed universe governed by a God who personally loves him. Those who say religion is only for children are usually those who have never tried *adult* religion.

Eighth, we want our boy to have ambition. This, too, is primarily an attitude or an appetite which parents can help create. They create it by holding before a boy the vision of the man they know he can one day be. The vision must not be too bright, not beyond his capacity of attainment. And it must not focus too soon. In early youth he wants to be a policeman, a cowboy, or a deep-sea diver. As he matures his interests change and so do his ambitions. Perhaps they turn to law, science, medicine, engineering, mechanics, aviation, or electronics. The important thing is to keep his searching "upward reach" scintillating and alive. A set of encouraging parents is the most vital single ingredient in this process. Parents who think they have problems might consider the case of Thomas A. Edison. Young Tom was expelled from the first grade because of his ambitions. Before he could read he wanted to study high school subjects. He was labeled incorrigible by his exasperated teacher and sent home to his worried parents. Even at home his ambitions soon created a neighborhood panic. He tried to inflate a small friend with gas so he would "ascend like a balloon!" Finally his mother decided to guide all these big ideas into more constructive channels. By the time young Tom was 9 he and his mother had carefully read Gibbons' *Decline and Fall of the Roman Empire,* Hume's *History of England,* Sears's *History of the World,* Burton's *Anatomy of Melancholy,* and *The Dictionary of Sciences.* Such was the early guidance of the career of a boy whose inventions later created industries worth more than twenty-five billion dollars.

Ninth, we will certainly not want to close this list of achievements without mentioning just one more—Junior's sense of humor. Most 21-year-olds have a fathomless capacity for humor, but like other human qualities it should have matured.

In his childhood days Junior responded to the "humor of absurdity." He loved the absurdity of slapstick comedy, pie-throwing contests, or seeing an elderly woman slip on the ice and crash to the sidewalk. Psychologists say that such humor is rooted in the warm satisfaction that *he* would never do anything so stupid. This warm feeling bubbles over into laughter, and the more ridiculous the situation the louder the laughter.

In later years Junior tastes enough of life to feel sympathy for people in unfortunate situations. Usually, he no longer laughs at people slipping or falling. He identifies his own feelings with those of the victim. His sense of humor now requires more subtle things. He graduates to the level of "hidden meaning humor."

By age 10 or 11 this is already beginning to appear. He is fascinated by the hidden meaning of anything sacred, private, or secret. Sex and excretory processes are referred to with loud guffaws even though his so-called jokes are otherwise pointless. A little later on he is fascinated by the double meaning of words. "Puns" now become an important source of laughter.

Finally, however, Junior should attain the rich, warm glow of grownup humor. Adult humor is hearty but not boisterous. It is not laughter to be heard but laughter to be felt. It grows out of the deep, golden depths of the human personality, which reflect the vast richness of life. It is the laughter of a father who is smothered under an avalanche of welcoming arms as a bevy of little people shout, "Daddy's home!" It is the laughter of the happy hunter as he brings home the game at the end of the day. It is the joyful laughter of the athlete as he leads his team to victory. Adult humor is the music of the heart—tuned in on the universe.

REFLECTIONS OF A PARENT

But whether our son has attained all of these desirable things or only part of them, the important thing is that suddenly he is 21! It seems almost impossible to realize it. He grew up so fast. Now we are sorry we didn't take time to enjoy him more. Perhaps in the twilight of a quiet summer evening we thumb through the pages of the family album. It sparks some happy memories for a mom and dad. As a baby he was the cutest little fellow in the town. At 4 he was like a monkey on wheels—all over the place. At 6 the camera caught him proudly grinning without his two front teeth. Age 10 was truly his golden year.

And wasn't he sprouting out of his Sunday suit at 13! Then there are all those wonderful high school pictures. You can almost see yourself in every scene and remember how it used to be in your day, at your school. The college pictures are great, too, but not quite so sentimental. And there is his picture in uniform. He made a handsome serviceman! No wonder the girls fell for him. Funny how he seemed sort of oblivious to it. Except, of course, for Jo Anne. She floored him. How lovely she looks in her wedding dress. They make a marvelous couple. . . .

As a mom and dad look back over the past fifth of a century they seem caught between the sentimental flood of happy memories and the relief they feel for a mission accomplished. They know they made some mistakes, but they marvel how well it turned out after all. One thing they can't help mentioning—how some of Junior's childhood vices turned out to be his grownup virtues. They remember how they worried over his destructive proclivities—how he took the family clock apart, unstrung the bedroom radio, wrecked the first family TV. Now he earns his living mending such things! Or they remember worrying about his reading so much but now they are proud as punch that he made the national honor fraternity. They think of Nancy Hanks Lincoln gently scolding her boy for being a dreamer and not splitting the rails for the farm fence. And all the time she was raising one of America's greatest presidents! Mother Nature surely has a way of fooling parents.

Perhaps this is why raising a boy so often seems like a chore. Only when the job is practically completed does it suddenly seem like the greatest happiness of a lifetime. And how great the reward of parents who were blessed with a boy who really tried. It makes a mom and dad know that it was all worthwhile, and they cannot help but say with the wisdom of the ages:

"It's better to build men—than mend them!"

Part II   PARENTS AND PROBLEMS

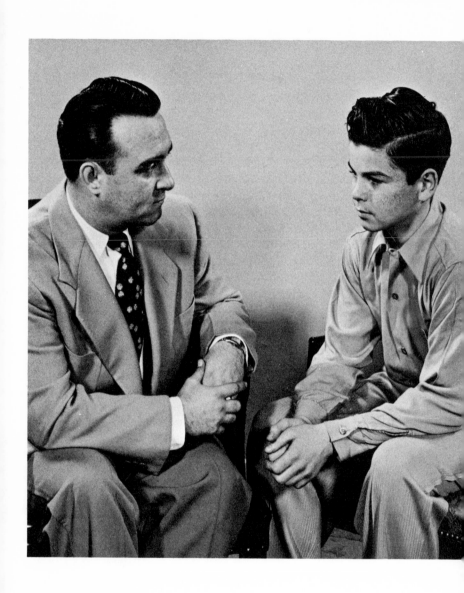

CHAPTER 24

SHARING THE FACTS OF LIFE

As we have already pointed out, questions about babies come sooner than most parents expect. When a little fellow asks, "Where do babies come from?" his folks must not assume that this is merely morbid curiosity. Questions about babies are normal at 4; often they come even earlier, so a parent needs to be prepared. It helps to keep in mind that such questions are desirable and wholesome at this age. It is an excellent opportunity to begin cultivating sensible attitudes in little people.

A child's education involves two fronts. First, he wants to know the plain, simple facts. Secondly, he wants to know the meaning or interpretation of those facts. For example, he wants to know about the sun. He sees it rise in the morning and set in the evening. This seems to be a plain, simple fact. Then he learns the exciting truth that the sun doesn't rise and set at all! He is now in the secondary stage of interpreting the facts.

Because adults have preceded him up the pathway of life, a child looks to adults for an honest and accurate interpretation of what is happening. This becomes a most important part of his education. But when we are discussing sex education, the question inevitably arises, "Are parents the right ones to teach it?"

WHO SHOULD BE RESPONSIBLE FOR SEX EDUCATION?

During the past two generations, parents have tried to get out from under the responsibility of sharing the facts of life with their children. It is easy to understand why. Discussing human love life is different from answering questions about the sun. This important part of life is entirely subjective and personal. It involves delicate human relations, easily misunderstood. It is like opening the door to a part of life which to most people is sacred and therefore secret. Many parents felt this called for the "professional treatment."

Unfortunately, however, the only two professions which could possibly qualify for the assignment are the physicians and the schoolteachers. Both turned out to be too far removed from the scene of action to do much good during the all-important early stages. If a boy asks, "Where do babies come from?" and a parent says, "The doctor will have to tell you," or, "Wait until you get to school to ask such questions," the child immediately gains the impression that for some reason his parents cannot, or will not, discuss babies with him. This pours fire and fuel on his childish curiosity, and may result in a morbid preoccupation with the subject.

The second difficulty involved in delegating sex education to physicians and schoolteachers is the problem of interpretation. A doctor or schoolteacher will often prove tremendously effective in teaching a child the plain functional facts about procreation, but they may prove entirely inadequate when it comes to building attitudes and disciplines which are compatible with those of the parents. In fact, many teachers point out that they absolutely will not become involved in the moral aspect of sexual behavior, since teaching ideals and moral responsibility is the primary function of the family and the church. They therefore restrict their classes to the physiology of sex. This is extremely dangerous if a parent then assumes that his child's education is complete. The fact is that, rightly or wrongly, a child will learn the physiology of the sexual function whether adults tell him or not. The more important aspect, however, and the key to normal sexual maturity, is understanding these functions so they become a wholesome part of life and not a morbid obsession.

Parents should be aware that, even among professionals, there is a wide variety of "interpreting" going on, and many parents would strenuously object if they knew what their children are being told in some of the so-called "sex education" classes. There are those who openly advocate non-suppression of the sexual urge as normal and desirable. Their theory is Freudian in origin. They think the release of sexual tensions is a prerequisite to sound mental health. They frequently condone practices which are pointedly condemned by the Judaeo-Christian culture of modern civilization. This libertine philosophy is gaining momentum, even though its advocates are under vigorous criticism by many of their own profession.

There has also been the fad in recent years of using nudity as a means of educating children about sex. The idea was to encourage a certain amount of nudity by both children and adults around the home so as to take the mystery out of sex and "make everything seem natural." The fallacy of this theory was soon demonstrated. As one writer recently said: "Seeing the nude bodies of grownups often arouses a child's interest in touching, exploring, and fondling. This may start feelings and desires in him that can't be satisfied and they are disturbing in many ways."

These are just a few of the problems connected with professional classes in sex education. The trend, therefore, is to return the task to the home where it more properly seems to belong. This means that parents need to prepare themselves so they can do it well. The job turns out to be less painful than many parents had supposed.

THE IMPORTANCE OF USING THE RIGHT WORDS

Every parent knows the sneaky hush-hush words used by many adolescents and even some adults to describe the reproductive process and the reproductive organs. All of these words have the common quality of being sexually exciting. They also have the quality of being crude words which cannot be used in the open without embarrassment. Parents who know only these slang expressions to describe the reproductive process are under serious handicap when they get ready to discuss the facts of life with their children. Very likely they have punished their children for using these very terms. How, then, can they use these slang terms to teach their children a wholesome understanding of sex?

A mother or father gets a chance to teach a child the right terminology the very first time their little 5-year-old comes in the house using a number of four-letter words he has picked up around the neighborhood. When this happens parents must be careful not to go into a state of shock. If they do, the child learns that these "shock words" are good bullets to fire when he wants to exhibit defiance or put his parents on the spot.

It is best to just simply count to five and then tell this little dimpled darling that the word he had just said is an ugly word which *"we* don't use." He should then be given the right word. It should be explained to him in simple language so as to satisfy his curiosity and eliminate the mysterious fascination which obscene terms usually provoke.

Here are a few of the terms taken from the family doctor book. It will be observed that all of these words are technical rather than descriptive. This is their chief value. They are neither obscene nor sexually exciting. If a child learns their meaning early in life, he finds it easy to use them without self-consciousness or embarrassment.

Male Terminology: Genitals: All of the glands and organs involved in the reproductive process. In the male these are the penis, the scrotum, the testicles, together with their related tubes, tissues, secretions, and cells.

Penis: The male organ for urinating and sexual expression.

Glans Penis: The terminal end of the penis, covered by the foreskin unless this has been removed by circumcision.

Scrotum: The pouch or sac in which the testicles are suspended.

Testicles: Two oval glandular bodies suspended in the scrotum by the spermatic cord. These are the reproduction glands. They produce the sperm cells and the semen fluid in which the sperm cells are suspended.

Sperm: The male reproduction cell. It is very tiny and is shaped like an apostrophe ('). The sperm has a threadlike tail which whips back and forth to propel it up through the uterus and into the Fallopian tubes. The sperm is an "incomplete" cell of only twenty-four chromosomes (half the regular number) which struggles to meet and combine with the female ovum or egg cell. The female ovum is also an "incomplete" cell of only twenty-four chromosomes. When the sperm and ovum combine, they make a complete cell of forty-eight chromosomes.

Seminal Emission: This is usually referred to simply as an "emission." It is the involuntary discharge of accumulated semen which occurs during sleep.

Ejaculation: The discharge of semen which comes at the climax of sexual activity.

Insemination: Transfer of the semen from the male to the female to produce conception. Sexual intercourse is the natural method of insemination.

Prostate Gland: A small round gland situated near the bladder and at the base of the penis. Its secretion forms part of the semen.

Female Terminology: Genitals: In the female these are the uterus (or womb), the ovaries, the Fallopian tubes, the vulva (or labia), the clitoris, and the vagina, together with their glands, tubes, secretions, and cells. Beginning from the outside of the female body, these genital organs are individually defined as follows:

Vulva: or "labia" are the fleshy folds that cushion the opening to the vagina. These constitute the only visible portion of the female genitals.

Clitoris: A small elongated organ situated in the upper part of the vulva, capable of erection under sexual excitement.

Vagina: The passageway or canal of the female sexual organs leading to the uterus or womb.

Uterus: Often referred to as the "womb," which is the female organ that becomes the home for the baby during gestation and prenatal development. It is a pear-shaped organ situated in the lower abdomen which is reached through the vagina. The larger portion of the uterus is uppermost, with the Fallopian tubes extending from it, one on each side. The uterus is like the stomach in that it is very flexible. It is capable of accommodating a single baby or expanding to accommodate twins, triplets, or even quintuplets. After the birth of the baby or babies, the uterus returns to its former size and shape.

Fallopian Tubes: These tubes connect the ovaries to the uterus. There are two tubes, one on each side of the uterus. The male sperm must travel up the vagina, through the uterus, and into one of these Fallopian tubes to meet the female ovum or egg cell which will have come down to this point from the ovary. When the union of the sperm and the ovum has taken place (called conception), the fertilized egg then travels slowly down the Fallopian tube to the uterus where it attaches itself to the uterus wall and the development of the baby continues there.

Ovaries: Two small almond-shaped glands, each of which is connected to the uterus by a Fallopian tube. Each ovary produces the female ovum or egg cell, which is projected into the Fallopian tube to meet the male sperm. If no male sperm is present to fertilize the egg cell, it is flushed away.

Hymen: This is often referred to as the maidenhead. It is a thin fold or membrane which protects the entrance to the vagina. It is ruptured at the time of the first intercourse, although it may be accidentally broken before.

Menstruation: This is usually referred to as the "monthly period." It consists of the discharge of the blood from the uterus when there is no pregnancy and the blood is not needed. This flushing of the blood from the uterus carries with it the cast-off lining of the uterus, which is renewed each month. The discharge usually lasts from three to five days. It is repeated approximately every twenty-eight days unless pregnancy occurs. This is a female function which commences with puberty. It usually starts around age 12 but may begin sooner.

Other General Terms Frequently Used: Coitus: The scientific term for sexual intercourse or cohabitation.

Orgasm: The climax of pleasurable sensation in sexual intercourse which culminates in the discharge of semen by the male. The orgasm of either male or female is followed by complete relaxation.

Copulation: Literally means being joined or linked together. It is another word to describe uniting in sexual intercourse.

Continence: Refers to habits of self-control. Sexual continence is the capacity to control personal sexual behavior.

Embryo: The name given to the unborn child from the time it begins as a fertilized ovum up to the end of the third month.

Fetus: The unborn child from the fourth month until birth.

Erection: Refers to the reaction to sexual stimulation of the male penis or the female clitoris.

Masturbation: The act by either male or female of stimulating sexual excitement and securing an orgasm by means other than sexual intercourse.

Puberty: The time of life when youth begin to acquire the physical maturity of manhood or womanhood. Sexually, puberty means the beginning of menstruation for girls and the beginning of seminal emissions for boys.

TYPICAL QUESTIONS OF CHILDREN

Numerous books are now available to suggest answers to the questions which children usually ask. These are some of the questions which most children ask while learning about sex. The suggested answers follow each question:

1. Where do babies come from? *They come from their mothers. They grow in a special place in the mother's body which is called the uterus. The baby starts out as a tiny cell and then gradually grows until it is ready to eat food and breathe air, then it is born.*

2. How does the little cell which grows into a baby get into the mother? *A baby grows from a cell which was already in the mother's body. It is called an egg cell or an ovum. Egg cells are produced in the mother's body by two small glands called ovaries.*

3. How does the baby get out? *Babies are born through a special passageway in the mother's body called the vagina.*

4. How does the egg cell know when to start growing into a baby? Can a mother just start making a baby any time she

wants to? *No, a mother has to wait until a sperm cell is given to her by the father. It is the sperm cell from the father which joins with the egg cell to start the baby growing.*

5. How does the mother know when the baby is ready to be born? *She can tell by the movement of the muscles in her body which are getting ready to push the baby out into the world through the special passageway.*

6. Does it hurt to have a baby? *Yes, all of the muscles have to stretch and push to help with the baby's birth. The stretching and pushing is painful, but when it is all over and the mother gets to see her baby she feels it was worth all the trouble and pain.*

7. When a baby is growing inside its mother, how does it breath? *A baby doesn't have to breathe air until after it is born. Before birth it is able to get all the oxygen it needs through its mother.*

8. When a baby is growing inside its mother, how does it eat? *It doesn't have to eat because there is a little tube which connects the baby to its mother, and when she eats the food gives strength to her body and the nourishment which she has received passes through the little tube into the baby. This little tube is called the umbilical cord. It is attached to the baby's stomach at the navel or belly button.*

9. Why don't I have a tube attached to my belly button any more? *Because now that you have been born you can eat with your mouth, so you don't need to be fed through the tube any more. That is why the doctor took it away after you were born. Anyway, you couldn't eat ice cream and lots of good things through the little tube and enjoy it as you can when you eat it through your mouth. It is lots better this way now that you have been born.*

10. When I grow up, will I have a baby? *Well, you will grow up to be a man and then you can be a father, but babies only grow inside a mother. That is why you will want to find a sweetheart when you grow up. After you are married to your sweetheart, she can have some children for you.*

11. If the mothers have the babies, what are fathers for? *The mother can't start growing a baby unless the father gives her*

a sperm cell from his own body. The mother can't grow a baby by herself. That's why fathers are so important. And anyway, while the mother is growing the baby she has to depend upon the father to go out and earn the living so the family will have a house to live in and food to eat. Fathers are very important.

The above questions usually come during the earlier stages of childhood. They are the questions children usually ask between 4 and 8. Beginning around 8 or 9 a child will ask these questions:

12. Where do fathers grow sperm cells? *These are made in the testicles. However, boys do not grow sperm cells until they begin to grow up and are getting ready to be fathers.*

13. How does the father give the sperm cell to the mother and start the baby growing? *This is done during mating. The sperm passes from the testicles and up through the penis. It enters the vagina of the mother and then makes its way up through the uterus to the Fallopian tube, where it meets the egg cell or ovum and joins with it. This is called conception. (If you have a family doctor book, this process can be traced on the sketch of the female reproductive organs.)*

14. Where is the place where the baby grows? *A few days after the egg cell has been met by the sperm in the Fallopian tube, it slips down into the uterus or womb and attaches itself to the soft wall. That's where it grows into a baby—in the womb.*

15. How long does it take to grow a baby? *It takes nine months for the baby to develop fully. Kittens and puppies can be grown by their mothers in a lot less time.*

QUESTIONS DURING ADOLESCENCE

As a boy matures he hears many things which excite his curiosity. If his parents have retained his confidence, he will usually come to them with questions about the things he has heard: Many of these questions will be extremely personal.

16. What is self-abuse? *This is usually called masturbation. It is an attempt to secure sexual stimulation by some artificial means. Sometimes boys get into bad sex habits during their*

early teens. This should be avoided. Every boy should know that masturbation may be the first step toward homosexuality.

17. What is a homosexual? *This is a person who tries to get sexual satisfaction from someone of the same sex. Of course, this is unnatural and all kinds of problems can arise from it. Frequently it starts out with masturbation, and then the individual seeks a partner for mutual sex play. These practices are destructive to the personality, and frequently this type of individual disintegrates to the point where he becomes involved in various types of sex crimes. In fact, the moral degenerate is responsible for some of the most vicious and sadistic sex crimes on record.*

18. Aren't some people born homosexuals? *This is so rare that whenever a case occurs it is considered a medical phenomenon. In practically all cases, homosexuality is cultivated. Individuals who get into abnormal sex habits during early youth can develop them into such a fixed pattern that they soon think these deviations are perfectly normal. When homosexuals are arrested, they try to excuse their conduct by saying, "I guess I'm just made this way."*

19. What does it mean when "a homo makes a pass"? *This usually refers to a situation where a young boy is approached by an older boy or by some degenerate who tries to get him to engage in sex play. This may happen in a theater, a public park, or public rest room. Boys in early adolescence should be aware of this type of individual and report him to the nearest policeman or other responsible adult.*

20. What do older boys mean when they talk about wet dreams? *This merely refers to a physical reaction called an emission. When the genitals have stored up a quantity of semen, the body gets rid of it during sleep by an emission. The sexual stimulation incident to the emission sometimes results in strange dream situations. This shouldn't worry you. It happens to all boys.*

21. Why do girls have "monthly periods"? *This is called menstruation. It occurs about every twenty-eight days. It is nature's way of getting rid of the extra blood supply which*

has accumulated in the lining of the uterus or womb. This is the blood supply which would be used to nourish an embryo if one were forming, but when the blood is not needed it is flushed away about once each month. That is why it is called the "monthly period." The process takes from around three to five days.

22. If a boy and girl are really in love, is it all right to have relations even though they are not married? *No, it is not right, and there are many important reasons why it is forbidden both by civil and divine law. Sex relations are part of family relations, and a boy and girl are in no way prepared for the responsibilities of a family until after they are married. Furthermore, a marriage is cheapened and elements of distrust are introduced when young people have indulged in sexual relations before marriage. When a boy and girl are really in love their affection for each other is greatly strengthened if each one makes sure that their intimate expressions are never allowed to go beyond certain prescribed bounds. Happy marriages depend to a large extent upon the respect a boy and girl develop for each other during their courtship days.*

23. What happens if a fellow is with a girl who throws herself at him? *This is likely to happen to almost every boy. And it may knock out his reasoning powers. Unless he has figured how he will deal with such a situation in advance, he is very likely to get trapped by his own feelings. Therefore he should be alert to such an eventuality. When it happens his task is to avoid fooling around with the situation. As one youth advisor said, "That's the time to pack up and git—git the girl home, and leave her there!"*

24. Is sex an important part of a happy marriage? *Yes, it is. It represents the culmination of love and unity between husband and wife. However, it is not an isolated aspect of marriage. Love is expressed in every moment of the marriage relationship, in kindness, consideration, and courtesy throughout each day.*

25. How many children should a couple plan to have? *The "big" family is coming back into style. More and more mar-*

riage counselors are answering this question by saying, "As many as health and circumstances will permit." There are many advantages to the big family if the parents have made up their minds to take the time to give each child the necessary ingredients of love and attention so he doesn't get lost in the crowd. It is a tragedy, however, for one parent to want a big family and the other parent to want few or none. The subject of "how big a family" should be discussed by every couple before marriage.

CHAPTER 25

THE PROBLEM OF STEALING

One of the most baffling problems confronting the parents of a boy is when he begins a pattern of chronic stealing. It is not so difficult when it is just a prank, a stunt, or an incidental slip; but when it is deliberate, premeditated, and defiant, both parents and their son are in for some heartaches.

Chronic stealing is complicated by the fact that it usually develops into a whole complex of related problems. What starts out to be just a little sneaky snitching soon blossoms out into neighborhood raids. Instinctively the tyro thief begins constructing a constellation of custom-built alibis. He makes lying an art. He begins establishing criminal contacts to "fence" or sell his loot. He promises himself he will never carry a gun, but in the course of a few burglaries he is bound to run into a gun. He steals it but promises himself never to use it on a job. Shortly, however, he carries it "just in case." Some dark night while committing a routine burglary or theft, he is suddenly confronted by a night watchman, a deputy sheriff, or a police officer. Almost without thinking he goes for his gun.

Many a young criminal has ended up on death row in a state penitentiary just by following this trail.

THERE ARE MANY KINDS OF STEALING

Parents would do well to train their children to respect the

laws against stealing because the penalties are severe. Stealing strikes at the very foundation of society. There can be no security where homes, stores, or other businesses are frequently looted by thieves. And there can be no safety on a highway where hijackers and road robbers operate.

Because the criminal code in each state lays great stress on the seriousness of stealing, it might be of interest to list some of the different kinds of thievery mentioned in the state statutes. We will choose those from a state which is rather typical of most states. In each case note the severity of the penalty.

Robbery: This kind of stealing consists of taking property from a person or from his immediate presence by means of force or fear. Robbery usually involves the use of "strong-arm" methods, a gun, a knife, or explosives. The penalty is very severe, usually five years to life.

Grand Larceny: This consists of stealing something which is worth more than fifty dollars or stealing something (regardless of value) from a person or from his presence (such as picking his pockets), but without putting him under force or fear. For example, stealing a hundred-dollar watch from the counter of a jewelry store would be grand larceny. It would also be grand larceny to pick it from the jeweler's pocket without his knowledge. However, if the jeweler suddenly realized what was happening and the thief had to pull a gun to get the watch, it would no longer be grand larceny but robbery because it would now involve "force or fear." The penalty for grand larceny is usually one to ten years with fines ranging from fifty dollars to a thousand dollars.

Petit Larceny: This includes other types of stealing not listed under grand larceny. It usually refers to such thefts as minor shoplifting, chicken stealing, taking a bicycle, etc. The penalty is imprisonment in the county jail for a period up to six months and fines up to three hundred dollars.

Burglary: This consists of breaking into a building, a trailer, or railroad car to steal or otherwise commit a felony. Sometimes burglars use nitroglycerine or other explosives to open safes or storage vaults. A wave of such thefts in private homes, stores, and banks can create community hysteria. Burglaries with explosives carry very heavy penalties—twenty-five to forty years. Nighttime burglaries without explosives carry one to twenty years. Daytime burglaries (but not involving explosives) carry a penalty of six months to three years.

Forgery: This usually consists of getting money by altering the amount of a check or putting a false signature on it. This is a felony. The penalty is one to twenty years.

Fraud: This is a method of stealing which might be described as obtaining something of value or gaining an advantage of some kind by deceitfully misrepresenting the true facts. There are many kinds of fraud, such as writing checks on a bank where the check writer has no account, or having an account but writing a check for much more money than is in the account. The penalty for this type of fraud may go as high as fourteen years. The fraud of burning property to collect insurance carries a penalty of one to ten years.

Confidence Games: This is a special kind of "stealing by trickery." The victim is told that he can make a fortune overnight by following certain instructions. The usual procedure is to ask the victim to put up a lot of money to show his "good faith" or financial ability to participate in the scheme. The operators take his money and disappear before he realizes what has happened. Many young people get involved in these schemes, some as operators, others as victims. Young people should be warned never to deal with a stranger who claims to have a marvelous scheme for getting rich quickly. The penalty for stealing by means of a confidence game is up to ten years in the state penitentiary.

Extortion and Blackmail: This kind of stealing is usually done by writing a threatening letter or otherwise inducing a victim to "pay off" because of force or fear. The penalty for a state violation is up to three years. If the mails are used it is a federal violation, carrying a penalty of as much as twenty years plus a heavy fine.

Embezzlement: This is the kind of stealing in which a person takes money or property which has been entrusted to him. If the value of the property which is taken is over fifty dollars, then the penalty is one to ten years with a fine up to a thousand dollars. If the value of the property is under fifty dollars, then the penalty is up to six months in the county jail and a fine up to three hundred dollars.

Impersonation: This type of stealing is getting money, property, or some special advantage by pretending to be an officer or a person with special authority. The penalty is up to one year with a fine as high as a thousand dollars. If a federal officer is impersonated, the penalty is up to three years' imprisonment and up to a fine of a thousand dollars.

Kidnaping: The stealing of either children or adults is one of the most vicious of all crimes. Sometimes the person is kidnaped for ransom, sometimes for a revengeful beating, sometimes for a life of vice and debauchery. After the kidnaping and slaying of the Lindbergh baby in 1932, the United States Congress passed a law against kidnaping which permits the jury to recommend the death penalty where the kidnap victim has been injured or killed. Almost immediately the number of kidnapings for ransom fell to an all-time low.

Espionage: This is stealing information which will endanger the security of the nation. In peacetime the penalty may be as high as twenty years. In wartime, the crime of espionage is particularly serious and the court may impose the death sentence.

Many youths are under the impression that the juvenile laws protect them from these heavy penalties which we have cited. The fact is that the juvenile law in most states permits the judge to decide whether a boy shall be handled as a youth or an adult. The juvenile is not automatically dealt with as a ward of the juvenile court. This comes as a privilege, not a right. Anytime the adult court wishes to assume jurisdiction, it can do so. Young hoodlums have sometimes carried on a spree of serious thefts because they assumed that even if they were caught the consequences would not be too serious. It has come as a great shock to them to suddenly discover that they were going to be tried as adults.

WHY DO PEOPLE STEAL?

Seldom does a person deliberately plan a career of crime for himself. He just starts out "taking a few little things." The sly and furtive habits of the professional criminal usually reflect the sneaking stealth of former days as a petty thief. It means that he has developed the habit of giving in to the pressures which lead people to steal.

What are these pressures?

First, there is the natural instinct of acquisition; the instinct to want "things." Like other instincts and appetites, the inborn desire to want things is a wholesome drive. Think how dull this life would be for a person who did not want anything. However, just as all human appetites must be controlled, so must the "passion for possession." Except for gifts or loans, the law says we are only entitled to possess what we can produce or pay for.

Second, there is the pressure of life's inequalities. We are all born equal before the law, but in all other respects we are unequal. We vary as to intelligence, physical attributes, material circumstances, and as to the so-called "favors of fortune." However, the successful citizen is the one who learns early in life to make up for any inequalities through hard work and personal initiative. He also learns to become reconciled to life's limitations. He accepts himself for what he is and then strives to make the most of it.

But some people never quite catch this point of view. Instead, they develop grasping, pinched-up personalities. They covet other people's property, and constantly lash out to acquire it by some devious means. Because of life's inequalities, they justify themselves in becoming thieves. It is important to get over to a boy early in life that the joys of life come from working for things, not stealing them. Furthermore, inequalities are the by-product of freedom. As long as men are free, there will always be those who excel above their neighbors, some in one thing, some in another. This means he also has the chance to use his freedom to excel—but not by stealing or cheating.

Third, there is the pressure of wanting to show off. This is not a desire for equality, but superiority. Many youngsters who are caught stealing admit they were trying to get a car, some clothes, or some money so that it would make them look like big shots. Many adults steal for exactly the same reason. Behind such stealing patterns will usually be found an inferiority complex. Two fronts must be attacked simultaneously. On the one hand, he must be made to realize that he lives in an orderly world and when he breaks the law he must face the music. On the other hand, he should see tangible evidence that the people around him want him to succeed; that they want to be friends and will help him if he is willing to try himself.

Fourth, there is the pressure in some people to make a game of stealing—to match wits. Some youngsters get a thrill from stealing just to prove they can do it without getting caught. Some adults are the same. Often the thing which is taken is neither needed nor wanted. The theft doesn't make sense to the casual observer, but the police and the psychologist have come to recognize this type of stealing for what it is—thrill stealing. It is not the thing being stolen which is important, but the excitement of successfully stealing *anything*.

Persons who follow this pattern of stealing are called klepto-maniacs. Years ago it was thought that the kleptomaniac had "an irresistible impulse to steal." Now it is recognized that his impulse to steal is like anyone else's impulse except that he does not resist it, he exploits it. He revels in it. With him it is an adventure, a game which completely ignores fair play and the rights of others. Kleptomania is very common among persons of low intelligence. It may be present, however, in an otherwise normal personality. The cure sometimes requires psychiatric treatment. It also requires a firm program of restitution and a penalty sufficiently strong to shock the individual into recogniz-ing the realities of his problem. It is necessary to increase the element of risk for the kleptomaniac until he realizes that his stealing is a crime, not a game.

STEALING IS A DIFFERENT PROBLEM AT DIFFERENT AGES

All four of the instinctive pressures which boys fall victim to during their years of development must be met by parents with other pressures designed to develop respect for property and the rights of other people. In the process of achieving this, parents find that age makes a difference.

At the early age of three to four a child has a very shallow sense of property rights even under the most favorable circumstances. To him, "his" property is whatever happens to be handy. He wears the older children's clothes, plays with their toys, and feels a certain sense of proprietory rights in everything which happens to be in his hands. This is the reason he is often reluctant to share a favorite toy. He thinks giving it up means losing it. With him, title goes with *possession*.

For this reason "wanting" something and "taking" it seem very reasonable to a 3-year-old. Therefore, one day his parents are shocked to find him dragging home all the neighbor boy's toys. Some parents immediately sit down and give Junior a long talk about his not becoming a "thief." They tell him he must not steal these things. To the 3-year-old this does not make much sense. He didn't steal anything. He just saw something, wanted it, and brought it home. In fact, what is stealing anyway?

Psychologists say that it is a good thing to stress property rights at this early age, but it is a mistake to call a boy a "thief." It has been found that likely as not he will take pride in this new title and start wearing it like a badge. It becomes a new source of notoriety and attention getting. It feeds his ego. Therefore, the wise parent will just simply tell him how badly he would feel if someone took his favorite toy and then stress the fact that the neighbor boy feels brokenhearted when Junior takes his things. The mother may conclude by saying, "You can play with Bobby's truck until I finish the dishes, and then you and I will take it back to him so he won't feel badly."

By the age of 6 most youngsters have a pretty good sense of property rights. They can also display the necessary discipline to go with it.

Between 9 and 11 another stealing streak may show up. By this time a boy knows precisely what he is doing. The parent can handle it accordingly. Because much of the stealing at this age is mostly "smart-alecky" and designed to match wits with the neighborhood store clerk, it is time to start laying it on the line. Stealing must not be allowed to develop into a game.

Between 14 and 16 some boys become involved in stealing when they are behind in other aspects of normal development.

A boy at this age is insecure and inadequate. He often thinks he would solve all his feelings of inadequacy if he just had lots of clothes, a car, money, sports equipment, etc. and etc. Stealing by a teen-ager should not be taken casually. Even when it is a prank, parents and police should let him know that this is something which must come to a screeching halt. A teen-ager is quick to detect the attitudes of his elders in a situation like this.

DEVELOPING SOUND "BUILT-IN" ATTITUDES

During a boy's development his parents should try to build into his thinking a strong aversion toward stealing. He should realize that in this country it is certainly no mark of cleverness to be able to steal. Our culture is built on the assumption that most people are decent and honest. Storekeepers spread their merchandise out on tables and trust people to pay. Grocery stores, department stores, cafeterias, and self-help gas stations all depend to a considerable extent on the honor system. Businessmen have learned that most people can be trusted. This is a great achievement in any society.

By way of contrast, there are many countries where people live behind high walls and barred windows. A car parked on the street must be continually guarded or it will be stolen. If people gather in large crowds, they are often victimized by pickpockets. In such countries, nothing is safe unless it is watched. People live under a cloud of constant fear and apprehension. We do not want this in our country, but already it is becoming evident in some of our larger cities. It must be stopped.

Most boys will respond to this approach if it is stressed over the years. There should be a built-in feeling that stealing is sneaky, stealing is cheating. Once these attitudes are firmly planted, they become the basis for appealing to a boy when he lets down and goes along with the gang on a snitching party. It becomes easy to revive the image of stealing as something tarnished and cheap, not heroic or adventurous.

Thus human motives are guided and shaped.

HOW TO BREAK THE HABIT OF STEALING

I once saw a 17-year-old boy interviewed by a well-known criminal psychologist. The boy had been stealing since he was 5. The psychologist said something like this:

"Did you know that in some ways people are like plants? Did you know that if a plant is neglected and begins to wither from lack of water and nourishment, you can still make it produce a fairly good crop of fruit IF you catch it during the GROWING stage?"

He then pointed out that once the growing stage is completed, no amount of water, fertilizer, and cultivation can make a neglected plant produce a crop of fruit. Once the growing period is over, it is too late. Then the psychologist continued:

"I have found that people are like plants in this respect. I have found that if we can help a boy get straightened out while he is still growing and developing, we have a very good chance of coming out with a good citizen. But, by the same token, the longer a boy postpones correcting his bad habits, the less likely he is to break them. If he waits until he has finished developing, the likelihood of his being rehabilitated is so low that it is almost a lost cause."

The boy said, "How long have I got left to break my habits?"

The man replied, "You are already becoming set in your ways. If you postpone getting straightened out for another 3 or 4 years, I will expect you to become an habitual criminal."

Then the boy said, "I always feel terrible when I get caught, but it isn't long before I go right ahead and do it again. What can I do to break the habit?"

"Well," the psychologist replied, "I can suggest several things. But remember, it's your problem. I'm like a physician. I can tell you what medicine to take but I won't always be there to see if you take it. That's your job."

The boy said he would appreciate any suggestions and try to follow them.

"First," the man said, "I want you to pick out someone whom you admire and trust very much. It may be a leader at your church, a scoutmaster, or a neighbor. I want you to tell that one person all about this problem of yours. Then I want you to go to him every Saturday afternoon and report to him whether or not you have kept a clean slate for the week. If you ever fail to show up, he will probably know you have slipped. If this happens he can then look you up and give you this sealed envelope."

"What's inside the envelope?" the boy asked.

"It is the dose of medicine you will have to take if you ever steal again. I warn you, it's nasty medicine and you won't like it. Nevertheless, it will help you break the habit if you really want to. And, of course, if you don't want to, then that's your business and I'll be seeing you up at the state penitentiary."

The boy said he really wanted to break his stealing habit and promised to have one of the men from his church call the psychologist and pick up the sealed envelope.

I later learned that the envelope never had to be opened. This boy made good. But if by chance the boy had slipped and the envelope had been opened, he would have received this dose of medicine: "Take it back!"

Any person who has ever stolen anything knows that there is no more bitter pill than "taking the stuff back." In fact it usually requires the encouragement of a parent or a police officer to achieve it. Nevertheless, the psychologist knew that, in the majority of cases, when a boy takes stolen loot back to the owner and apologizes for his mistake, it somehow makes it easier for him to resist future temptations and never steal again.

But this was not the only advice the psychologist had for the boy. He knew this boy had never had much money, and part of his temptation was the fact that he wanted things "like the other guys." So the psychologist made arrangements to help him get a job. It wasn't a fancy job, but it kept the boy busy and gave him some spending money. Later he obtained a better job on his own initiative.

Finally, the psychologist told the boy to "keep busy." He said, "A constructive life helps to keep a boy from living a destructive life. I want you to get so busy doing good things that you break down your bad habits by sheer neglect!"

On one occasion I heard this psychologist say, "You know,

honesty builds happiness. It is a wonderful feeling to know you are right with the world; that you haven't cheated anybody; that you haven't taken money or property that didn't belong to you. In fact, it isn't possible to be at peace with yourself unless you're honest. That's why God included this law of happiness among the Ten Commandments: 'Thou Shalt Not Steal!'"

CHAPTER 26

THE PROBLEM OF NARCOTICS

When any member of a family is hit by narcotics addiction, the family ties are strained to the limit, often broken. The addict surrounds himself with mysterious comings and goings, unexplained sources of money, lies to cover up his activities. The normal living pattern of the addict falls apart. He becomes nervous, irritable, cannot hold a job, cannot be trusted, cannot eat, has difficulty sleeping. His health is poor, normal physical functions are sluggish, he lacks ambition, initiative, or a zest for life.

Parents are appalled when a boy falls into this type of problem because they know so little about it. Often they try to keep it a secret instead of seeking professional advice. They try to use threats, discipline, or "talk" their boy out of it. They do not know that he has lost all capacity to do anything about it. He is "hooked"! Without some kind of outside help, his case is hopeless.

HOW SERIOUS IS DRUG ADDICTION?

Ever since World War II drug addiction has been an increasingly serious problem. However, any discussion of the problem is usually confined to heavy narcotics—opium, morphine, heroin, with only fringe concern over such things as marijuana,

barbiturates, benzedrine, bromides, and cocaine. Many other types of habit-forming substances get no consideration at all.

For parents to realize the hazards of narcotics addiction, it is first of all necessary to realize that we are raising the present generation in a psychological atmosphere which makes habit-forming substances a cultural fad. If we are honest with ourselves, we will admit that ten cups of coffee a day are not "for food," two packs of cigarettes a day have nothing to do with nourishment, daily consumption of alcohol gives no food value to the body whatever. Nevertheless, parents will excuse these "minor vices" while condemning the use of "any kind of habit-forming drugs." It is important to realize that most drug addiction occurs in a cultural setting where it is considered the thing to do. This is the way cigarette smoking begins—everyone is doing it—a boy is then urged to try a marijuana cigarette because everyone is doing it. The next jump is to try heroin, because "all of us have tried it just for kicks." But the evolution from cigarettes to heroin is dynamite; one of the best known ways to destroy a happy, constructive, well-adjusted human being.

Dr. Victor H. Vogel points out that the chemical age in which we live can be disastrous if we do not restrict the pain-relieving drugs and tension-relieving chemicals to medical purposes only. To use them as escape hatches from the routine disappointments, failures, frustrations, and fears of life can only lead to the bottomless pit of addiction.

Obviously some people are much more prone to use drugs as a crutch than others. These are people who are unhappy, insecure, or who feel inadequate. They are the ones who find themselves to be anti-social, lonely, supercritical, and at odds with the world. The vast majority of the patients at the federal hospital for narcotic addicts at Lexington, Kentucky, were found to be of this type. That is why persons of this temperament are called "addiction prone." They are attracted to narcotics and get "hooked" more easily than other people.

This perhaps explains why so many teen-agers have become involved with narcotics. During those years when they are trying to become independent, well-adjusted citizens they go through a series of defiant, belligerent stages which make them reach out for anything that might relieve the pain of having to face life and grow up. The dream life of a drug jag is sometimes used to escape the ordeal. When this crutch is used, the youngster stops growing up—emotionally, socially, professionally.

Drug addiction affects the memory, it destroys will power. It makes a boy feel like he can't concentrate, think, or reason. Ambition is killed. His only object in life is to get the needed supply of drugs. He may become a psychopathic liar. There is a deadening of the sexual instincts which often leads to failure in marriage. He must seek out criminal companions for "contacts" and sympathy. The average addict finds himself putting out at least twenty-five dollars every single day for his drugs. He fears the shakes—the withdrawal pains—above everything else in the world and will bleed his family and friends of all their resources to keep him going. He will beg, borrow, steal, cheat, and sometimes even kill to get the money for his shots, bundles, or caps.

THE DIFFERENT KINDS OF NARCOTICS

In the popular sense, any drug which affects the normal functions of the body either by overworking them through stimulation or putting them to sleep by sedation is included among the "narcotics." For the purpose of this discussion we will eliminate the habit-forming drugs in alcohol, tobacco, coffee, tea, and cola drinks and go to those drugs which are prohibited by law unless administered under direction of a doctor or sold in government-approved formulae.

Opium: This is obtained from a certain variety of poppy which is grown in India, Turkey, China, and Mexico. In the field the seed pods are scratched or cut and a dark brown or black gum forms on the surface. This is tediously scraped from the pods and is then processed in a variety of ways to be eaten in a candy paste, drunk in a kind of tea, or smoked in a pipe. In the beginning an opium user experiences hallucinations and very pleasant dreams. As he continues, the pleasant dreams require heavier doses to bring them on. Finally the body has not only built up a tolerance for the drug but *depends* upon it for normal functioning. Now the addict must consume large quantities of opium even to maintain a state of normal well-being. An increased dosage is necessary to get the pleasant sensations. Before long, he may have increased his consumption fifteen times. Long before, however, the addict will have learned that he lives under the constant threat of "withdrawal sickness." This is the most excruciating convulsion of practically every cell in the body. If the addict cannot get his opium supply, the withdrawal commences. The eyes and nose begin to run, the body perspires heavily, the pupils of the eye enlarge, and goose pimples cover the skin. This is followed by the convulsive spasms —terrible cramps in the legs, back, and stomach. He screams with pain. There is vomiting, diarrhea, fever, and general dehydrating. The addict fears he will die; though very few do, the withdrawal sickness is a nightmare of pain. If left to himself, he will abandon his resolution to "kick the habit" and will run frantically out to steal or do whatever is necessary to get money so he can buy more drugs and get relief.

Morphine: This is a drug which is made from opium. It is a white, feathery powder. It is odorless but has a bitter taste. It is sold as a powder, in pills, capsules, cubes, or in folded papers. Criminals buy the morphine and then mix it with some other white powder so they will make more profit. The addict never knows the strength of the supply he is buying but must take the word of the pusher who sells it to him. Morphine is a very powerful drug and only a quarter grain is required to kill pain. Doctors consider a half grain a very heavy dose, and use that amount only in the most severe cases. However, addicts find that their body tolerance for the drug builds up so fast that before long they may require ten grains of morphine three times a day! As with opium there is the constant threat of withdrawal pains. The moment an addict begins to get the symptoms of withdrawal, he has the desperate urge to get a "fix." The addict's method of taking morphine is usually a crude one. It consists of dissolving the drug in a small amount of water in a spoon, heating it with a match, and then drawing it up into an eyedropper or hypodermic syringe through a piece of cotton. A safety pin or razor blade is then used to open up a main vein and the fluid is squirted in. Often large sores and infections develop along the arms and legs of a "main liner" who has been shooting himself over a period of time.

Heroin: This is made from morphine, but it has three times the strength of morphine. It is a colorless, odorless, crystalline powder with a very bitter taste. Because the body tolerance for this drug builds up with astonishing speed, the dangers of addiction are greater with heroin than with either morphine or straight opium. For this reason the government saw no advantage in using it for medicinal purposes and therefore in 1925 it was made illegal for anyone to possess, manufacture, or use heroin in the United States. Today all heroin must be smuggled in by criminals from other countries.

Heroin may be used by sniffing it up the nose where it can be absorbed into the blood stream or it may be taken by injection. Addicts usually refer to it as "H." Heroin has such a grip on its victims that practically none of them are permanently cured once they have become addicted to it. Even those who have gone through the pain of withdrawal and have been pronounced "cured" will usually return to it eventually. Both parents and youth should know the dangers of this drug.

There are other drugs which are derived from opium such as dilaudid, metopon, codeine, pantopon, paregoric, and laudanum, but they are not as strong as their better known cousins, morphine and heroin.

We should also mention that experimental laboratories have developed several synthetic narcotics which are substitutes for morphine. Two of the most common are Demerol and Methadone.

Cocaine: This drug appears as a colorless or white crystalline powder. It is obtained from the leaves of the coca plant which grows in the higher altitudes of South America and Java. Cocaine is a stimulant rather than a sedative, and is used by some criminals to bolster them before committing a major crime. It has an intoxicating effect which releases inhibitions and takes away the sense of time or distance. It may give the addict hallucinations. He may think insects are crawling all over him or he may think he has a foreign substance under his skin. The characteristic symptoms of this drug are the most injurious to an individual, since it affects his moral and mental qualities with alternating periods of exultation and despondency. There is a loss of appetite and a loss of weight, there is a pallor of the skin and he suffers from insomnia and general deterioration of health. Under the influence of this drug the individual is very dangerous, often with maniacal tendencies.

Cocaine is usually sniffed up the nostrils or placed inside the lower lip and slowly picked up by the salivary glands. Cocaine is habit-forming but does not have the same violent withdrawal pains when it is discontinued. However, the likelihood of committing serious crimes under this drug is greater than that of opium, morphine, or heroin.

Marijuana: This drug is an intoxicant sedative similar to the alcohol drug. It comes from the resin found in the flowers and leaves of Indian hemp. As a general rule, marijuana plants which supply the illicit market are grown in Mexico or the southwestern part of the United States. As with alcohol, marijuana affects people in different ways. It has been considered of no medicinal value because of the unpredictable reaction which it produces. People who are normal and well adjusted to life do not get pleasure from smoking marijuana. In fact, they may have a rather violent reaction to it.

Marijuana tends to make people irresponsible, lose their sense of reality, and give them hallucinations and delusions. There are often temporary mental disturbances and some people engage in violence while under the influence of marijuana. Marijuana is smoked in the form of homemade cigarettes and smells something like the pungent burning of dried weeds. The most dangerous aspect of this drug is that it conditions the user to depend upon a drug for pleasure. Later on, he often wishes to enjoy greater pleasure and turns to a more powerful drug such as heroin. Heroin and marijuana are frequently sold by the same pusher.

Marijuana is considered a dangerous and intoxicating drug. However, it does not result in withdrawal sickness when discontinued.

Barbiturates: These drugs are manufactured from chemicals

and are sold in sleeping pills. Addicts often call them goof balls. They are sedatives and when taken in quantity give the addict an effect similar to alcohol. There is very little effort to control the use of these drugs, and as a result they are not difficult to buy. The seriousness of their use is reflected in the fact that more people in the United States die of barbiturate poisoning each year than from any other kind of poison. This often happens when a person is intoxicated, has a few barbiturate pills on hand, and in his fuzzy state of mind foolishly gulps down a lethal dose without realizing what he is doing.

The barbiturates are not only addictive, but when a person has taken large amounts over a period of time the withdrawal sickness is even more violent than with morphine, opium, or heroin.

Parents should be aware that the capsules in which barbiturates may be purchased are often colored, and therefore they should know what young people are talking about when they refer to "yellow jackets," "blue angels," or "pink ladies."

Benzedrine: Like cocaine, the benzedrine drugs are stimulants rather than sedatives. They are used illicitly to "get high," but this is not so much a pleasant feeling as it is a feeling of nervous, jittery excitement. Students or others who use a "benny" to stay awake and cram for an exam find it difficult to concentrate, and their brain has a dullness that makes the practice less than satisfactory. When used over a period of time, the user finds himself unable to sleep and may resort to barbiturates to put him to sleep. This cycle of taking too much benzedrine and then too much barbiturate is extremely dangerous and can lead to acute mental disturbance in mental illness or death from poisoning.

TREATMENT FOR DRUG ADDICTION

Whenever a family is suddenly confronted with the problem of a drug addict in the house there are several basic things to keep in mind: first, the addict is sick. He will need treatment of a special kind just as though he had cancer or some other serious illness. Second, he is a source of contagion. If left to his own devices, he will try to get others to take drugs and thereby spread the addiction process. Third, the addict has an absolute terror of the "withdrawal pains," therefore no matter how good his intentions or how profound his promises, he will rush out for "just one more fix" the moment he feels the pains coming on.

For these reasons it will be obvious why real drug addiction cannot be treated at a clinic or doctor's office. The cure absolutely requires that he be confined for a period of four to six months in some institution, such as the U. S. Public Health Hospital in Lexington, Kentucky. If the addict is of minor age, he cannot be released without the consent of his parents. If it is an adult he can commit himself voluntarily and leave voluntarily, but if he leaves against the advice of his doctors he can never be re-admitted unless he gets a court order which places him in the custody of the institution "until cured."

The first step in the treatment at an institution is withdrawal. No matter how this is achieved, it is a nightmare. A patient will do everything in his power to get relief. Most hospitals do what they can to alleviate the violent spasms, but there is no way of avoiding so-called withdrawal sickness. Withdrawal usually lasts several days but even after the spasms have stopped the effect continues for several weeks.

The second step in curing an addict is to build up his health. After he has gone through withdrawal, he will discover that he is in a very rundown condition. He needs good food and rest for about two weeks of convalescence. During this period he is very susceptible to various illnesses and diseases and would like to use these as an excuse for more narcotics.

The third step in the cure of the addict consists of another four to six months of custodial care, during which time an effort is made to change his whole attitude toward drugs and keep him so busy he doesn't have time to feel sorry for himself. If he goes through this period successfully, he should be ready to return home.

There is a tremendous challenge to the addict and his family when he returns home. The addict must realize that only a minority of addicts are ever cured permanently because they *deliberately* choose to go back to the drug even though they have regained their will power to resist it. Those who stay cured usually do so because they have lined themselves up with a group like Alcoholics Anonymous or Narcotics Anonymous. In any event, the addict must get his interests and his activities so completely diverted away from his old haunts, his old worries, and his old associates that it helps him resist the temptation to revert. The family can be of great assistance during this re-habilitation process. Sometimes a trip with the family or a visit with some understanding relative is in order.

THE PROBLEM OF THE ACCIDENTAL ADDICT

The accidental addict is usually a member of the family who has undergone major surgery and has become addicted while in the hospital. This is usually the easiest type of addict to cure. He usually has a normal, well-adjusted personality, and once he realizes his problem he responds to treatment and then stays cured. Even some of these, however, require custodial care before they can reconcile themselves to the physical pain of withdrawal.

In any event, whether the addiction is self-imposed or accidental, it has been found that the cure depends almost entirely on the capacity of the addict to "get back into the swing of life," and shift his attitude 180 degrees away from drugs. He must discontinue thinking of them as something pleasant or an escape. He must look upon them with the same kind of abhorrence which the alcoholic successfully develops as a member of Alcoholics Anonymous. This organization teaches its members to accept the fact that they will never drink again. This must also be the hard-core conviction of the addict: "I will never return!"

CHAPTER 27

WHAT ABOUT ALCOHOL?

Recently this conversation took place between a worried mother and the desk sergeant at a metropolitan police department:

"Hello—are you the person in charge?"

"Yes."

"Please don't ask my name. Just tell me what to do about my boy who drinks."

"How old is your boy?"

"Twenty-two. He's an alcoholic at twenty-two!"

"Tell me about it."

The voice on the phone was nervous and emotional, but the story finally came out, including the name.

"I guess my boy isn't really an alcoholic," she said, "at least not yet. But if he keeps drinking as hard as he's been drinking lately, he'll end up in the gutter. Dave didn't use to drink at all. He claims he got started two summers ago when he went away to work. Someone told him a stiff shot would kill a cold. After that he got to drinking just for the kicks. Now he drinks all the time. What can I do?"

The officer told the mother that a great deal could be done.

"But what makes him drink?" she asked. "It's getting so he can't control his alcohol and I can't control him. Things are getting hopeless for both of us."

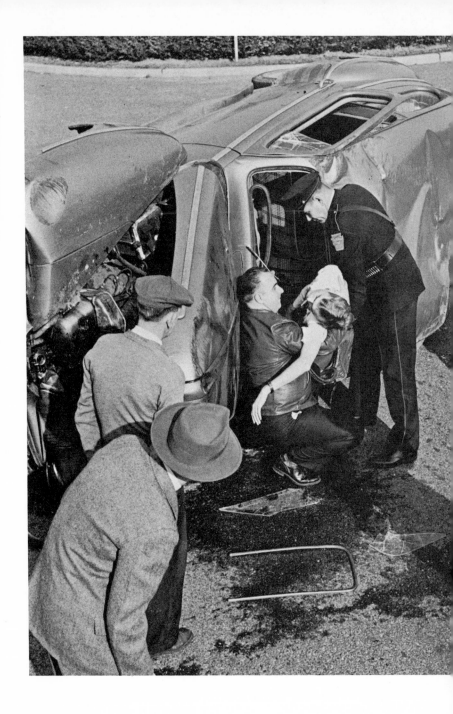

WHAT MAKES PEOPLE DRINK?

The police sergeant promised to send an officer out to talk to her. He said maybe the officer could find out what made Dave drink.

It didn't take the officer from the crime prevention squad very long to figure out why Dave did his drinking. His parents separated when he was a child. Dave was all his mother had, and she had been so anxious to protect him and help him that he had never learned to do many things for himself. As he approached manhood he found the world too big and too difficult. He felt inadequate, incompetent, and insecure. So Dave was drinking. And he was drinking for the same reason most people do—it made Dave think he was a better man.

"But it hasn't made him a better man," the mother complained. "He can't keep a job, his fiancée threw him over, and when he comes home all liquored up he's almost too mean for even me to put up with. Why would Dave think drinking makes him a better man?"

"Perhaps we should ask him."

Dave admitted that drinking hadn't made him a better man. "But, Mom," he said, "at least it makes me *feel* like a better man." And here was the magic secret of alcohol, not only for Dave, but for most of the five million people in the United States who are called "alcoholics."

Dave described how he first learned to drink, how it made him feel, how miserable he was now without a drink. He said it made him forget his worries. It changed him from a bashful, retiring nobody into a boisterous, easy-talking somebody. Dave said he hated liquor but couldn't seem to get along without it any more.

He said his pals were now calling him a "plateau drinker"— meaning he nipped the bottle right along to maintain a state of semi-intoxication. He said some of the other fellows he knew were "peak drinkers"—meaning they could go for several weeks without any serious drinking and then suddenly go on a bender for three or four days.

The officer knew it was unusual for a 22-year-old to get caught this early on an alcoholic merry-go-round; usually this comes later. But he also knew it was not unusual for a certain percentage of young people to have trouble with alcohol. He knew that some start drinking just to be sociable, some hear it's a good way to cure a cold, as Dave had done, some try it out for the kicks because they think they might be missing something. But, regardless of how they get started, all of them soon learn that *alcohol makes life different*. It creates a world of make-believe. That is what it had done to Dave. As he grew up Dave knew he had to overcome a lot of problems, and he knew this would take a lot of effort. Then he discovered alcohol, and alcohol seemed to solve his problems *without* any effort.

"Dave's problem," said the officer, "is twofold. First, he didn't know enough about alcohol, and, secondly, he didn't know enough about himself. Now he'll have to learn about both."

LEARNING ABOUT ALCOHOL

Several years ago Yale University set up a special institute to study alcohol and its effect on the mind and body. This study revealed that there are many popular misconceptions about alcohol:

Some people think alcohol is a food. It is not a food in the ordinary sense. It has no vitamins, no hormones, no minerals, and it cannot be stored by the body for future use. Neither can it build or repair body tissue.

Some people think alcohol is a medicine. Unfortunately, it is not. It will not cure a cold, an infection, or a disease. In fact, it may act to aggravate a disease.

Some people think alcohol is a stimulant. It turns out to be just the opposite. It is a depressant or a sedative. It has an effect on the brain and body similar to ether. It first dulls the frontal portion of the brain which is the center of judgment and discrimination. It gives a person the feeling of "not caring." He may become hyperactive, talkative, and want to sing. He acquires an air of reckless abandonment and irresponsibility. As the quantity of alcohol increases it deadens the other centers of activity in the brain. Motor reflexes are numbed, muscular co-ordination becomes awkward and slow, peripheral vision decreases, speech becomes thick, balance becomes difficult to maintain. Finally, when the quantity of alcohol becomes even more excessive, it reduces the brain to unconsciousness. In acute alcoholism it can result in death.

Some people call alcoholism a disease. But it is not a disease in the ordinary sense. It is actually an addiction. This is because alcohol is a drug. Habitual use of it affects the cells of the body to a degree which is similar to other narcotics. The cells come to depend upon the alcohol. A gnawing appetite for alcohol develops. If the alcohol is taken away, there is a narcotic withdrawal period with spasms of pain and convulsive disturbances in physical functions. This painful withdrawal period lasts from thirty-six to forty-eight hours, but the complete "drying out" of an alcoholic at some rehabilitation center usually requires from 80 to 120 days.

HOW ALCOHOL WORKS

When ordinary food is taken into the body, it has to be digested before it goes into the bloodstream. This is not true with alcohol. As soon as alcohol arrives in the stomach, it begins passing immediately into the bloodstream by penetrating the stomach wall. What the stomach does not absorb is absorbed in the first four feet of the small intestine. The blood carries the alcohol to every tissue of the body, which accounts for its fast impact very soon after consumption. As the alcohol bathes the brain it begins to have its narcotic effect.

The ability of the body to get rid of alcohol is rather slow. A small amount is eliminated through the saliva, breath, and urine, but 98 per cent of it has to be reduced to carbon dioxide and water and thereby eliminated through the liver. The liver can only reduce alcohol at the rate of about one half ounce per hour. This is why the intoxicated person takes several hours to sober up.

Alcoholic addiction has psychological effects which we have already mentioned. It can have powerful "escape appeal" to a person in pain, a person who is worried, frustrated, frightened, ashamed, insecure, embarrassed, or just plain bored. Where people are emotionally or socially immature they can easily get addicted to alcohol. They come to lean upon it as a crutch. They use it to create their make-believe world of strength, confidence, and skill. When the alcohol wears off they find their strength, confidence, and skill were just an illusion of the mind. It is easy for one of these to say, "What a fool I've been. I need a drink!"

The physical effects of alcohol are also becoming better understood. We have already mentioned that it is not a food—that is, it contains no fat, protein, carbohydrates, minerals, vitamins, or hormones. An ounce of alcohol does contain two hundred calories—units of energy—but they are of little practical use to the body. They can only be burned up and eliminated from the body in the form of heat.

This physical process of burning up the calories in alcohol gives a person the feeling that he is loaded with energy. He therefore tends to avoid regular food. In process of time an alcoholic literally starves himself to death. Cirrhosis of the liver and several other diseases associated with alcoholism are actually diseases of *malnutrition*. That is why one of the first steps in rehabilitating an alcoholic is to get him back to a steady, nourishing, vitamin-filled diet.

Alcohol addiction puts a heavy load on the heart and can lead to heart disease. It also inflames the throat and stomach, and acute alcoholics are prone to gastric hemorrhages. The serious lack of vitamins through alcoholic addiction eventually affects the nervous system which can bring on mental sluggishness and mental diseases. In fact, every intoxicated person goes through a period of temporary mental disturbance, for he partially loses contact with reality.

The most shocking aspect of alcoholism is the DTs—delirium tremens. The body is attacked by a series of violent spasms. The victim complains of wild hallucinations. He sees fantastic and grotesque creatures in his mind which may set him to screaming with terror. After it is all over he may not be able to remember anything about it.

HELPING THE ALCOHOLIC

Therapy for the alcoholic addict is gradually becoming an accepted routine. Many physicians are becoming schooled in the proper treatment for alcoholism, and a growing list of hospitals will accept an alcoholic for treatment like any other illness.

Immediately upon admission the alcoholic is treated as a person suffering from an uncontrollable compulsion just as any narcotic addict would be treated. Therefore he is kept safely restricted to his own quarters. For his own safety, he is literally locked up. He is treated with certain drugs to ease the discomfort of the withdrawal pains and to avoid a seizure of DTs. A general examination is given to discover what physical abnormalities exist as a result of his protracted drinking. Sometimes there must be emergency treatment for hemorrhaging, heart attack, or hallucinations.

After two or three days the management of the alcoholic requires a restoration of the proper fluid balance, the restoration of the electrolyte balance, and the correction of his acute vitamin depletion. He must be made to realize that the prescribed physical therapy will require many months.

Equally important is the attack on his psychological problems. Immediately after withdrawal the alcoholic is at a low ebb. He wants advice and suggestions. A plan for his long-term rehabilitation should be presented. As soon as he is able he should be kept occupied—physically and mentally. He should be introduced into some warm group identification. He doesn't want pity. He wants friends—people who understand and like him. Here is where Alcoholics Anonymous so often helps. The two main assets of this organization are motivation and fellowship. But the recovering alcoholic must realize one thing, his drinking days are over. Unless he will accept this premise, the AA cannot help him.

During the critical "drying-out" period the doctor may prescribe a drug to help the patient resist taking a drink during some low moment. This type of drug will react to alcohol. Therefore, the patient is told that he will become violently ill if he takes a drink. The principal advantage of the drug is that during a moment of weakness it eliminates the problem of making a choice. When the patient asks himself, "I wonder if I shouldn't have just one drink?" the drug is a noisy little reminder which says, "Brother, you just *can't* drink!"

Each alcoholic must receive his own special course of treatment, but, with good therapy and the help and understanding of family and friends, he can make it.

ALCOHOL AND ADOLESCENCE

Because alcohol is a drug, it needs to be respected as such, especially by youth. Parents need to remind themselves occasionally that adolescence is a period of learning and much of it involves frustrations, failures, backtracking, new adjustments, new social patterns, and acquiring many new skills. Every so often an adolescent will therefore feel the urge to abandon the battle and escape from it all. This being the case, alcohol is a loaded beartrap for adolescents. A perfectly normal, wholesome personality with only the average amount of adolescent problems can suddenly be turned upside down by getting involved with alcohol. And it is even worse for an adolescent with complicated problems.

This is why the law is so strict in trying to keep alcohol and youth separated.

Numerically speaking, because alcohol is so readily available, it is a more universal problem for youth than other types of narcotic drugs. However, the boy or girl who gets involved with alcohol can be much more easily led away from it than if he or she had become "hooked" with some heavy narcotic. Therefore, the task of the parent is to be alert to the problem so that if it becomes apparent it can be handled promptly. In fact, the better way is to prevent it.

Because drinking gives a strong sense of togetherness in the group, a young person may feel compelled to participate just so he won't be a square. Or he may participate just to find out what it is like. Parents know this will eventually happen, and so it is best to help a boy or girl *think out in advance* what they will do to handle the situation when such an occasion arises.

It also helps if parents have taken the time to explain just what alcohol really is and how it works. This takes away much of the glamour and most of the mystery. And glamour and mystery are two of the things which a curious and adventuresome adolescent would otherwise find it difficult to resist.

ALCOHOL AND THE AUTOMOBILE

Studies by Forrester in Buffalo, Holcom in Evanston, and Heise in Milwaukee all show that a drinking driver is involved in from 45 to 58 per cent of injury-producing accidents. Therefore, the role of alcohol is far more serious on the highway than many have supposed.

Studies also show that very frequently the drinking driver involved in injury-producing accidents is not actually "drunk." He has had just enough to make him an *indifferent* driver and therefore far less competent than he imagines.

Alcohol content of .03 per cent in the blood is enough to affect nerve and muscular reactions, but the driver does not actually begin to "feel his liquor" until the alcohol in his blood has reached about .05 per cent. When it reaches .15 per cent he will be staggering drunk. It is therefore in the lower range of alcohol intake that drivers can be particularly dangerous because the impact of the alcohol has started to work without the subject being able to realize it. By the time the alcohol in the bloodstream has reached .05 per cent a driver is definitely dangerous even though three times as much alcohol is generally required to classify the person as a prima-facie drunk.

An American Medical Association Committee, with Dr. Fletcher D. Woodward serving as chairman, reported the following: "It is the opinion of this committee that it should be unlawful to drive a motor vehicle with an alcohol blood level at .05 per cent or greater on public roads. . . . Last year, some 21,000 people died and some 800,000 people were injured by drinking drivers" (*Law and Order*, May 1958, p. 10).

ALCOHOL PREVENTION

Vast quantities of time, money, and energy are being spent on the treatment of alcoholism. More energy needs to be exerted in the direction of alcohol education as a preventive measure.

A person should not have to become an alcoholic to discover that he should have left alcohol alone. This is especially true of youth. The goal held up to them by their parents should be the goal of Alcoholics Anonymous—total abstinence.

Civilizations tend to go through cycles of resisting or controlling alcohol, then of tolerating its abuses, and finally of exploiting it. Modern civilization is in the third stage. Every possible commercial appeal is used to promote and expand the consumption of alcohol. A certain amount of control is exercised by the law, but it is part of our culture to make it appear "smart to drink."

Parents usually find it difficult to hold up a stricter rule for their youth than they themselves have been following. Studies therefore show that drinking parents tend to raise children who become drinking adults, while abstaining parents tend to raise children who become abstainers as adults. Occasionally, a young person is so repelled by his parents' excessive use of alcohol that he is motivated to follow strict abstinence. Usually, however, he will follow their example.

So the most effective prevention program for alcohol could originate with parents. They have a greater power of persuasion than they may have known—their own example.

CHAPTER 28

THE PROBLEM OF BUILDING
BALANCED PERSONALITIES

One final phase of raising boys remains to be treated. This will consist of making a summary analysis of the major building blocks out of which a human personality must be developed. During the previous chapters we have touched on most of these qualities as they influence the various maturation periods, but in this chapter we will cover them in a single composite treatment.

All individuals have the same variety of building blocks but they are not all of the same mortar. It is the task of the parent to see that each human quality or building block is developed, shaped, and balanced to meet the needs of life.

The psychologists point out that human qualities can be grouped in three general classifications:

1. *Qualities related to the SURVIVAL INSTINCT.*
2. *Qualities related to the SOCIAL INSTINCT.*
3. *Qualities related to the REPRODUCTION INSTINCT.*

THE SURVIVAL INSTINCT

The first group we shall consider are those qualities which are designed to help us stay alive. Actually life on this planet is a very fragile thing. Except for the built-in defensive devices which each person possesses, the race would have become extinct long ago.

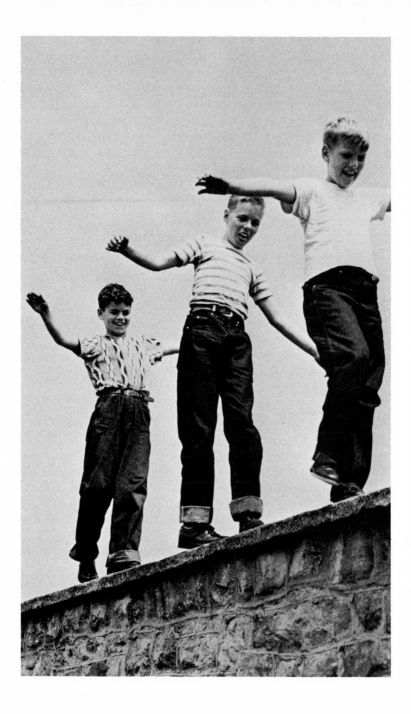

Here are the major elements of our survival machinery:

(a) *The need to satisfy hunger and thirst.* From birth to age 2½ the appetite is a rhythmical, clear signal. At approximately 2½ it begins to fade, and for three years a child may have the appetite of a sparrow. This would seem to be a violation of the law of survival. The truth, however, is that the child is temporarily living off of himself. He is using up all that extra baby fat to build new sinew and bone. As soon as the process is completed the ravenous hunger of a bottomless pit will return. And from here on it is not only the problem of satisfying a gnawing hunger but meeting the demands of special tastes. In childhood it is best to keep these tastes simple. They fan out soon enough.

(b) *Fear.* This is a fundamental part of the survival instinct. It gives the individual a healthy respect for the unknown and a bitter recollection of some things which have become known. The task of parents is to help the child distinguish between warranted fears and imaginary fears. To the child, both are extremely real. Unwarranted fears are generally dissolved through familiarity with the source of such fears. For example, fear of the water can be overcome as the child becomes accustomed to it. Fear of riding horses can be overcome by learning on some plodding, gentle mare. Some types of fear are overcome or reduced by just being told what to expect. This is why the doctor takes the time to explain to his patient what he has found in his diagnosis and what the treatment for such an ailment is. A third method of dealing with fear is to have the person recognize that, while there are elements of danger involved, the risk is not nearly so great as the individual had thought.

(c) *Acquisition.* To feel secure, human beings instinctively reach out for the things which are considered "needed." Unless this instinct is controlled by moral or legal values, it can play havoc. The fact that this instinct is difficult to control is demonstrated by the fact that theft of property is by far the most common crime on the books. To protect both the child and the community, it is important to teach him respect for property at an early age. A sense of property rights will still be rather weak at 6 but should be rather firmly fixed by age 12. As part of his training on property rights a child should be taught how to "own" things for himself. He needs to know that he is entitled to own any legitimate thing he desires just so long as he gets it by (1) making it, or (2) going out and earning the money to buy it.

Sometimes a child whose sense of acquisition has been starved (or who is suffering from neglect or rejection) will turn to stealing for no other reason than to acquire things just for the sake of having them. The stolen objects are very often useless items which are carefully stored away. This kind of senseless stealing, as we have said, is called kleptomania. With careful guidance it can be cured.

(d) *Resistance to pain or discomfort.* Survival is dependent upon physical well-being, and therefore a person instinctively searches for relief from pain, tension, or discomfort. With all of these, children have an extremely low endurance quotient. Their most common source of discomfort is having to sit still for any length of time. Their growing muscles literally shout for activity. In school or church about the only remedy for a youngster who is a jumpy, squirming wiggle-wart is to somehow focus his interest and attention. Excitement and interest can hold him glued to his seat. In the absence of these, expect action!

(e) *Sleep.* After fourteen to sixteen hours of wakeful activity the machinery of the human body instinctively drifts into a state of suspended animation so it can recharge the battery and get rid of the waste material. Children tend to fight sleep. Every excuse under heaven—and some heaven never thought of—will be used to postpone the inevitable. The main problem is getting a youngster to wind down. This always takes from thirty minutes to an hour. If nothing else works, the parent will find two or three stories can serve as tranquilizers. The first one needs to be sufficiently interesting to get the child settled down and then the next two can be dull and prolonged. Being bored is part of going to sleep.

(f) *Anger.* This is the alarm signal or emotional reaction to a situation which threatens a person's reputation, loved ones, beliefs, or personal well-being. Anger has a chemical reaction which affects the entire body. It paralyzes the digestive tract and prevents the mind from functioning logically and clearly. Because anger is a defensive reaction, it is more likely to be a problem with those who are defensive and insecure. They need to learn to avoid those situations which trigger their anger. They also need to learn that it is possible to resist something, even resent it, without actually becoming angry. It is the threshold of that blind flash of rage which robs them of their power to think that must be avoided. Often when children learn what anger is they can control it better.

(g) *Appeal.* In time of crisis a human being instinctively reaches out for help. A parent needs to be available when childhood crises occur. However, it is a mistake to rush forward and continually insist on helping a child even though he has not appealed for help. An oversolicitous parent can become bitterly frustrating to a child who is trying to learn how to do something for himself. Most parents discover that a child's appeals usually come right when the parent is busily involved with something. Part of the training of parenthood is becoming reconciled to the necessity of answering appeals when they are made and answering questions when they are asked.

(h) *Confession.* Survival requires a sense of affinity with or acceptance by the powers that be. Therefore when a person has guilty knowledge of something he has done he feels the instinctive desire to confess. It is an act of reconciliation. This is a wholesome inclination which needs to be encouraged. The FBI learned that, by treating criminals fairly and honestly, 85 per cent of them would frankly confess their crimes. Parents need to keep this in mind when dealing with problems of lying and stealing. Naturally, the instinct to confess will be suppressed if the child is dominated by a fear that his confession will result in an excessive or unreasonable amount of punishment. It is best when a child learns early in life that, "I get off easier when I tell the truth."

THE GREGARIOUS OR SOCIAL INSTINCT

The second group of human qualities relate to social adaptation. Human beings are instinctively gregarious. They like to be with people and get along with people. Of course, social adaptation depends to a large extent on whether a person's outlook is introverted or extroverted.

An introvert is one who enjoys things inside himself. He likes to meditate (mentally talk to himself), read books (mentally talk to the author), solve problems (mentally engage in a contest). He enjoys mathematical problems in many instances. He likes research, philosophy, and often engages in some form of artistic expression. The social instinct of the introvert is satisfied primarily through mental associations with people rather than physical associations. He is very sensitive to the social blunders which he makes. He tends to be bashful and may be considered by associates as anti-social. Because he is sensitive, analytical, and introverted, he is also distressed by his lack of knowledge on any subject. He is also troubled by difficulties which need to be solved. Therefore, as one might expect, the introverts have turned out to be the problem solvers of the world.

An extrovert, on the other hand, is one who by natural inclination looks outside of himself for pleasure. He wants lots of people around, lots of activity, lots of music, noise, excitement. He is not so much a spectator but a participator, not so much a thinker but a doer. He is generally well liked but may not be much of a student. He tends to solve problems by ignoring them, laughing them off. This gets him in some difficulties, but it is amazing how often he can laugh them off too!

Now, obviously, the tendency to be an introvert or an extrovert is merely the beginning of life. It is the task of the parents to take an introvert and gradually bring him "out of his shell" so he can attain proper balance. An extrovert, on the other hand, must be encouraged to keep his happy, boisterous self under control and gradually learn to enjoy studying, thinking, and problem solving. Whenever parents are successful in this process of building a balanced personality from an introvert or an extrovert, we call the finished product an *ambivert*.

An ambivert can move into a social situation and be a hearty, outgoing, gregarious participant. Or he can pick up a book and start the mental processes going like a regular introvert. In fact, when parents have done a good job rounding out a boy, it is difficult to tell whether he was an introvert in the beginning or an extrovert. His original tendencies are hidden behind the façade of a balanced personality.

SOCIAL PROCLIVITIES

Now we treat the social instincts of human nature. The development of these qualities in the introvert and the control of these qualities in the extrovert become the task of parents as they strive for balance.

(a) *Self-assertion.* When one human being meets another they both have a desire to participate in "being sociable." Therefore, unless there is an opportunity for both to assert "self" into the relationship, it is a failure for at least one of them. The rules of polite society are designed to let everyone participate in any social setting. Experience soon reveals that human relations are often spoiled by a "gabber" who monopolizes the conversation, a leader who has to do everything himself, or a follower who is always taking over. All of these are forms of excessive self-assertion.

In children there are several periods when parents may expect excessive self-assertion. We have mentioned these in the previous chapters. One of the most exasperating is during the "Me Stage" of 4, 5, and 6. It is particularly evident at the dinner table, where Junior will get on a talking jag and dominate the entire dinner hour. Older children will sit slumped in their chairs in bored disgust. Parents have to intervene. While it is good to give Junior a chance to find his place in the sun and practice his vocabulary with all his exciting reports, nevertheless it will probably be necessary to stop him after telling about "Johnson's cat that had kittens," and make him eat his first course before he unloads the latest on "Johnny Jensen who has chickenpox."

(b) *Submissiveness.* It may surprise some parents to learn that their child has any built-in appetite for submissiveness. Nevertheless, it is there. Every human being wants to be under some leader. He actually searches for some personality to whom he can give his admiration, respect, and submissiveness. In children this

will naturally gravitate toward their parents. In later years they
will look for others to follow. Sometimes they have several ideals
or leaders to whom they feel submissive. It may be a teacher,
a movie star, a political leader, a businessman, or a youth worker.
This quality continues to manifest itself all through a lifetime.
Each person enjoys having someone to whom they can give their
loyalty and support.

(c) *Affection.* The capacity to like people is a great human
attribute. However, it is easily scarred. A child's capacity for affection and love has to grow on a two-way street. He has to see
his uninhibited and spontaneous gestures of affection reciprocated by those around him. Otherwise, he will gradually withdraw. It is a great tragedy when a human being has become so
burdened with feelings of rejection and heartbreak that he loses
his capacity to have affection and confidence in others. This
happens to a few children. Fortunately, the spark can be re-
kindled, but it is sometimes a long and tedious task. The ideal is
to have a child raised to give and receive affection in a natural,
happy setting. Happy, affectionate children generally come from
happy, affectionate homes.

(d) *Consistency.* In his relations with others a person likes to
feel he is "filling his proper role." This effort to be consistent can
have all kinds of consequences—constructive and destructive. It
depends upon the role he thinks he is playing. Once he has
made up his mind what that role is, he will make his behavior
fit it whether for good or for evil. It is important to take a positive
approach with a child and constantly paint the image of his best
self. His role must always be heroic and promising, but it must
also be realistic and attainable. The image projected by parents
must be a role which their boy wants to attain and can attain.
Therefore, parents have to put the image in a different uniform
every so often. At one stage it wears a policeman's uniform, then
a cowboy outfit, next a space suit. It may finally end up in a
doctor's gown or a judge's robe, but the main thing is to keep a
bright uniform on a bright image, so that he is motivated to be
consistent with the very best of what he hopes to be during each
stage.

(e) *Migratory instinct.* Another quality of human nature is the desire to explore, travel, and investigate. Most of the satisfaction gained from such adventures is the thrill of coming back and telling friends all about it. The migratory instinct therefore contains a strong social element.

This instinct is manifest on three different levels, each of which is generally controlled by the age of the person involved.

First, there is the youth phase when the migratory instinct expresses itself in vast quantities of exploratory adventure. Youth says, "I want to go places, see people, and do things!" And that is precisely what happens.

Second, there is the phase of middle life when the individual is beginning to talk about "favorite" places rather than new places.

Third, there is the phase of the mature life when the individual just wants to sit and reflect on all the wonderful places he has been. This is so pleasant that elderly people often have to force themselves to get out and explore around so the ole rockin' chair won't get them.

From this it can easily be seen why there is often a conflict between youth and adults when it comes to going places and doing things. Often parents have to trade off with their children by telling them that if they will go to a "favorite" place this time, we can go to that exciting *new* place next time.

(f) *Constructive instinct.* Building and inventing just come naturally to human beings. Beginning with the time when a baby first starts playing with pebbles, pots, pans, rattles, beads, and blocks, he will go through life trying to see how everything can be remade, rearranged, and reconstructed. One of the problems with many modern toys is the fact that a child can't *do* enough things with them. When a father comes home and finds an expensive electric train all dismantled and strewn around the floor, he may count it wasteful DEstruction. However, his son, who worked on the project all day, may have considered it strenuous CONstruction. He was just simply trying to see what else he could do with this contraption besides make it run around on a silly little track.

If a father wants to see a boy really have fun, he should give him a dozen empty fruit crates, a hammer, and twenty-five cents' worth of nails. When the boy is finished it may look like a rattle-trap monstrosity to the father, but it will be a flying saucer to his son.

A boy can also get endless delight from a cheap alarm clock and the necessary tools to take it apart. What happens may not be considered constructive, but it actually is. The constructive instinct is like the two sides of a coin. One side is the fun of taking the thing apart. The other side is the fun of putting it all back together again. Later this boy may learn to construct motors, TVs, and radios by following the same procedure.

(g) *Curiosity.* This is a built-in appetite to become omniscient, to know everything. But curiosity is more easily satisfied in some people than in others. Some are satisfied with a superficial knowledge while others insist on probing the most intimate details. This second kind often make good detectives, good scientists, good researchers. The first kind are effective in other fields by reason of the very fact that they don't get bogged down in details and trivia.

(h) *Disgust or repulsion.* This instinct is a positive reaction to a negative situation. Parents have the responsibility of building into their children a fine sense of values so that their reactions of repulsion or disgust are aimed at deserving targets. Sometimes children grow up and find that they have been taught to feel antagonistic toward something which was not inherently bad at all. This is the way we discover and eliminate our own prejudices. Some parents are so fearful that they might prejudice their children that they refrain from giving them any code of values at all. But ignorance is just as great a vice as prejudice. The better course is to give a child the very best thinking his parents can provide and then let the child test it for himself. Some elements of prejudice are bound to slip through, but the child's experience will eventually reveal it. Parental advice and counsel is important even if it isn't perfect. "Better to have bread with a little grit than no bread at all."

(i) *Laughter.* The social instinct to share laughter together is a warm, stimulating, and satisfying communication between people that might well be called the only existing universal language.

Some of the most pleasant associations people can recall are occasions when "we got together and all laughed a lot."

Laughter is not always easy to come by. In fact, comedians on TV, radio, and the screen draw some of the top salaries. In every crowd the fellow who has developed the capacity to produce a few chuckles is soon rated as a popular and valuable asset.

As with all virtues, of course, the extreme becomes a vice. Thus, the fellow who not only laughs but who laughs so much that he becomes a nuisance is not so likely to be popular as he is to be labeled a "giggling idiot."

The psychology of humor and laughter is an interesting study. It has been found that laughter is stimulated by five different factors:

1. Physical exhilaration. This ranges all the way from chucking a baby under the chin to taking an adult for a ride on the roller coaster. Physical exhilaration can produce squeals and shrieks of laughter and delight.

2. Ridiculous situations. This is where a person sees something happen to somebody else which is so stupid and ridiculous that he feels sure it would never happen to him. His sense of superiority bubbles over into laughter. This is what happens when some young boys see an elderly person slip on the ice and fall. They break out in gales of laughter without recognizing the seriousness of the situation at all. Slapstick comedy also falls in this same area of humor.

3. The play on words. This usually takes the form of a pun or the clever turning of a phrase. This is often rated as "adolescent" humor, but it is the kind most frequently used by professional humorists on radio and TV.

4. The obscene. For some mysterious reason, the subjects of sex and the excretory processes have always been successful in stimulating laughter. Even in small children the things which they have been told "aren't nice" often will be used as topics of conversation and bring on uproars of laughter and cackles of delight.

5. The sacred. To poke fun or profane sacred matters also produces laughter, although psychologists have never discovered the reason why. It somehow tickles the fancy to hear subjects which are ordinarily held in the most serious respect portrayed in a humorous light.

Telling jokes can be a two-edged sword. A good rule to remember is, "If the victim of the joke can't laugh, too, don't tell it." Everybody likes to laugh but nobody likes to be laughed at.

One final thought on laughter is the need to be careful around 2- to 3-year-olds because they often pull some cute antic that causes grownups to laugh heartily. A quiet chuckle is taken in good humor by a child at this age, but a loud belly laugh will often be interpreted as ridicule. He thinks the rest of the family are laughing at him and therefore bursts into tears at the very moment when the rest of the family consider him the life of the party.

THE REPRODUCTIVE INSTINCT

Finally, we come to the third group of human qualities which are considered part of the reproductive instinct. To refresh our memory, the first group was related to the survival instinct, the second group was related to the gregarious or social instinct. Now we come to those built-in qualities which attract the two sexes together and result in the reproduction and raising of that "next generation."

(a) *The desire for companionship with the opposite sex.* From about age 3 there is a natural inclination of an individual to seek companionship with members of the opposite sex. This inclination therefore exists long before puberty and continues long after the powers of reproduction are gone. It is called "a natural affinity between opposites" and appears in various ways all through nature. Companionship between the sexes is therefore a state of balance in nature.

Children need to be trained to respect the members of the opposite sex and learn the psychological differences between the two. A boy who has never been around girls until he suddenly falls in love and gets married may have a difficult time adjusting. The same is true of a girl who has never been around boys. Male and female characteristics are something to be recognized and "lived with." Sometimes a man may complain because his wife is so tenderhearted and sensitive. This is not only true, but if the facts were known, this is probably the very reason he married her!

(b) *Courtship.* The affinity between the sexes leads to a pattern of conduct we have come to call "courtship." It originally related to the courtesies of courtly ways. Courtly ways in a boy usually consist of generosity, kindness, and doing little thoughtful things for a girl. He buys her flowers, candy, tickets to shows, and so forth. It may also make him clothes conscious for the first time and result in his getting dressed up "just for her."

The courtly ways of a girl involve clothes, perfume, hair-dos, manicures, and manners which are simultaneously flirtatious and coy. She is sweet and demure but subtly demanding. It is confusing to a boy but he generally likes it. He finds himself chasing the girl until he is caught.

In both boys and girls the courtship instinct starts out by "playing the field." In other words, the individual shows forth his or her courtly ways toward a number of the opposite sex. Gradually, and sometimes without realizing just why, the field is sharply narrowed. Then comes the whirlwind campaign of concentrated effort to win over completely the chosen object of affection.

It is during the final stages of this campaign that the tides of instinct and emotion rise to a level where they become a "ferocious hunger." The mating instinct is never stronger, and the most powerful personal disciplines are essential to preserve the propriety of both moral and sacred law.

(c) *Marriage.* The vortex of all the instinctive satisfactions relating to the reproduction of the race can be found only in the family relationship. Any attempt to secure them by any other means always turns out to be disappointing and impossible.

The well-adjusted marriage has many components. The satisfactory relationship between the sexes is one of them, but when a married couple celebrate their golden anniversary they look back and realize that the joy of living together came from many things:

Sharing time, talk, and common interests with each other.
Doing things for each other.

Working out problems together.
Sharing crises together.
Having someone to share sorrow with.
Having someone to share pleasure with.
Having someone to go places with.

The list could go on, but these are examples of the things which draw a man and woman into an orbit of harmonious unity which literally make them "one" just as they were promised in the Genesis of the race.

The parental instinct. Born in each of us is the desire to care for, guide, and protect the weak or the helpless. This is the parental instinct. It manifests itself long before an individual becomes a parent—in fact, a small child may exhibit it—and it survives with continuing vigor long after a brood of children are raised and gone.

Like all other instincts this one must be kept under control or it becomes destructive instead of protective. This is what the psychologists mean when they tell a mother not to smother her child with her love. Sometimes, to satisfy her parental instinct, a mother not only "protects the weak" but she so dominates every waking moment of her child's life that she *keeps* him weak. Mother love is so strong it sometimes requires concentrated restraint so a child has a chance to reach out into life and achieve independence.

CONCLUSION

So now we have considered all of the more important building blocks of human nature. Each one makes its own specific contribution to the well-being of the individual. It impresses the student once again with the fact that we are obviously creatures of purposeful design and precision engineering. Having been given these instinctive qualities as a providential gift, it then becomes our task to shape them and refine them to the peak of utmost enrichment. And having done this for ourselves, we become that much more competent to guide our children in shaping theirs.

CHAPTER 29

WHAT IS AN IDEAL MOTHER?

I am sure you will agree it takes a lot of reckless courage to write a chapter on this subject. Who would dare describe the heavenly attributes of an ideal mother? Surprisingly, however, the experts tell us the ideal mother is not an angel. At least not the traditional kind. She is not a radiant being of unearthly sweetness who sweeps blissfully through each crisis and tribulation as though it were the winning ticket on the Irish Sweepstakes. She is not a model of austere puritanical perfection with finishing-school manners. Nor has she the majestic piety portrayed on her children's lovely, lacy Mother's Day cards.

Experienced mothers know that little boys would drive such a woman mad! No, the ideal mother is a barometer of life for little boys. They watch her react to life, sometimes portending stormy weather, sometimes fair. From her they learn there is a time for joy and a time for sorrow, a time to work and a time to play. They also learn what is right and what is wrong and the blessings or penalties that go with each.

The ideal mother is very much of the earth, earthy. A being who is struggling toward heaven and drawing her children with her. The ideal mother is a housekeeper, a washwoman, a cook, a seamstress, a bookkeeper, a purchasing agent, a home decorator, a teacher, preacher, policeman, child psychologist, disciplinarian, nurse, gardener, hostess, conversationalist, storyteller, good listener, PTA officer, church worker, barber, sliver-puller-

outer, diaper changer, and superintendent of the Saturday night baths. In addition to all of this she is the sweetheart and wife of her husband, the constantly available source of sympathy and affection for her children, and a friend indeed to her neighbors in need.

No doubt the Bible was portraying just such a woman when the mother of King Lemuel declared:

Who can find a virtuous woman?
For her price is like rubies.
The heart of her husband doth safely trust in her . . .
She will do him good and not evil all the days of her life. . . .
She seeketh wool, and flax, and worketh willingly with her
   hands. . . .
She riseth also while it is yet night, and giveth meat to her
   household . . .
She considereth a field, and buyeth it:
With the fruit of her hands she planteth a vineyard. . . .
She stretcheth out her hand to the poor;
Yea, she reacheth forth her hands to the needy.
She maketh herself coverings of tapestry;
Her clothing is silk and purple. . . .
She openeth her mouth with wisdom; and in her is the law of
   kindness.
She looketh well to the ways of her household,
And eateth not of the bread of idleness.
Her children arise up, and call her blessed;
Her husband also, and he praiseth her.
Many daughters have done virtuously,
But thou excellest them all!

PROVERBS, 31:10–29

THE IMPERFECTIONIST

The ideal mother is not a perfectionist. In other words, she knows that in a good home for children there has to be a healthy margin of tolerance which may leave much to be desired as far as adults are concerned. This means a reasonable amount of tolerance for clutter, noise, and deterioration of furniture. It is the expectation that walls will sometimes become a garish gallery of surrealistic crayon art, that the household must occasionally give way to the adoption of a pet. (And a brand-new puppy is as much trouble as an additional child!) It means that family books will be pored over, pictures scrutinized, pages occasionally wrinkled or torn, backs accidentally bent. It means that every so often there will be a broken mirror, spilled milk on a fresh table-cloth, a slice of bread with honey and peanut butter plopped on the living room rug.

The ideal mother is a deliberate imperfectionist in other ways, too. She has to be willing to express interest and enthusiasm in childish things—childish games, childish stories, childish parties.

She learns to cope with crises—nails in bare feet, huge splinters in palms or seaters, bleeding fingers, swallowed marbles, bumped craniums, and beans in nostrils.

She adjusts her irritability quotient to allow for a certain amount of Indians and cowboys, squeals of pleasure, fussing, and bickering. She also accepts as more or less normal the painful wail of a screeching violin in the hands of a learner, the hesitant and repetitious plunking of piano scales, even the rattling and cymbal crashing of a drum practice in the basement.

By design the ideal mother is a perfect imperfectionist.

HOW A BOY LOOKS AT HIS MOTHER

When it comes to analyzing mothers, little boys have a special point of view.

They know, for example, that mothers were made by God to be loved, almost worshiped, by little boys. Of course, mothers are equally loved by little girls, but in a somewhat different way. A girl senses early in life that she is very much like her mother and will grow up to be even more like her. A boy, however, sees in his mother something marvelous and mysterious, something totally different from himself. He looks upon her as that vitally necessary supplement to life which seems to make up for all of his own deficiencies. She therefore becomes his pillar of inspiration as well as his protector against the storms of life.

A little boy often says to himself, "Nothing must ever happen to my mother!" He worries about this a lot. He cannot imagine how he could possibly survive without her. This fear shows up in his dreams. He dreams that his mother is the victim of some wild and breathless adventure with many narrow escapes from disaster. If he actually loses her in one of his dreams, the nocturnal adventure turns into a terrifying nightmare. He panics with the thought of being alone. The fact that his father is still with him is a little comfort, but his pearl of great price is his mom.

Of course, some little boys lose their mothers in real life—by death, divorce, or abandonment. For most boys, losing a mother is accompanied by a period of abject sorrow. Then, if a boy is fortunate, other women will gradually come into his life. If they are the right kind of women, he will discover in them the same wonderful qualities possessed by his own mother. Deliberately, he makes them "stand-ins" for his mom. But, for substantial periods of time, he will favor one over all the rest. It may be an aunt, a Sunday school teacher, a day school teacher, a kindly neighbor lady, or a foster mother. If this woman does not let him down, she can *almost* fill the gap of his missing mother. This indicates that little boys are made of pretty tough stuff and can develop a wholesome "mother image" if given half a chance.

THE IMPORTANCE OF GETTING A GOOD "MOTHER IMAGE"

Psychologists have found it extremely important that a boy get the proper respect, affection, and understanding of his mother because this is the way he develops an understanding of women in general. The experts call this, "getting a good mother image." They know that he will tend to take whatever image he gains of his mother and superimpose it on all other women later in life. Under normal circumstances she becomes the model or standard by which he will judge women. A mother is therefore representing her side of the human race and occupies a highly strategic position in making a warm, pleasant, and satisfying impression on the mind of her son.

Furthermore, a mother can capitalize on the fact that a boy's love makes him feel very much a part of her—both biologically and spiritually. He wants to be sure that she feels the same way. If a mother is playing her role well she can use this warm relationship, which is so precious to a boy, to keep him moving in the right direction.

What are some of the things which build an "ideal mother image" and make a boy feel that his mom is the greatest?

A MOTHER'S LOVE

From the moment a mother first cuddles her baby boy in her arms the ingredients of love are being nourished. Love is a two-way street which requires assurances of affection from both mother and son. Within days after a baby is born he looks up at this wonderful creature who cuddles and coos at him and wrinkles his face into a dimpled grin to show his appreciation. Actually, his eyes cannot distinguish too much detail as yet and a psychology lab researcher may say it is only a gas pain, but a mother knows that her baby's smile came from his soul and was meant just for her.

Later this little fellow learns to hold out his arms to her, to nestle his head against her cheek, to pat her gently with his pudgy little hand. It is the way a boy's love for his mom gets off to a wonderful start.

The next step in the cultivation of this relationship is to make love the foundation for teaching and discipline. A mother treads the narrow trail between exploiting her boy's love on the one hand while not destroying it on the other. Her task is made so much easier if she has taken the time to learn a few fundamentals about child development. For example, to expect that a 2½-year-old will obey as well as he will at 3½ is to fly in the face of nature. On the other hand, he will not usually obey as well at 4½ as he did at 3½. The ebb and flow pattern of a child's development is the key to a mother's peace of mind as she uses his love to nurture this little fellow up the path of wholesome childhood development.

If properly handled a boy interprets discipline quite differently from what a mother might think. When he teases her unmercifully and deliberately violates her wishes in spite of several warnings, he fully expects her to do something about it, if she really loves him. In fact this is his way of testing her love. As a little 4-year-old was heard to remark, "I wish somebody around here could make me mind!" This meant he wanted the barriers firmed up, to assure him that he lived in an orderly world, to be certain that his folks really cared about him and what he did.

A final word about love is the fact that a little fellow likes it to be demonstrative. He wants to *feel* his mother's love. Every so often he wants her to pick him up, hold him in her arms, and give him 100 per cent of her time and attention. This only requires a few minutes through the day but they are precious minutes. The experts call this a time for T.L.C.—tender, loving care. Even in hospitals, nurses are required to administer regular doses of T.L.C. to younger children with the same regularity as pills or medicine. This spreads a perfume of security in the mind of a boy which bathes his hurts and constantly assures him, "You are wanted, you are loved, you are needed!"

A MOTHER'S AVAILABILITY

In the tender years of childhood, time is a seemingly endless and painful extension of duration. A day is like a week or even a month of later life. Therefore, a little fellow feels the need to check in with his mom every few minutes because it seems such a long time. He also wants to know where she is every moment. If she is in the house, he wants to know what part of the house. If she is going away he wants to know why and for how long. If at all possible he wants to spend a lot of time with her. If she is in the kitchen that is just where he wants to set up his train, or build his blocks or experiment with his skates. If he has been playing outside, he has to hurry in to report every significant development.

It means a great deal to a boy just to have his mom around. This need continues with amazing intensity all through the growing period. Even in high school a boy who comes home to an empty house gets a sinking feeling. He may not say anything, but he feels it.

Of course, when a mother has to be away, a boy can usually understand and rationalize it satisfactorily. But he still feels a certain unspoken anxiety until she returns. What really leaves a vacuum in his solar plexis is the feeling that his mother *wants* to stay away and uses any flimsy excuse to leave home. Unfortunately, our fast, modern living competes with the home. If a mother is not careful, she may find her children growing up without a mother.

THE MOTHER AS A TEACHER

An important part of a boy's image of his mother is in the role of a teacher. He likes her in this role. She answers questions, she solves problems, she uses language he can understand. Furthermore, she tells him stories and helps him understand life by fitting into the stories explanations and editorial comments. A boy is fortunate if he has a mother who has cultivated her own mind and seeks to share with him the exciting things he can expect as he grows up.

A small boy has an almost unlimited appetite for interesting information. He is capable of being held spellbound for long periods of time by carefully prepared and interestingly presented material. The key to good storytelling technique is to play on people or "things in action." Children do not like preaching, but principles and morals can be worked into the action. A mother is an almost immediate success if she looks at her little brood just before bedtime and says, "How would you like to hear about the little boy who got caught in a cave by a bear?"

THE FORMING OF CHARACTER

When a boy grows up he asks himself whether his mother helped build his character or weakened it.

Sometimes he can see that she gave him his way too much, or failed to counsel him when he was obviously headed for disaster. On the other hand, he might come to appreciate that his troubles in life are really the result of his failing to heed his mother. He says to himself, "I had a good mother. I just didn't have sense enough to listen to her!"

A mother has to raise her son in terms of the long pull. She has to use her wits continually to get the right reaction from her son during his early years. But if this fails, she has to go right ahead and do what she knows time and life will teach her son to be right. Therefore, many mothers who rate themselves as a failure in raising rebellious sons find themselves a success in later years when their boys have grown a little older, have come to their senses, and say, "Gee, Mom, you were great!"

THE BUILDING OF GOOD HABITS

The key to good character is forming good habits. This is the primary task of a mother. Habits are motivated by attitudes, and a boy picks these up from his parents, especially his mother. Habits of cleanliness, order, thrift, friendliness, courtesy, hygiene, punctuality, honesty, and work are all part of the heritage a mother helps pass on to her son. A mother is particularly successful if she practices all of these things herself. This gives a boy the feeling that it is the thing to do. Otherwise, he listens to his mother's teachings and then watches her violate them and says to himself, "What Mom says is a good idea, but hardly anyone does it—not even Mom!"

THE CHAIN REACTION PRINCIPLE

This leads us to the next major premise which says that, "As goes the mother so goes the child." This is not always true, but it is true more often than not. A father can be rated a success by all normal standards and still raise a weak family if the mother is weak. She is closer to the children than he and therefore a greater influence for good or for ill.

The children pick up her attitudes and methods of solving problems. For example, marriage counselors point out that this is true in divorce problems. If a quarreling, nagging mother allows her marriage to collapse, it establishes a pattern in her children and tends to make their married lives unstable. This is why it is sometimes true that "divorce runs in families." On the other hand, a wise mother finds herself in a key position to guide the entire family toward unity and solidarity. Her children watch her as she patiently passes by the minor inconveniences and disturbances of life and they thereby learn to do the same.

This is just one example of why a mother is described as the spark which produces the chain reaction that will often reflect itself in her descendants for generations to come.

THE CHANGING CLIMATE

Up until a little fellow reaches 11 he is pretty much his mama's boy. Then the climate changes. Suddenly he begins to get too big for his mother to handle. He begins asserting himself with a certain defiance. A mother should expect this changing climate. It will be a dominant characteristic in their relationship for five or six years. Gradually, however, it will subside. A boy begins to come around when he is 16 or 17 and soon his mother discovers that, while it is not the same relationship she enjoyed with him as a child, nevertheless, it is warm, affectionate, and wonderful. By the time her son is 20 or 21 he should have developed a sense of adult equality with his mother and treat her as "the best mom a fellow ever had."

If this does not happen, Junior may be a little behind in his maturity schedule, or, if that is not the case, it may be a reflection of problems in early childhood.

SCARS OF THE TWO EXTREMES—NEGLECT AND "MOMISM"

When a boy has won his sense of independence and equality during the middle or late teens he usually wants to restore the happy relationship which he used to have with his mother as a boy. But if the mother never took the time to create a happy relationship or wholesome "mother image" during the earlier years, then there is nothing to restore. A mother therefore has the heartbreak of seeing her son go on trudging through life as though she were practically non-existent.

At the other extreme is the mother who tries too hard, who hovers over her boy like a cloud, constantly protecting him, continuously reminding him, lavishing him with love whether he reciprocates it or not, fighting all his battles, making all his decisions, doing all his work. This is called "Momism." It smothers a boy. He is not allowed the normal opportunities to learn his own lessons, fight his own battles, make his own decisions, or grow from a baby to a man. He therefore enters adult life unprepared, timid, dependent, afraid. And he soon identifies the source of his trouble—an overprotective mother.

THE UNITED FRONT

As a boy is growing up he visualizes his mother and father as a team with his father carrying the leadership role of being "the first among two equals." The wise mother will capitalize on this. She will teach her boy to respect and love his father, to look to him for leadership, and seek his companionship and counsel. She will set the example for this herself. When she disagrees with the kind of discipline her husband administers, she will not argue in front of her children but will counsel behind the scenes if she thinks it is necessary.

It does something to the heart of a boy to see a strong bond of love and companionship between his mother and father. This does not create jealousy but gives a boy a deep sense of satisfaction. He learns many things from the courtesies, the hello and good-by kisses, the gestures of affection which he sees his father express for his mother. It makes a boy feel like their home is a castle and inside that home there is a united front.

By way of contrast, open quarreling between parents can so upset a boy that he may fail in school, resort to belligerent behavior himself, or even indulge in youthful crimes. He is also disturbed if his mother constantly complains about his father and tries to arouse the boy's sympathy with a continuous barrage of woeful wails. When a mother is genuinely abused, a boy is quick to sense it, but even so, if she handles him correctly, he can be motivated to grow up and be a better man than his dad without nurturing a hatred for his father.

THE TASK OF BEING BOTH FATHER AND MOTHER

Sociologists have pointed out that when a brood of children lose their father, they nearly always lose their mother, too. Usually she has to get a job, and the entire family must somehow limp along under far less than ideal conditions. Such a family can be a success, however, and usually is, but it takes a truly great woman to serve the double role of both father and mother. Such circumstances call for as much encouragement and help as possible from the church, community agencies, and neighbors. It is surprising how many leaders and outstanding personalities have come from widowed mothers, but whenever this happens it is usually because a mother was willing to go the extra mile—sometimes many extra miles—to make up for the handicap of a missing father.

TRIBUTE TO AN IDEAL MOTHER

Several years ago a wonderful woman in Southern California who had raised eight robust children under very difficult circumstances was selected as "the Mother of the Year." At a special program in her honor I was given the privilege of paying this brief tribute to her. Because she was my mother I called it, "My Mother and I."

Even before I was born she knew me, planned for me, and gave me a name.
After I was born she nursed me, taught me, tended, and prayed for me.
She was my first sweetheart, my first baker, my first tailor.
She was my first doctor, my first judge, my first teacher.

> *She shared her life with me—*
> *Even risked losing hers for me.*
> *She asked God to let her be*
> *My creator.*

When cuts and falls and ailments came,
She shared the shock and tears with me;

With every scratch and bruise and burn,
She felt the pain vicariously.

She took the mystery out of the things I saw.
She made me feel at home on earth.
She helped me see the road of life
As the way to God—and Paradise.

She watched me grow up and away from her.
She saw me cut the apron strings and stand alone.
It broke her heart, but she knew that time
Would bring me back again.

Now, in the twilight of her life,
As the years weigh heavily and long,
I would like to tell her how I feel—
But the sacred words, I cannot speak.

I can only look deep in her heart
As she looks into mine
And both of us know the love we share—
My Mother and I!

CHAPTER 30

WHAT IS AN IDEAL FATHER?

Ideal fathers come in a great variety of sizes, shapes, models, and makes. Therefore, from a distance, it may be difficult to spot one. Naturally, he cannot be identified by nationality, education, profession, church, lodge, political party, or social set. Neither can he be labeled a successful father even though he may appear to be a very successful man. A man might be a great scientist, a financial genius, a popular movie star, a world-famous musician, even an authority on child psychology, and still be a failure as a father.

In the final analysis, an ideal father is the one who develops the attributes of being a great "next generation builder." It means he is not egocentric and selfish but has cultivated a willingness to invest money, energy, training, and time in those who are next in line to inherit the earth.

WHAT IT'S LIKE TO BE A FATHER

Becoming a domesticated, well-adjusted father is no accident. In fact, it takes many years to raise a good father. And his wife and children do most of the raising.

It all begins when a young husband makes that first fearful pilgrimage down the long, antiseptically pure hallway of the hospital to the window marked "Nursery." Inside he can see several rows of pink and blue bassinets full of babies. Even through the glass the nurse can tell he's a new father (new fathers are easy to pick out), so she gives him special attention because the hospital has never lost a father yet.

She hunches her shoulders as though to say, "Which one?" and he hunches right back, "How should I know!" She points to a card on the nearest bassinet and he can lip-read her question, "What's your name?" He blurts it out through the glass and startles himself with the noise of his own voice echoing down the silent hallway. The nurse turns away to search around and finally wheels over a very special bassinet bearing the family name. She uncovers the little wonder package and, sure enough, it's a baby—a real live baby. The nurse gently lifts up each of the tiny hands and then each of the feet.

As the young man looks through the glass he can't help scrutinizing each fragile feature—the eyes, nose, lips, chin, fingers, and toes. Truly, it is a miracle. Suddenly, out of the cosmic void from a hundred million light years away there comes a booming message. It strikes him in the forehead like a ten-pound sledge hammer. It says, "Boy, you are a father!"

Of course, he knew it all along; at least, he knew it in an abstract, intellectual sort of way. But looking through the window makes a difference. He quietly says to himself, "Gosh, this is for real."

Thus the mantle of fatherhood settles on the young in heart. In the days, months, and years that follow this business of being a father becomes more real with every passing hour. As seasons come and go the family grows. Instead of one baby there are two, maybe three, four, or even more. With each one a new chapter of "How to Become a Better Father" begins. Each child is different, and the father finds himself taking his home-study course on the basis of "learning by doing." However, he finds that the role of being a father actually suits his secret fancy rather well. It isn't as tough as he thought it would be. He learns that the biggest job of solving family problems is simply "getting at it." Once he has settled down to "working things out," he usually finds each riddle easier to solve than he had suspected. Consequently, when someone asks him how he became a successful father, he replies rather quizzically, "Oh, I really don't know—exactly; just working at it, I guess."

HOW A FATHER LOOKS TO A LITTLE BOY

Little boys have their own special slant on fathers. To most little boys a father seems like a combination of a big bear, a dray horse, and Superman. The big bear is only evident on special occasions when Junior finds he has fouled up with the head of the house. But once he has come under the shadow of the big bear's paw he makes a strong mental note, "Dad is a great guy, but don't rile him." He knows that sometimes sweet talk will melt Mom, but not so much with Dad. "Once Dad's mad, wow!"

This mental note is good for a growing boy. It makes him feel his dad cares enough about him to want him to mind. As long as a dad is reasonable, a boy likes it that way.

The dray horse facet of a little boy's father is evident every morning when he gets up from the table and says, "Time to go to work!" A little boy feels that the drudgery of Dad always going to work is a nuisance. He and his dad could have so much fun—if he would just stay home.

This desire to have Dad as a playmate comes from the feeling that this big fellow who presides over the family is just about the most tremendous, colossal thing that ever happened. He's a superman. He can ride a horse, shoot a gun, play a par game of golf, tie Scout knots, fix a tire, bandage cuts, clip hair, and, when necessary, pull teeth. In addition to that, he has money in fabulous quantities; at least, he has more than little boys have.

It is no wonder that a boy with that kind of a dad might assume that his father could also whip any other father in the block; maybe in the whole world!

Unfortunately, this heroic dream soon fades. As time takes its toll, Junior gradually learns the truth. He finds his father is a wonderful, lovable person, but his game of golf is lousy. He also gets buck fever every time he sees a deer and might just as well sell his rifle. He can ride a horse but jiggles in the middle if the horse goes faster than a walk. There is some proof that he did get a few merit badges in Scouting, but now he ties granny knots in everything but his shoelaces. He can fix a tire, but takes out service insurance so he won't have to. As for being a fighter, he is the most non-provocative, peace-loving man in town. And he isn't so rich either.

If the little boy only knew it, his father is happy and relieved to be debunked. It gave him the jitters to be put up on a wobbly pedestal where his hero-worshiping son had perched him. Now the two of them can start out fresh, building a real father and son relationship on a man to man basis.

GETTING A GOOD "FATHER IMAGE"

It takes several years for a boy to really know his dad. In his early years he has many happy associations, but his closest ties are with his mom. Somehow his dad rather puzzles him, seems always on the go, sort of preoccupied, has a worried, weary look when he comes home sometimes. He remembers his mother's quiet warning, "Don't bother your father tonight, he's tired."

After several years a boy gradually gets the idea that life is not such a jolly bowl of cherries for Dad. He becomes aware that the house, the car, the food, the clothes, taxes for schools, money for vacation—somebody has to go out and earn enough to pay for all of those things. He becomes conscious of debts and bills and wishes he could strike uranium in the back yard to help out. All of this is good for a boy.

He learns something else about his dad—the patience and plugging that it takes to raise and run a family. He sees the "big bear" image once in a while, but most of the time he notices that Dad gets what he needs with patience, hard work, and cheerful persistence.

And when Mom warns the family that Dad is pretty worried about something, he notices how well his father can usually hide it and frequently joke and play as though everything were all right. In fact, he likes to see his father cut loose with some guffaws of laughter once in a while. He also likes to feel the physical impact of wrestling with him or being tossed around. Dad calls it "getting roughed up." Junior feels better after one of these tussles. There is a strong masculine sense of adventure with the matching of muscles, daring to be thrown high in the air, or being whirled about at a dizzy pace.

Sometimes there are bumps or minor accidents, and Junior learns that among us men there's a lot of give-and-take and "men don't bawl." He also learns to provide his share of roughness with cub bear tactics that really don't hurt. He learns that Dad is a boy at heart with a wonderful sense of humor, and when circumstances permit it he can really be fun. These are among the memories of a boy with his dad.

THE IMAGE OF AUTHORITY

Another thing a boy should learn from his father is the image of judicious authority. From this he deduces that he lives in an orderly world and that the center of his boyhood world is presided over by his father. This does not mean he is a dictator, monarch, or blind authoritarian mogul. He learns that authority merely means that final decisions are usually left up to Dad. He notices that Mom is often asked for her ideas and suggestions and she gives them freely; but after all the discussion is over she defers to his decision and supports it once the decision has been made.

In many homes there is a confused image of authority because a father does not carry his normal division of labor, which is to preside and take the initiative in family leadership. It therefore becomes necessary for the mother to assert her leadership, and it can be very confusing to a boy who is trying to get a picture of the father's role in the family. When such a boy marries, he may distort his own family pattern by playing the role of Casper Milquetoast and lean pathetically on his wife the way his father used to depend upon his mother.

THE IMAGE OF DISCIPLINE

Juvenile judges have not only been saying, "Let's put Father back as head of the family," but they have also recommended a much more sound and consistent pattern of discipline for children. Some parents have been led to believe that any form of discipline is primitive and archaic, that it inhibits a child's outgoing personality. As a result their children frequently fail to develop normal personalities and become social monstrosities.

Discipline simply means a reasonable set of standards or rules, administered with discernment and judgment, and consistently enforced where necessary. The form of the discipline depends upon the child and the circumstances. Obviously, discipline should never be harsh or brutal, and a parent with a temper should wait until he has cooled off before handling his boy's problem.

THE IMAGE OF MASCULINE ADVENTURE

Women can often be quietly courageous beyond the point achieved by most men. Nevertheless, a boy usually learns physical courage and the spirit of adventure from his father.

There is a certain spirit of reckless abandonment which a boy loves to see in his father and which he tries to emulate. Actually, as a boy eventually learns, his dad only *appears* to be reckless and his courage is calculated, not blind. Still it's that great spirit of masculine adventure which sets a little boy's eyes to shining and his heart to thumping. Even in big cities, dads should work it out so their boys get some father-and-son adventures—at the beach, in the mountains, along some trout stream, or just camping somewhere. In later life it is this same kind of spirit which makes a man a great jet pilot, a good civil engineer, or a fine corporation president. Experts have observed how many leaders in business, industry, and government come from farms or small towns. Many of them feel that the boy tends to develop a stronger spirit of adventure and achievement in a rural setting. The same thing can and does happen in the city, but a boy's father has to cultivate it. And that takes time.

The kind of time a father spends with a boy is important. What he needs is "quality time" rather than quantity. To answer a boy's questions when he asks them, to give him undivided attention when he's trying to explain something, to help him with his problems at the moment they arise, these are what a boy rates as "quality time" with his dad.

THE IMAGE OF A LEADER

It doesn't take a boy very long to identify the qualities of a leader, especially in his dad. Leadership means "pointing the way." It makes a boy feel confident and secure if he has a father who knows the way and isn't afraid to help others find it. Leadership therefore means taking the time to study things out and gaining the foresight to anticipate trouble. It means having the answers in a crisis. And this is important to a boy who constitutes a crash bag full of crises. Of course, a good leader has to be teachable himself. He pushes his curiosity on any problem to its bedrock foundation so that he can gain some opinion concerning it. A good leader therefore develops opinions on many subjects but tries to avoid being opinionated about any of them. If there is a chance to learn he becomes a good listener. Still, he takes a firm position on facts and is not easily persuaded otherwise unless somebody comes up with more facts or sounder conclusions. It makes a boy proud of a father who is big enough to say he was wrong or change his view on something.

A boy also likes to see the quality of initiative in his father's leadership. When a group is fussing over a problem, a boy often gains the impression they are all equally confused and just milling around waiting for some guidance. He takes great pride in the fact that quite often it is his father who seems to come up with a helpful answer and is not afraid to express it.

THE IMAGE OF EXEMPLARY MANHOOD

A boy tends to see in his father the man which he, himself, will some day be. Whatever his father is, whether good or bad, the boy usually seeks to emulate him. A cursing father therefore usually raises a cursing son. A drinking father is likely to have a drinking son. A lying father is practically certain to raise a lying son. The boy who sees his father steal will justify himself in similar conduct almost immediately.

Naturally, such behavior may arouse the anger of a boy's father. He therefore orders his son to "do as I say, not as I do."

With most boys this is like setting the torch to ten tons of TNT. In the father's presence the boy may pretend to comply but when he is by himself he glories in the riotous example of being "just like Dad."

It is a low order of civilization when adults force a code of citizenship on their children which they will not practice themselves. It creates burning resentment in the hearts and minds of the youth of that generation. They feel imposed upon and are easily agitated to strike out against adult society. In fact one authority has written: "The hour of revolution comes at the moment when the youth of a particular generation find the hypocrisy of their elders totally intolerable."

THE IMAGE OF SPIRITUALITY

A boy has a hungry spirit. He is anxious to hear about God and the meaning of life. He wants to feel a part of the vast universe in which he seems to be the very center. He likes to have it explained over and over again.

A good father will not send his boy to church. He will take him. Too many fathers are unwilling to give adult religion a place in their lives. They think of religion in terms of the simplified version which they received as a child. They remember it was helpful and want their children to have the same help, but they are unwilling to go back to church as an adult and try to understand the profound and inspiring point of view of great spiritual instructors like Moses and Paul who never could be understood completely by children.

The father who makes religion an exciting and inspiring topic in the home and leads out in matters of prayer and devotion is likely to realize the literal meaning of the beatitude: "Blessed are they that hunger and thirst after righteousness for they shall be filled." They say that families who pray together stay together, and a boy from this kind of home usually remembers the strength he derived from it.

A few years ago it was considered smart psychology in some circles to deny children any religious training so they could "choose for themselves after they grow up." This proved to be a tremendous blunder. As one expert recently commented, "It was like making a child go naked until he grows up so he can choose his own preference in clothes. Likely as not he will prefer to go naked!"

WHAT BOYS SAY ABOUT THEIR DADS

Recently a group of boys were asked to evaluate their fathers. Most of these boys were in their late teens and were first asked: "What character trait do you admire most in your fathers?" The following qualities were rated by the boys in this order:

1. *Love*
2. *Example*
3. *Patience and even temper*
4. *Kindness*
5. *Organization ability*
6. *Courageousness*

Next the boys were asked: "What character trait do you admire least in your father?" These were mentioned most often:

1. *Quick temper*
2. *Impatience*
3. *Lack of attention or interest in children*
4. *Tenseness*
5. *Worry*
6. *Lack of thrift*

When asked what the boys considered the most important qualities in an ideal father, they nearly all agreed that there were three essentials: love, ability to discipline, and willingness to set an example. In commenting on a father's love, the boys defined it as:

"Interest in his children and their children."
"Not too lenient, yet not too harsh."
"Willingness to spend time with his children."
"Firm, but not too strict."
"Understanding."

"*Not a dictator, anxious to help a boy do things the right way
instead of just bossing him around.*"

Commenting on ability to discipline, they said:

"*Make a fellow stick to what is right.*"
"*Constant control over children.*"
"*He should speak softly but carry a big stick.*"
"*He should be the disciplinarian and head of the family.*"

The general feeling about setting an example is summarized
by one boy's comment: "He should be everything he expects his
boys to be."

CONCLUSION

Nearly all fathers have aspirations to be "ideal" dads, but I
doubt that any father would admit achieving it. Ideal fatherhood
is a perpetual struggle, and most fathers find themselves capable of wearing a champion's crown for only brief periods at a
time. This chapter is therefore dedicated to all the fathers who
are trying.

CHAPTER 31

WHAT IS AN IDEAL FAMILY?

I suppose nearly all young newlyweds approach a marriage
career with the firm expectation that theirs will be the greatest.
Shortly, however, they find themselves in one of three groups.
Some find themselves among the hurdy-gurdy newlyweds. These
are they who approach marriage like a little boy who says to the
organ man, "I've paid my nickel, now let's hear the tune!"
To such as these, marriage is sort of a circus. It has to be noisy,
colossal, and tremendous. When the noise dies down and the
novelty wears thin, so does the marriage.

There is a second group which might be called the "Marriage
Muddlers." These are they who never completely crack up, but
neither do they become a sensational success. They just muddle
through. These are the kind who don't seem to find themselves
until about their fiftieth wedding anniversary. As the quiet twilight of life gradually makes them senior citizens and grandparents they suddenly look at each other and say, "Well, look
what we did!" They decide that life did not treat them badly
after all. In fact they really could have been enjoying it all
along!

Finally, there is the third group, the ones who approach marriage with as much excitement as any of the others, but, either
by instinct or by training, sense that they are "kingdom builders."
Perhaps some day all young couples will be trained to think of

themselves as kingdom builders, because that is what Providence intended them to be.

At the head of this tiny empire is a king and queen who have power to rule generously or selfishly, lovingly or harshly, wisely or stupidly. The true kingdom builders are those who learn early in their married life to govern themselves and their somewhat helpless subjects in a warm, happy spirit of generosity, love, and wisdom. From the sidelines, observers will say, "There is an ideal family!"

WHAT IS THE FORMULA?

But when newlyweds are encouraged to create an ideal family life they come up with the obvious question, "What is the formula?"

After several thousand years of human civilization, a formula should now be available in a scientific, foolproof package. But, unfortunately, this is not the case. And there is a good reason. It turns out that nobody achieves "ideal" family life status for any extended period of time. Everything will be flying along beautifully for a while, and then unexpectedly there is a tremendous mid-air crash and the family pattern goes into a tailspin. What was once a model of happy living is exploded into confusion as the entire family struggles to meet the new situation and restore order. The crisis may be a financial setback, a serious illness, a burnout, moving to a new town, the loss of a parent, a call to military service, loss of a job, in fact any one of several dozen serious problems.

Building an ideal family is therefore not a goal but a *process*. It is a pattern of living which centers around a mother and father who are willing to quickly shift with the currents of life. It is a passion to preserve their own little kingdom with its binding bonds of love between father, mother, and children and to do it in spite of all adversity—poverty, war, crime, accidents, disease, disaster, even death.

Accepting, then, the fact that ideal family life is a *process* rather than a goal, we cannot help asking, "What is the best process?" What pattern is most likely to produce happy family living? Experts suggest the need to remember three things:

1. *Getting off to a good start.*
2. *Providing built-in stabilizers for the family.*
3. *Being willing to fulfill the* total *family role.*

GETTING OFF TO A GOOD START

On this point we should mention that even those who do not get off to a good start can usually get themselves straightened out, if they try, but it is far more pleasant to do it right in the first place.

A good marriage begins with a well-matched couple who have love *and* respect for each other. Woe unto the marriage where a gay young blade says, "I am getting married to the most luscious blonde, but boy is she dumb!" Or the girl who says, "I am embarrassed to be seen with Joe, but I love him, and I guess that's all that matters." Such matches don't usually stand the strain of the long haul. They often start falling apart before the honeymoon is over.

On the other hand, we should emphasize that even well-matched couples will have some adjustments to make. They will learn that a happy marriage is built on a foundation of "sharing things and sharing each other." In addition to sharing each other's companionship there is the sharing of the treasures of life—first, of course, their children, and after that good books, favorite friends, special foods, relatives, recreation, hobbies, religion, conversational interests, intellectual pursuits, sports, and travel. Even at best, some few differences will remain, but it greatly helps to have "all things in common," if possible.

Getting off to a good start is sometimes made difficult because one of the partners is out to reform the other. A bride will sometimes tell a girl friend, "Just wait until I get John married to me. I'll soon change him!" The experts will wish her luck, but statistics are against her. If a boy does not respond to her pleas for personal improvement during courtship, he is even less likely to respond after marriage.

Nevertheless, accepting the fact that a girl cannot remake her husband completely, at least she can promote certain refinements as long as he doesn't become *defensive.* He must be allowed to feel that overcoming a problem is his own achievement and not the victory of a nagging spouse. Some newlyweds trade problems. One will agree to try to overcome a certain weakness if the partner will agree to overcome one. As long as a spirit of good humor and mutual improvement prevails, much can be achieved.

Getting off to a good start is also enhanced by some fundamental things like living away from parents, having a job with a future, having plans for a home and a car, having ambitions for a good-sized family, having plans to continue with an education and setting up goals which will some day lead to independence and security. These are gravitational centers which draw the souls of a boy and girl together and thereby motivate them to work with all their might to make their little kingdom a reality.

THE BUILT-IN STABILIZERS OF A FAMILY

As soon as a young couple have launched their marriage successfully, they will want to provide some built-in stabilizers to protect their little kingdom against the storms of life. Their object is to take the gamble out of life—to reduce the margin of risk. Here are just a few things they can do:

START A SAVINGS ACCOUNT. Francis Bacon wisely said, "It is not what you earn that makes you rich, it is what you save!" Most young couples do not have ambitions to become wealthy but they do have a desire to feel secure. The most important key to security is having a savings account, and the genius for creating a good savings account is simply putting aside part of each paycheck and then spending the remainder. Too many people spend what they have and then wonder why there isn't any remainder for savings. Their formula is backward. During a lifetime most young couples will earn a quarter of a million dollars. As the years go by they may find practically all of this slipping through their fingers. At least one-tenth should have been held back in a savings account.

TAKE OUT SOME LIFE INSURANCE. Life insurance should be taken out primarily on the husband or breadwinner.

However, there is such a thing as being "insurance poor." It is better to start out modestly and then build insurance plans which make it possible to carry maximum insurance when children are growing up and then taper it off later on when less will be needed. The cost is spread over the years so that it is not a hardship when the need is greatest.

TAKE OUT HOSPITALIZATION INSURANCE. This usually includes a plan for medical and surgical services. What a blessing this can be when that first baby arrives. Furthermore, unexpected illness can wipe out the security of the entire family and leave them under a mountain of debt. Sometimes hospitalization will not pay the entire bill but at least it will absorb the major blow.

TAKE OUT SOME LIABILITY INSURANCE. This is primarily for the members of the family who drive automobiles. Modern traffic problems being what they are, even the most careful drivers can become involved in accidents. Damages for inadvertent carelessness can cost a family thousands of dollars so some protection is needed.

START BUYING A HOME. This is becoming more and more feasible for young married couples as time goes by. Low down payments and long-term contracts make homeowning easier to achieve in many parts of the United States than any place in the world. No young couple should pay rent any longer than is absolutely necessary. It is important, however, that they buy a modest home to begin with and trade or sell it for a larger home as their need and financial status increase. A family is a lot better off in a home they can operate with economic comfort than in a fancy place where the monthly bills for insurance, taxes, utilities, upkeep, and the mortgage are a back-breaker to a harassed father and worried mother.

FULFILLING THE TOTAL FAMILY ROLE

Families, like people, have personalities. Some families are nothing more than a group of people sharing board and room. Other families are like little kingdoms with courts and customs that leave the fragrance of happy memories for all who dwell therein. There are a number of important functions which the institution of the family is expected to provide.

First, the family is supposed to develop a magnetic center of social solidarity or security. Both parents and children need to feel that "home is a refuge." No matter how serious the trouble or how far they roam, children should feel the invisible golden threads pulling them back to the family circle. This is possible only when there is unity between father and mother.

Each set of parents should develop a single gravitational center of unity for all the little people who orbit around them. If parents begin pulling apart, it confuses children. The family solar system becomes wobbly. It has two suns instead of one. This is why parents must be extremely careful about criticizing one another in front of their children or seeking the sympathy of the children after some quarrel or disagreement. Children should see constant expressions of thoughtfulness, common courtesy, kindness, and love between their parents. They find it easier to love their parents if the parents love each other.

And if parents are united and are willing to expand their unity and love to include each of their children, it is amazing how much a family can successfully endure. Through all adversity the core of security remains. Unity is therefore the indispensible ingredient for happy family living.

THE FAMILY IS A PLACE TO BE APPRECIATED

Second, the family circle is a place where each member of the family should feel appreciated.

If all the world is a stage, then Mom and Dad are the grandstand audience as far as growing children are concerned. They hunger for the approval and appreciation of the two most important people in their lives. Children from three years and up do not need to be tended as much as they need to be tolerated. They like to bring their noise and toys right into the middle of the adult circle.

"Get rid of those kids!" I heard an angry father say recently. His children were having a wild and woolly time trying to get his attention. All they got was his goat. He was trying to read the paper after a hard day. Only a few moments before he had arrived home with the warm expectation that now he could relax. Then the kids had discovered him. With a whoop and a holler they had descended on him. He had taken time out to process their hugs and kisses one at a time and had told them to go outside again. But they didn't. They stood around wishing something would happen. They wanted this wonderful lovable dad to come alive, react, join the gang for a frolic. It wasn't something they reasoned out, it was just something they felt. When they didn't get his attention peaceably they used the tactics of war. That was when their dad exploded.

Because parents feel the terrific tensions of modern life they need moments of quiet privacy to collect their wits. But it helps if they have saved a little·time, energy, and humor for their home-front fans.

To meet the competition of the outside world, each home has to have its own private grandstand where Mom and Dad frequently preside in royal splendor. If families feel they are falling apart, they might call a council and all of them determine to:

Talk together more.
Play together more.
Read together more.
Travel together more.
Work together more.

A weekly "home night" is the ideal way to make sure that time is reserved for this kind of togetherness. Families which have regular home nights build precious memories, never to be forgotten. It is difficult for a child to wander from his own home grandstand if things are happening there which are just too good to miss.

PROVIDING BASIC NECESSITIES

Third, the family is responsible for providing basic physical necessities. These include three wholesome meals per day; a clean comfortable place to sleep; clean and adequate clothing; transportation; heat; light; and housing. In many countries the law also requires that the children receive a certain amount of education in public or private schools, and that certain health standards be maintained in the home.

These physical needs of a child are not cheap. It is estimated that the average child's share of all the things he receives up to the time he is twenty-one costs his parents and the community over $35,000. Each child is a major investment!

Some parents deprive their children of physical necessities without quite realizing it. It is amazing how many children go to school without an adequate breakfast, and the National School Lunch Program is the result of teachers and principals watching children nibble at soggy, badly prepared lunches which were neither tasteful nor nourishing. In some homes, there is also a tendency for the whole family to "just grab a bite" instead of eating the meal together. Under these circumstances children tend to get left out insofar as healthful, vitamin-filled foods are concerned. They get their food by nibbling—munching on cookies, jam sandwiches, and whatever else strikes their fancy in the family larder.

Other areas of neglect often include inadequate clothing for cold weather, an inadequate place to sleep, lack of cleanliness, and failure of parents to provide their children with available services such as dental care, eye examinations, vaccinations, and "shots."

By way of contrast, we should mention that in some homes physical necessities are overemphasized, so that parents keep themselves and the children in a state of threatened bankruptcy because they are trying to provide too many things. The world's most prosperous nation has recently learned a bitter lesson—namely, that luxury spoils children, cultivates criminal tendencies, and breeds heartbreaks for parents. The better plan is to keep life simple; avoid overindulgence whether it is malted milks, chocolate bars, motorboats, sports cars, or mansions. As the psychologists point out, children should grow up "wanting things" —not essentials, of course, but other things. When a person wants something for a long period of time it becomes precious to him— something to work for. It winds up a boy's mainspring of action and teaches him to appreciate what he does get. On the other hand, if his appetites have been satiated and his tastes dulled by lavish indulgence, he usually grows up to be a soft, spoiled, uninspired adult. Studies show that rural life, where children get stars in their eyes just from looking at mail-order catalogues, tends to produce more leaders in business, industry, and government than urban life where children often get things almost as soon as they think about them. America is becoming a "cityfied" civilization. To produce leaders and happy human beings, parents should tighten up on their children to keep their appetites well whetted for "wanting things."

"HOME, SWEET HOME"

The fourth role of the family is providing a home. This means a great deal more than providing an apartment or a house. It means providing a place where there is a chance for happiness and growth by every member of the family. It is a "place to go" because one is loved and wanted. It is a place where there is not only security but pleasant associations and exciting things to do. This means that somebody is "home" most of the time. At least one of the parents should be there. Brothers and sisters add to the excitement. It is a place where pals are welcome.

They say it takes a lot of living in a house to make it a home. Every nook and corner should reflect the personalities of those who live there. A picture drawn in school by a member of the family is far more significant as a temporary fixture on the living room wall than an expensive print of some classic. Baseball bats, fishing rods, tennis rackets, and riding boots are more important to growing boys and girls than fancy vases, delicate tapestries, and mahogany furniture. When a boy occupies a room he is delighted to be told he can fix it up to suit himself. When he is through, it won't look like an ad in a homemaker's magazine, but it will certainly be the boy's pride and joy.

Of course, some parts of the house have to appeal to the parents, too; a place where visitors can be invited without breaking their necks on skates, scooters, or toy trains. In the old days, the sanctum 'sanctorum was the parlor. Children entered it at the risk of getting their breeches tanned. Today the parlor is family headquarters for TV, hi-fi, teen-age gab fests, and is otherwise the focal center of traffic congestion for the entire family. Parents therefore may have to set up adult headquarters somewhere else. Parents, like children, need a little privacy once in a while.

Sometimes parents get discouraged because the home they are able to afford isn't as fancy as they would like. It should be recalled that some of the best remembered "home, sweet homes" of famous men have been shacks by modern standards. A home is not underprivileged as long as the attitudes of those within it are right. When necessary, satisfactory homes have been set up in log cabins, tents, or even covered wagons. It is not "the place" which makes a home, but the attitude of the people who inhabit it.

HOME—THE CHILD'S FIRST SCHOOL

The fifth role of the family is to provide education for those within its circle. A child will do far better in school if he gains the zeal for learning in his own home. This is unlikely unless the parents have a thirst for knowledge. If parents talk about mathematics, science, music, art, history, current events, political problems, sports, and business, then the children are likely to catch the spark and absorb a tremendous amount of basic knowledge on these same subjects. A child also does much better in school if he has acquired good social attitudes from his parents. A child is fortunate who comes to school with a deep-rooted sense of appreciation for honesty, fair play, sobriety, morality, and thrift.

A few years ago there were those who discouraged parents from helping children with homework. This proved to be a mistake. One of the richest associations parents can have with their children is refreshing their minds on some of the rusty rules of English and mathematics or the highlights of geography and history. Of course, no parent should actually do a youngster's homework, especially if it is "to help him get good grades." Likely as not, he would flunk! Helping with homework is of the greatest value when it provides both parent and child with the satisfaction of "learning together."

THE HOME AS THE CHILD'S FIRST CHURCH

The sixth role of the family is providing spirituality. This is explaining to him his own significance and his relationship with his Creator and the universe. It is designed to give him a sense of responsibility in terms of permanent and unchanging values. It helps him learn that he has *duties* as well as rights and his acts are significant not only in this present life, but for his future life as well. These are concepts which will be further emphasized at church or Sunday school, but most churches have access to a child less than an hour a week, which falls far short of the time required to give a child a good religious education. So the parents must somehow make up the difference. In fact it may add to their own religious education, just learning enough to teach their children. It also helps if parents *take* their children to church instead of *send* them. A youngster who is sent to church gets the idea that religion is "just for children."

THE FAMILY AS A LABORATORY OF LEARNING

It is interesting that the expert management of a family is efficient in a different sort of way than the operation of an office or a business. The purpose of a business is to get certain *things* accomplished. The purpose of a family is to provide each member of the household with the maximum opportunity for self-realization. *Things* are therefore not as important as *people*. An efficiency expert from a factory might watch a family and rate it "total confusion," whereas a sociologist would see below the surface and say, "There is some confusion all right, but it is organized confusion." Wholesome family life leaves a margin for free-will expression around the border of all of the necessary tasks of daily living. A boy of 8 will not wash dishes like an adult. Parents are lucky if he is willing to go through several years of "just plugging." To force him to wash exactly like a grownup would be extremely disastrous. The same is true in cutting lawns, washing cars, or any other place a boy is asked to help. Perfection takes time. Learning takes time. Meanwhile, a certain amount of imperfection must be tolerated or there will be no learning. A mother who constantly picks up after her children will never motivate them to pick up after themselves. A mother who "can't stand" to let the children do things because "they are so sloppy about it" is depriving them of a chance to learn how *not* to be sloppy. It takes patience—sometimes cast-iron patience—to make home a "laboratory of learning."

This also means that the pace in a home is not top factory speed. If it were, the whole family would get ulcers. Mother knows that the kids come home from school and Dad comes home from work to get a little pleasant relaxation. She therefore usually gets her rest in the afternoon before they return so she can go into high gear and get dinner ready while the rest of the family members are recharging their respective batteries. Perhaps after dinner, they can step up their pace as they get to studying, doing the dishes, or attending to other household chores.

TO BE BORN OF GOODLY PARENTS

So we conclude by saying it is a great heritage to come from goodly parents. It is one of life's choicest blessings to be raised by a man and woman who truly tried to be a good king and a good queen; who presided over their tiny empire with diligence and humble anxiety; who did unto their children as they would like to have been done by.

And what parents of a successful family can help but exclaim, "Oh, the joy and blessing of obedient and loving children!" No matter how famous or rich a man and woman might become, it is tarnished fool's gold compared to the treasures of happiness which lavish their hearts and minds when they see the obedience, love, and success of their own well-raised children. In fact, it is in this kind of family circle that the total, cosmic fruition of all mortal existence finds its ultimate zenith of happiness and contentment. It is the nearest thing to paradise that human beings enjoy on earth.

INDEX